D0713321

CONQUISTADORS

SEARCHING FOR EL DORADO:
THE TERRIFYING SPANISH CONQUEST
OF THE AZTEC AND INCA EMPIRES

JOHN PEMBERTON

Futura

First published in Great Britain in 2011 by Futura

Copyright © Omnipress 2011

The moral right of the author has been asserted.

All rights reserved.
No part of this publication may be reproduced, stored in a retrieval system, or transmitted, in any form or by any means, without the prior permission in writing of the publisher, nor be otherwise circulated in any form of binding or cover other than that in which it is published and without a similar condition including this condition being imposed on the subsequent purchaser.

A CIP catalogue record for this book
is available from the British Library.

ISBN 978-0-7088-6746-4

Typeset in Great Britain by Omnipress Limited
Printed and bound in Great Britain

Futura
An imprint of
Little, Brown Book Group
100 Victoria Embankment
London EC4Y 0DY

An Hachette UK Company
www.hachette.co.uk

www.littlebrown.co.uk

The views expressed in this publication are those of the author. The information and the interpretation of that information are presented in good faith. Readers are advised that where ethical issues are involved, and often highly controversial ethical issues at that, they have a personal responsibility for making their own assessments and their own ethical judgements.

Contents

THE SEARCH FOR EL DORADO

EPILOGUE

NEW WORLD MEETS OLD

Introduction

In 1507, German cartographer Martin Waldssmuller scratched the name of 'America' on a hurriedly re-drawn map of the world which showed the 'New World' as a continent, separate from Asia, for the first time. It was a leap of faith, as reports regarding the new lands were contradictory and intermingled with fables. But by the end of the century the existence of the continent was confirmed, and England, France, Germany, Portugal and the Netherlands fought with the Spanish for domination of the vast freshly discovered territories. The exchange of the lands themselves would happen between foreign powers via the barrel of a gun, and would continue for centuries. The maps would be redrawn many times as new countries were sketched upon the blank parchment of *terra incognito*.

But the tales of how the borders of those countries

came to be drawn, astonishing as they are, seem trivial when set beside the epic story of those that first journeyed to the New World – the Conquistadors. Never again would two such alien worlds stare in wonder, joy, terror and awe at the sight of one another; after the discovery of the Americas the two previously separate halves of the world would forever more be fused together as one.

The story of the Conquistadors, then, is nothing less than the story of how the world that we know today was created. That is why it has been called 'the most important event in history'. It is a tale so full of drama and wonder that at times it reads more like myth than reality, with heroes and villains as compelling and improbable as anything the Greeks conjured from their vivid imaginations. Here, in full, is the whole astonishing saga of what happened when a small band of adventurers set sail from Spain in search of wealth and glory.

The most important event in history? Quite possibly. The most incredible story in history? Undoubtedly.

THE GREATEST EVENT IN HISTORY

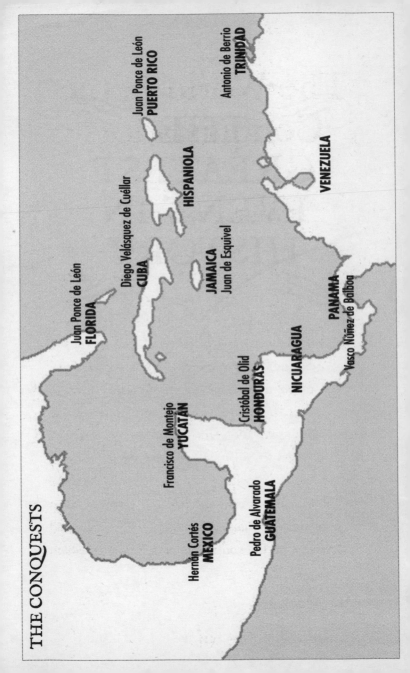

THE CONQUESTS

Juan Ponce de León
FLORIDA

Hernán Cortés
MÉXICO

Francisco de Montejo
YUCATÁN

Pedro de Alvarado
GUATEMALA

Diego Velásquez de Cuéllar
CUBA

Cristóbal de Olid
HONDURAS

NICUARAGUA

JAMAICA
Juan de Esquivel

HISPANIOLA

Juan Ponce de León
PUERTO RICO

PANAMA
Vasco Núñez de Balboa

VENEZUELA

Antonio de Berrío
TRINIDAD

The World of the Conquistadors

THE RECONQUEST

When Isabella I of Castile married Ferdinand II of Aragon in 1469, two of the most powerful Kingdoms of the Iberian Peninsula united to form a single mighty Catholic alliance. 'Espana' became a reality when Ferdinand ascended the throne in 1479, five years after Isabella was crowned Queen of Castile. Formal union under a single King would have to wait until 1516 when Charles V was crowned. He technically reigned alongside his mother, 'Joanna The Mad', but Charles called all the shots, as his mother's alleged habit of carrying her late husband's corpse around with her was considered too eccentric even for a Spanish monarch. Nonetheless, Isabella and Ferdinand were the controllers of a Kingdom which had great military power, and one of the first targets of that power was the Moorish Emirate of Granada.

Wars between Castile and Granada had raged for many years, but in-fighting amongst Christians had prevented the Spanish Kingdoms from launching a decisive campaign in the Reconquista of lands taken by the Moors. Isabella and Ferdinand united at a time when Granada was itself suffering from violent internal conflicts, and the Spanish exploited these divisions ruthlessly. It was a lesson they would not forget when later seeking to pacify the Americas.

A surprise attack from Granada in 1481 in response to a Christian raid shattered an uneasy truce between the two sides. Ten years of brutal warfare followed before Granada finally fell, to be annexed by Castile. During those ten years, the Spanish learned much about war, particularly concerning the devastating power of heavy artillery. One hundred thousand Moors were slaughtered or enslaved: the rest were given the choice to convert to Christianity, flee Spain or die. Once Granada had been subjugated, Spain was free to pursue a more aggressive foreign policy, secure in the knowledge that she would face no more major insurrections at home.

One of those inspired by the Christian victory was the explorer Christopher Columbus, who linked his own mission with that of the Reconquista, writing to Isabella and Ferdinand:

> On the second day of January I saw Your Highnesses' royal banners placed by force of arms on the towers of the Alhambra ... and in the same month ... Your Highnesses, as Catholic Christians and princes devoted to the holy Christian faith and the furtherance of its cause ... resolved to send me, Christopher Columbus, to the ... regions of India.

The particular brand of Christianity exported by Spain was characterised by extreme zeal and a frequent use of force. Isabella and Ferdinand had a problem: their military success and the union of their two Kingdoms had left them with a population that was a patchwork of different beliefs and cultures. In order to create a truly stable Kingdom, they had to find a way to unite their people in a shared set of beliefs. The plan was simple: they would ensure that the people of Espana were Catholic, and loyal to the Crown.

Many thousands of Jews and Muslims had been forced to convert, but there remained a suspicion that they had merely claimed to have adopted the 'one true faith' in order to escape death or exile. A rapidly expanding network of spies reported that these supposed converts were in fact carrying out their own religious practices and ceremonies in secret. Additionally, many 'true' Catholics had different interpretations of their faith, including beliefs considered heretical to the hardline court of the new monarchy. To ensure the orthodoxy of Christianity across their Kingdoms, Isabella and Ferdinand ordered a tribunal to be established. The Tribunal of The Holy Office of The Inquisition was to become notorious across the world for its brutality, and its more common name has since become a byword for religious intolerance and cruelty – The Spanish Inquisition.

THE SPANISH INQUISITION: MYTH AND REALITY

Much has been written regarding the barbarity of the Spanish Inquisition, and scholars disagree about how much of it is accurate and how much is exaggeration (it was common, in later years, to seek to demonise the Spanish, and the creation of the so-called 'Black Legend' is discussed later on in this book). Books such as *A Discovery and Plaine Declaration of sundry Subtill Practices of the Holy Inquisition of Spain* by Reginaldus Gonsalvius Montanus, published in 1567, describe the cruelty of the Inquisition in graphic, eye-watering detail. This was almost certainly the work of a Protestant Spaniard, however, and he may well have chosen to embellish the facts in order to suit his own agenda.

That said, there are countless reports (some of them from the Inquisitors themselves) which document the methods that the Inquisition used on a regular basis to extract confessions from the defendants hauled before them. The accused had their hands tied and were hung up for hours, or even days, until, in their agony, they admitted to whatever might best please their tormentors. Often they were strapped to a *potro* (variously described as being like a trestle table or step-ladder, with sharpened 'steps') with ropes that could be tightened so that they sliced into their flesh. Water was forced down their throats until they thought they would drown.

One official report by the secretary of the Inquisition concerns the case of Elvira del Campo, who in 1568 was tried in Toledo for not eating pork. The account shows that it was not enough for Elvira to confess to the crime she was accused of; she had to reveal her true reason for committing the crime in the first place, too. Elvira did not understand that her torturers wanted her to confess to being a Jew, so her torture continued without mercy:

> She was tied on the potro with the cords, she was admonished to tell the truth, and the garrotes were ordered to be tightened. She said 'Senor, do you not see how these people are killing me? Senor, I did it

– for God's sake let me go'. She was told to tell it. She said 'Senor, remind me of what I did not know – Senores, have mercy on me – let me go for God's sake – they have no pity on me – I did it – take me from here and I will remember what I cannot here.' She was told to tell the truth, or the cords would be tightened.... Another turn was ordered on the garrotes ... Then the linen toca was placed (in her throat) and she said 'Take it away, I am strangling and am sick in the stomach.' A jar of water was then poured down, after which she was told to tell the truth.... She was told that the torture would be continued till she told the truth and was admonished to tell it, but though she was questioned repeatedly she remained silent. Then the inquisitor, seeing her exhausted by the torture, ordered it to be suspended.... Four days were allowed to lapse, for experience showed that an interval, by stiffening the limbs, rendered repetition more painful... The interrogatory went on, when her replies under torture were more rambling and incoherent than before, but her limit of endurance was reached and the *inquisitors finally had the satisfaction of eliciting a confession of Judaism and a prayer for mercy and penance.*

There is little doubt, then, that the Spanish Inquisition's reputation for barbarity was well deserved. Nor is there any doubt as to the power the Inquisition had over ordinary citizens in the Spanish territories, or the fear they instilled in people whilst they wielded that power. None could feel truly safe unless they demonstrated absolute devotion to the Catholic faith. Indeed, a 'good Catholic' should not only practice their faith with single-minded determination, but should also inform the Inquisition of any heretical practices indulged in by their friends, family or neighbours. The net result of this was a widespread public religious fervour, and a hysterical mistrust of any behaviour that was considered different, or strange. The Conquistadors who sailed for the New World took this same intolerant attitude with them.

The Spanish Inquisition, it should be pointed out, was an instrument not just of religious control, but of state control. It differed from earlier inquisitions in that, from the very beginning, it was responsible to the Crown, rather than the Pope. Though the priests worked in God's name, Isabella and Ferdinand paid their wages and called the shots. Religion and patriotism rapidly became fused into one and the same thing – only those judged to be truly Catholic could be considered to be truly Spanish. The Inquisition worked to cleanse Spain of those who might pose a threat to her. Though they were priests in name and dress, in practice they were more like the state's secret police force.

Those known to have practiced other religions previously were, inevitably, the first to come under suspicion. Jewish converts were known as *conversos*, Muslim converts as *moriscos*. According to Andalusian priest Andrés Bernáldez in his chronicle *Memorias del reinado de los Reyes Catolicos* (1509), over 700 conversos had been burnt and more than 5,000 punished by the Sevillian Inquisition by 1488. Bernáldez may have been boasting – for like many at that time he clearly approved of the religious and ethnic cleansing of Spain – but what is beyond dispute is that the Inquisition very rapidly held the entire Kingdom in its grip of terror.

Even those Spanish citizens who initially approved of the Inquisition, however, soon came to realise that their fervour had spiralled completely out of control. Driven less by a desire to convert the ungodly than a desire to take the assets from those found guilty of heresy, those it did successfully convert to Catholicism were given no real religious instruction. In the words of Juan Antonio Llorente, who wrote a history of the Spanish Inquisition published in 1817 (widely considered to be more balanced than earlier accounts):

> *The Inquisition maintained and strengthened its hypocrisy, punishing only those who knew no better; but it converted nobody. The Jews and Moors were baptized without proper conversion.*

In 1559 even the Archbishop of Toledo was accused of heresy. The man in question, Bartolomé Carranza, had himself been a zealous Inquisitor just a few years earlier. His real crime was to fall out with a rival. Making enemies in Spain at this time was a dangerous business indeed.

It was from this Spain, then – a Spain hardened to cruelty and swirling with fanatical religious fervour – that Christopher Columbus set sail in 1492. Even today his voyage is celebrated by much of the world as a triumphant example of European exploration. But he also exported to the New World a great deal of what was worst about the Old World, murdering and enslaving all those with different gods to that of Spain. It was in his bloody footsteps that the Conquistadors would soon follow.

COLUMBUS AND THE NEW WORLD

The greatest event since the creation of the world (excluding the incarnation of Him who created it) is the discovery of the Indies.

Francisco López de Gómara, 1552

Christopher Columbus was a man with an obsession. Like so many who claim to be guided by the voice of God, his deep-seated convictions drove him to undertake extraordinary adventures that ultimately changed the course of history. And, ironically, proved all his fervent beliefs to have been entirely wrong.

In 1492 Columbus set sail in search of a Western passage from Europe to Asia, convinced in his own mind that the two continents were separated only by an easily navigable open ocean. He landed first in the Bahamas, and then in Cuba, which he took to be part of the Asian mainland. After stopping off in the Dominican Republic and Haiti (named 'Hispaniola' by the Spanish) he returned with a small amount of gold and a previously unknown plant that would later go by the name of 'tobacco'. Further voyages followed, which took him across the Caribbean to Central America and Panama, but whenever Columbus thought he might be within a day or two of the Ganges River, his hopes were dashed.

Spanish settlers in Hispaniola treated the natives there

so badly that they revolted, and the settlers themselves threatened insurrection at the lack of the riches they found in these new lands. Columbus got the blame, was stripped of his position as Governor and returned to Spain in chains.

This, perhaps, gives us the first clue that whilst these events are often described as 'the *discovery* of the New World' by Europeans, we might better describe these voyages as the first *encounters* between two separate worlds. The lands in question were far from uninhabited spaces; quite the opposite, indigenous cultures had flourished there for thousands of years. It was an encounter which would prove disastrous for huge numbers people and for many of the European discoverers too. Almost as soon as the first encounters took place, attempts at conquest followed.

> *As soon as I reached that sea, I seized by force several Indians on the first island, in order that they might learn from us, and in like manner tell us about those things in these lands of which they*

themselves had knowledge; and the plan succeeded, for in a short time we understood them and they us, sometimes by gestures and signs, sometimes by words; and it was a great advantage to us. They are coming with me now, yet always believing that I descended from heaven, although they have been living with us for a long time, and are living with us to-day. And these men were the first who announced it wherever we landed, continually proclaiming to the others in a loud voice, 'Come, come, and you will see the celestial people.' Whereupon both women and men, both young men and old men, laying aside the fear caused a little before, visited us eagerly, filling the road with a great crowd, some bringing food, and some drink, with great love and extraordinary goodwill.

Christopher Columbus' First Letter.

By 1511, Spanish slave traders had occupied Puerto Rico, Jamaica and Cuba. With this foothold established, the Spanish pushed further West and South. Other voyages along the coast of South America proved that there were further new lands, with potentially greater riches, for the Spanish to explore and conquer. A vast new ocean – the Pacific – beckoned them towards fabled worlds of infinite riches and infinite youth.

The Portuguese explorer Magellan, sailing under a Spanish flag, became the first to circumnavigate the world in 1522, finally finding the route from Europe to Asia that Columbus sought thirty years earlier. It was far too long a journey to form a viable trade route, but for the first time in history humankind had successfully explored the very furthest limits of the world's surface. All that remained afterwards, it seemed, was to fill in the gaps on the map. It is hard to imagine a more exhilarating time for men of adventure who yearned to travel in search of wealth and glory. The air in Spain was thick with tales of extraordinary new sights, sounds, people and places. Above all, the air was thick with tales of the staggering riches that lay waiting, like low fruit, to be taken back to Spain:

> *I promise this, that if I am supported by our most invincible sovereigns with a little of their help, as*

much gold can be supplied as they will need, indeed as much of spices, of cotton, of mastic gum.... also as much of aloes wood, and as many slaves for the navy, as their Majesties will wish to demand.

Christopher Columbus' First Letter.

It was a time of seemingly infinite possibility, for those brave enough to grab their opportunity. But Magellan's astonishing voyage also contained within it the clearest possible warning for those who set out in search of adventure. Of the two hundred and thirty-seven men who ventured forth with him, only eighteen returned alive. Magellan himself was not one of them. He was hacked to death by native warriors on an island in the Philippines. It was a battle that Magellan did not need to fight. He did so as a favour to a local chief who had recently converted to Christianity. Magellan refused all offers of help in the battle, preferring to use inexperienced volunteers from his own crew. He believed that God was on his side, and that his artillery would more than compensate for the fact that he was vastly outnumbered.

The received wisdom at the time was that the indigenous inhabitants of the New World were not only ill-equipped for war, but also too cowardly to threaten the invaders:

> *All these people lack, as I said above, every kind of iron; they are also without weapons, which indeed are unknown; nor are they competent to use them, not on account of deformity of body, for they are well formed, but because they are timid and full of fear. They carry for weapons, however, reeds baked in the sun, on the lower ends of which they fasten some shafts of dried wood rubbed down to a point; and indeed they do not venture to use these always; for it frequently happened when I sent two or three of my men to some of the villages, that they might speak with the natives, a compact troop of the Indians would march out, and as soon as they saw our men approaching, they would quickly take flight, children being pushed aside by their fathers, and fathers by their children. And this was not because any hurt or injury had been inflicted on any one of them, for to*

every one whom I visited and with whom I was able to converse, I distributed whatever I had, cloth and many other things, no return being made to me; but they are by nature fearful and timid.

Christopher Columbus' First Letter.

The battle proved conclusively that this view was wrong. The native chief had superior knowledge of the battle ground, and used that knowledge to his advantage. The battle proved to be a disaster for Magellan, with his warships rendered useless after beaching themselves on a reef. Later when pleas were made for the return of Magellan's body, not a single piece of it could be found.

The first of those brave soldiers sailing from Spain, the earliest of the men who called themselves Conquistadors, did not know of Magellan's fate. But they must surely have known that they were risking everything in their search for fame and gold, and that they might never live to see their homeland again. Many would find, as Magellan had before them, that their god would not protect them from the murderous fury of the people they sought to conquer. It is to those people that we must now turn our attention.

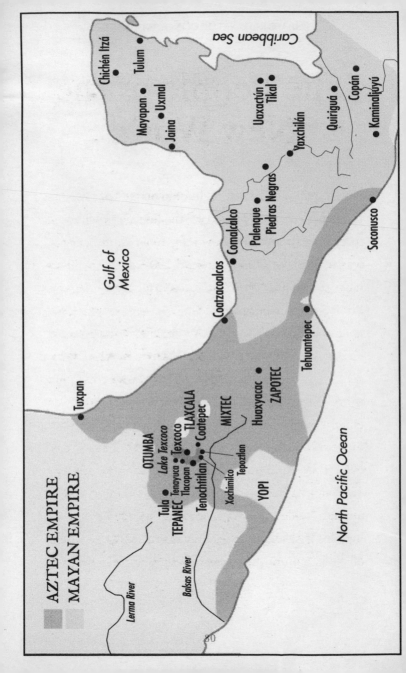

The People of the New World

Although it is believed that human beings have lived in the Americas since 35,000 BC, the first true civilisation to emerge in what we now refer to as Latin America was that of the Olmec, around 1500 BC. Excavations have shown that their largest centre, La Venta, was built on a small island a few feet above sea level, near the Gulf of Mexico. It was a skilfully planned city, with great mud and stone temples sitting in large plazas, suggesting that open-air religious ceremonies were commonplace. The Olmecs worshipped an enigmatic jaguar god, which they appear to have made offerings and sacrifices to. Absent from Olmec culture, in common with all other prehistoric cultures of Latin America, were the wheel, domesticated animals (aside from dogs), and any widespread use of metal. These absences severely restricted the evolution of their culture, but nonetheless it is clear that for their time they were a highly organised and culturally sophisticated people. Their settlements were to prove the blueprint for all future Mesoamerican cities.

One of the most famous such cities was Teotihuacan, which was mysteriously abandoned around AD 650. It is thought to have taken several centuries to build, and to have once been home to some fifty thousand inhabitants. Many of the gods worshipped at Teotihuacan would have been familiar to the natives that the Conquistadors encountered some one thousand years later. One in particular, the feathered serpent god Quetzalcoatl, would prove pivotal in the story that was later to unfold. It is not known what disaster befell the people of Teotihuacan, or the other great Mesoamerican cultures of the period, who, similarly, vanished. But their sudden dramatic decline ultimately allowed the rise of the mighty empires – the Aztecs and the Inca.

THE RISE OF THE AZTECS

We may never truly know the truth about the origins

of the Aztecs, as all of their sacred historical texts were burnt in the year 1430. This was done not by their enemies, but on the orders of their then ruler, Itzcoatl (though some sources say it was his nephew, Tlacaelel). In effect, he created a new set of myths for his people, one that suited a tribe of growing importance in the region. Itzcoatl never lived to see his people take full control of Mexico, but by the time the Spanish arrived the Aztecs, ruled over by Montezuma II, were the undisputed superpower in the region.

Claiming descent from the earlier Toltec civilisation (which itself claimed descent from the Teotihuacans) they built their capital city, Tenochtitlan, fifty miles south of the ancient Toltec capital, Tula. When the Conquistadors first laid sight on the Aztec capital, it so astonished them that many wondered if they were dreaming. And yet it was built by a band of natives who just a few generations earlier were considered by most to be the lowest of the low. For the Aztecs (or 'Mexicas', more accurately, at this early time) had been serfs, so brutally abused by their masters that they chose to leave their homeland in the north in search of pastures new. Even after they arrived in central Mexico, they continued to pay a monetary tribute to the Tepanec tribe who owned their new land.

The 'pilgrimage' that the Aztecs embarked upon was arduous and long, and their myths speak of great hardship during the many years that they roamed. They were searching for a 'promised land' where they would be wealthy and free – the land of their ancestors, the Toltecs, who they knew had once been a mighty force in the region. The Aztec language, Nahuatl, was derived from that of the Toltecs, and their myths told that one day they would rule Mexico as their ancestors had hundreds of years previously. Indeed they believed that just as they had once themselves been serfs to cruel masters, so in turn they would subjugate the people of the new lands and become masters of them. This was their destiny, foretold to them by their high priest (and later deity) Huitzilopochtli. The Toltecs had been led by the high priest Quetzalcoatl, named after the feathered serpent god worshipped by the Teotihuacans. It was from Quetzalcoatl himself that the Aztec nobility claimed direct descent.

Sometime around 1426, war broke out between the Aztecs and the Tepanecs of Azcapotzalco to whom they paid tribute. It appears that most of the Aztec people needed a great deal of persuading to wage war, with *macehualtin* (the commoners) preferring to opt for peace. The Aztec *pipiltin* (nobility) struck a bargain which stated that if the Aztecs lost the war then the nobility would obey the commoners for the rest of time, but if the Aztecs won the war then the commoners would serve the nobility. When the war with the Tepanecs was duly won, this deal became the backbone of the Aztec social structure. It meant the many served the few, and partly explains why rulers such as Montezuma were able to acquire such staggering wealth and prestige.

In order to defeat the Tepanecs, the Aztec leader Itzcoatl allied himself with Nezahualcoyotl, the exiled leader of the city state of Texcoco. This was the beginning of the 'Triple Alliance' that became the foundation of the culture we describe as 'Aztec'. The alliance brought together the Mexica of Tenochtitlan, the Acolhua of Texcoco and the Tepanec of Tlacopan. The senior partners in the alliance were the Mexica, and the centre of power was their capital, Tenochtitlan.

Under their legendary leader Itzcoatl, the new triple alliance of the Aztecs went from strength to strength. With the nobility having such a firm grip on the populace, huge amounts of resources could be thrown into building up the strength of the Aztec military machine. The Aztecs fought ferociously, believing victory in every battle was assured them by their gods. They took huge numbers of their enemies prisoner, and sacrificed them to ensure further victories. By the time Montezuma I began his reign (around 1440) Aztec rulers themselves had a semi-divine status, and by the end of his reign (around 1469) many neighbouring territories were already under Aztec rule or subjugation.

Although a sophisticated civilisation, the Aztecs ruled through fear, and at times with ruthless barbarity.

Many of the people they subjugated hated them for engaging in human sacrifice, and for the disrespect that they showed to their wives and daughters, who were often abducted and raped. This hatred would later be fully exploited by the Conquistadors. One rivalry would prove particularly significant − the rivalry between the Aztecs and their near-neighbours, the Tlaxcalans.

THE TLAXCALANS AND THE FLOWER WARS

The Tlaxcalans were never entirely conquered by the Aztecs, but they were dominated by the sense of menace that they generated and lived in fear of all out war and, potentially, complete subjugation. To avoid such a disastrous war, the two cultures appear to have agreed to fight in so-called 'Flower Wars', which were ritual pitched battles in which each side attempted to take prisoners rather than kill the enemy.

The tradition of the Aztec flower war began with

Tlacaelel, the emperor of the Aztec empire at that time. He decided to rewrite the history of the Aztecs, burning old history papers and emphasising that his people were the 'chosen ones' as decided by the gods. Even before the start of the flower wars, the Aztecs were already a warrior people with powerful religious beliefs. Their god of war was Huitzilopochtli and Tlacaelel made his people swear allegiance to this powerful deity. In addition, the Aztecs had to keep their god appeased by making up offerings of blood. Although the Aztecs occasionally provided their own blood, they preferred the blood of others which meant they were in a constant state of warfare and, as a race, were extremely feared.

To the East of the Aztec empire was the city of Tlaxcala. The Tlaxcalans were also a powerful people who shared their culture and language with the Aztecs. They made an arrangement with the Aztecs that any captured prisoners would be taken to a temple and sacrificed to Huitzilopochtli. Perhaps what is most shocking about these sacrifices, is that the person who was being offered to the god most often went of their own freewill, believing that they were about to enter the most glorious afterlife.

However, the theory behind the Aztec flower wars had its weaknesses and eventually backfired. As more and more people were being offered as sacrifices, so the strength of both cultures was considerably weakened. When the Spanish eventually arrived from across the sea, it was the people of Tlaxcala that would join them against the Aztec empire, bringing an end to the flower wars.

THE RISE OF THE INCA

From earliest times, South America has always been a patchwork of cultures and peoples. The area around the Andes has been particularly prized and has seen many great cultures rise and fall, one of the earliest of which was the Moche culture (AD 100 – AD 800). Named after the Muchik language spoken in ancient times on the north coast of present-day Peru, the Moche built the vast twin *Huacas del Sol y de la Luna* – temples of the sun and the moon. Looting carried out by the

Spanish in the seventeenth and eighteenth centuries (with full permission of the crown) severely damaged these structures, with Huaca del Sol especially badly affected, but the remains still offer a glimpse into the world of this mysterious ancient people.

Huaca de la Luna is a mud-brick structure measuring some 290 meters (951 ft) from north to south and 210 meters (689 ft) from east to west. Excavations have revealed it underwent at least six construction phases spanning a staggering six hundred years. The recurring image of the same god (the fearsome Winged Decapitator, to whom human sacrifices were dedicated) in the murals and the reliefs at the site points to the continuity of the cult over time. The Moche built miles of irrigation canals, making the coastal valleys they controlled fertile enough to support a vast population that thrived on bountiful harvests of maize, squash and beans. Although little is known about the Moche, we can be reasonably certain that they were a well organised and sophisticated culture – and one of the first such major cultures to emerge in

Peru. At its zenith the Moche sphere extended from Piura in the north to Huarmey in the south. Sometime around AD 800, however, the culture was wiped from the face of the earth. It has been speculated that this sudden decline was due to foreign invasion – perhaps by the Wari people – but it may equally have been due to a loss of prestige by the Moche elite, after some form of natural disaster, resulting in internal social unrest. Whatever the reason, later Moche settlements are characterised by fortifications and defensive works. The civilisation fell, leaving behind fertile lands that would inevitably become the scene of conflict as new waves of settlers fought for control of a prime piece of real estate.

THE WARI (HUARI)

The next significant culture to dominate the area was the Wari culture (named 'Huari' by the Spanish), who emerged around AD 500. Whether the Wari used military might or negotiation and trade to take over the lands is still debated – some conflict is almost certain, but the Wari seem to have been masters of agriculture and social organisation above all else. They created new fields using 'terraced field' technology, and built a network of roads in the region. These would both be used to great effect by later cultures, including the Inca.

The Wari culture began to decline almost as soon as it reached its peak of influence, however, and by AD 1000 their main settlements were suddenly and catastrophically depopulated. Since they made no written records, we cannot be sure what happened. Archaeological research has revealed evidence of high levels of violence during the final period of Wari control, however, so it has been posited that warfare between different Wari factions may have led to the collapse of the state apparatus.

CUZCO AND THE EARLY INCA

The Killke culture built much of Cuzco, later to become the capital of the mighty Inca empire. It is thought that the Inca culture evolved from a tribe within the Killke culture, and for archaeologists the Killke period is largely synonymous with 'early Inca' (AD 900 – AD 1200). We know very little about this period, for neither the Killke nor the Inca left any writings behind, and many Killke settlements were reused and expanded upon by the later Inca.

According to Inca legend, Cuzco was founded by their first Sapa Inca (or 'paramount leader'), Manco Cápac, who was told to build a settlement there in honour of his father, the sun god Inti. The Inca's main rivals at the time, the Chankas, later launched a massive attack on Cuzco with some forty thousand warriors, causing the elderly Sapa Inca Viracocha to flee into the mountains. His successor, Sapa Inca Pachacuti, made alliances with other local tribes and raised an army to retake Cuzco, eventually defeating the Chankas in an epic battle which left thousands slaughtered on both sides.

The retaking of Cuzco marked the birth of a new age for the Inca. Their sphere of influence grew rapidly, until, through a mixture of diplomacy and warfare, the Tawantinsuyu (or The Four United

Provinces) of the Inca empire was established. Cuzco became a major urban settlement, the administrative and religious headquarters of a new South American superpower. Some 20,000 km (12,427 miles) of roads connected it with the rest of the Kingdom. Unlike the Aztec capital Tenochtitlan, nobody thought to map the great city of Cuzco, and so we can only speculate on the scale and grandeur of the Inca power base during its glory years.

The Inca appear to have generally preferred persuasion to brute force when colonising their neighbours. Inca nobles would send messages and gifts to those they wished to assimilate into the empire, in an attempt to convince them that with Inca patronage they would be wealthier and better protected. No doubt there was a veiled threat behind these offerings, however, and we might reasonably assume that many cultures were intimidated into subjugation rather than truly embracing Inca rule. On the other hand, chronicles of the pre-Inca period suggest that it was a time of constant warfare, and thus smaller communities may well have welcomed the relative safety and stability that Inca rule afforded them. In the years before the Inca rose to power, chronicler Felipe Guaman Poma de Ayala relates that:

> ... the towns were depopulated... fearing war, they had to leave the good places mentioned.... They were forced to move from their towns to the higher places and now lived on peaks and precipices of the high mountains. To defend themselves, they had to build fortresses... ramparts and walls; the houses and hidden places were inside... They fought each other to death ... they took captives, even women and children. They took each other's lands and irrigation ditches and pastures....

Once the Inca had taken control of a province, they kept the nominal leader of that province on a very tight leash. One eyewitness from Chupaychu relates that:

> ... if some ethnic lord wanted to rise and rebel, they killed him and all his lineage so not one was left.

*When the Inkas were still alive, this witness was
young and saw some of it and the rest he has heard
from his elders and other old men who talked of it.*

The Inca's 'diplomacy backed by menace' approach
worked, and worked well. From 1438 to 1533, the Inca
expanded their territory to incorporate a large portion
of western South America, including large parts of
modern Ecuador, Peru, western and south central
Bolivia, northwest Argentina, north and north-central
Chile and southern Colombia. Some 4,000 km (2,485
miles) of new land was acquired in less than a century.
It was a vast empire, and it made the Inca leaders
wealthy and powerful. The one sizeable tribe that
chose to oppose the Inca, the Chimu (descendants of
the powerful Moche people) were soon crushed by the
invincible Inca army. Just as the Aztecs had risen to a
position of seemingly impregnable power in Mexico, so
the Inca had a similar vice-like grip on Peru. They were
the two undisputed superpowers of the New World.

The Aztecs and Inca were enjoying a meteoric rise at

the time of the arrival of the Conquistadors. But one other mighty ancient empire of the New World was spiralling just as rapidly into a terminal decline: the Maya.

THE RISE AND FALL OF THE MAYA

We found a large number of books.... and, as they contained nothing in which were not to be seen as superstition and lies of the devil, we burned them all, which they regretted to an amazing degree, and which caused them much affliction.

Bishop Diego de Landa

Had de Landa's Spanish Inquisition not burnt many of the Maya's codices and cult images (some twenty thousand in total, it is believed) we would know a great deal more about an ancient civilisation that, at its height, was one of the most advanced on earth. For uniquely amongst these early empires of the Americas, the Maya recorded their history in writing. As it is, the ceremonial burning of Mayan texts on 12 July 1562, has robbed us of the vast majority of the Maya's words, and we must rely on archaeological evidence and the accounts of the conquering Europeans to piece together their story.

One of the numerous great ironies in the tale of the Spanish conquest is that we must look to the man who ordered the destruction of the Maya's own historical documents, Diego de Landa, for many of our main insights into the Mayan culture. His work *Relacion de las Cosas de Yucatán* contains numerous eye-witness accounts which – he claims – came directly from the mouths of the Maya informants he interviewed. It is a chronicle undoubtedly coloured by de Landa's own prejudices, but when taken together with the Maya 'stelae' (stone markers bearing hieroglyphic texts) and the few surviving codices (just four, one of which may not be authentic) we can at least begin to assemble the key events in the history of this extraordinary civilisation.

The longevity of the Maya is nothing short of astounding: the culture is thought to have emerged around 1000 BC and continued until the arrival of the

lowlands of the Yucatán, in particular, remained as thriving centres of trade. The great walled city of Mayapan became the capital of the empire around 1220, and appears to have exerted control until around 1450. It may be from this city that the Maya got their name (the term 'Maya' only became popular in the nineteenth Century). A local nobleman became incensed at living under the rule of the Cocom family, who had held ultimate power in Mayapan for almost two hundred years. He launched a savage attack on the Cocoms, resulting in the death of the entire family and the total destruction of the city they ruled from. After the revolt, the lands occupied by the Maya degenerated into relatively small city-states that competed against one another for resources and influence. It was this patchwork of smaller tribal lands that the Conquistadors encountered in 1533.

Ironically, the fractured and incoherent nature of the Maya culture, and the lack of a strong central control structure, made it far more difficult for the Spanish Conquistadors to conquer the Maya territories. It would not be a short deadly campaign, as with the campaigns against the Aztecs and the Inca. Instead, the Conquistadors would have to fight a long bloody war of attrition against perhaps the most determined and resilient of all the American peoples. It would take them one hundred and seventy years to subdue the Maya, and they would pay dearly for their victory.

Warfare:
Steel versus Stone

Both the Spanish invaders from the Old World and the native defenders of the New World were well used to the blood and tears of war. The Spanish had learned not only from their campaign against the Moors, but also from war with France, which began in 1495 and rumbled on until a peace accord was signed in 1515. This peace would only last until 1521, but the cessation in hostilities was long enough for trained Spanish soldiers to start looking for fresh adventures in the lands newly discovered by Columbus. By this time the Spanish had enjoyed two decades of almost unbroken military success, and so the Conquistadors were confident of their own invincibility.

The Aztecs and Inca had enjoyed similarly spectacular military success. Their empires had suffered few serious setbacks and their armies were better trained and organised than any previously seen in the Americas. They conquered their neighbours more or less at will. The Maya were admittedly already in decline, but their warriors were hardened by battle too – often battles fought amongst themselves. What the South Americans had in common was a lack of metalworking skills, and domesticated animals. These deficiencies would prove fatal in the epic struggle for control of the New World.

SPANISH STEEL

The messengers said... 'Their trappings and arms are all made of iron. They dress in iron and wear iron casques on their heads. Their swords are iron; their bows are iron; their shields are iron; their spears are iron. Their deer carry them on their backs wherever they wish to go. These deer, our Lord, are as tall as the roof of a house.'

From the Aztec *Codex Florentino*

The 'deer' that inspired such awe in the Aztecs were, in fact, battles horses; and the 'iron' was Toledo steel. Both were entirely new to the native people, and both were used by the Spanish to lethal effect. The swordsmen of Spain were, at this time, the most feared in Europe, having honed their skills against the Moors and the French. Their blades were fashioned in Toledo and made to the most exacting standards. Each sword was tested by being bent into a semi-circle, and struck with full force against a steel helmet, before being declared fit for service. The Toledo craftsmen produced swords that were famed across Europe for being strong, flexible, light, and razor sharp.

The straight Spanish sword was about a metre long and double edged, with a sharp point, allowing the swordsman to slash and thrust at the body of his enemy. The blade ended with an S-shaped crossguard designed to both protect the user's hand and help him trap an opponent's weapon. This was paired with an iron shield or 'buckler' which protected the swordsman from attack without impinging on his ability to wield his own weapon. Shields made from hide were also popular with the Spanish, being strong enough to deflect the arrows and obsidian blades of the native armies whilst also being light and easy to manoeuvre.

All Conquistadors were required to provide their own weapons and some form of basic armour. Captains and wealthier nobles might have three-quarter armour, consisting of a closed helmet, *cuirass* (breastplate), arm defences and leg defences that ended at the knees. Those of lesser means made do with a helmet and some form of leather or cotton armour. In time, however, the Spanish began to favour the native-style quilted cotton armour, which was far more comfortable to wear in the humid climate of the New World, yet still afforded protection against the majority of native weapons. One report states that a Spanish Captain emerged from an especially savage battle with some two hundred arrows lodged in his cotton armour. Even if this is an exaggeration, it is clear from the Conquistadors' reports that the native armour was extremely effective against stone and wood. It was next to useless against the Toledo blades of the Spanish, however, or the lances carried by the most terrifying of the Conquistador forces – the cavalry.

SPANISH CAVALRY

The peoples of the New World had never encountered horses prior to the arrival of the Conquistadors. The sight of the Spanish cavalry terrified them. Initially it is reported that they did not know whether the man and the horse he rode were two separate entities or one. The Spanish recognised at once the effect the horses had upon the natives, and they exploited their fear at every available opportunity. The terror the horses inspired comes through in every Aztec account of the strange new creatures ('stags' or 'deer') that faced them:

> *The stags came forward, carrying the soldiers on their backs.... These animals wore little bells, they are adorned with many little bells. When the stags gallop, the bells make a loud clamour, ringing and reverberating. These stags snort and bellow. They sweat a very great*

deal, the sweat pours from their bodies in streams. The foam from their muzzles drips onto the ground... They make a loud noise when they run; they make a great din, as if stones were raining on the earth. Then the ground is pitted and scarred where they set down their hooves. It opens wherever their hooves touch it.

Spanish horses were prized throughout Europe for their strength, stamina and agility. Cavalry had been used extensively by both sides in the battles between the Spanish and the Moors, and the Spanish cavalry had adopted many of the tactics of the Moors to create a highly mobile and manoeuvrable fighting unit. Men on horseback had several significant advantages when facing the armies of the New World, who had no strategy for dealing with such an attack. Although in time the Aztec and Inca would evolve such strategies, nonetheless the horse remained a potent weapon through the campaign in the Americas.

Striking downwards allowed a man on horseback to gain extra force with every blow. Lances were aimed at the faces of native warriors as the cavalry thundered into their ranks. It was difficult for an enemy on foot to reach upwards to strike back at his assailant. Those not decapitated by lances or slashed in two by swords were liable to be crushed beneath the hooves of galloping beasts. In addition, the horse could transport a fighter around the battlefield at much greater speeds than a man on foot. The Spanish charges caused chaos amongst the ranks of the native armies. Horses could be used to launch surprise attacks across long distances. Men carried on horseback arrived at the battlefield relatively fresh compared to those who had been forced to march long distances across difficult terrain. All of these advantages, combined with the sheer terror of being faced with an unfamiliar, almost supernatural-looking beast, led the natives to fear the horse above any other Spanish weapon.

It was not the only deadly new force they would face, however. The Spanish also deployed another weapon entirely alien and terrifying for the people of the New World – the cannon.

SPANISH GUNPOWDER

Montezuma was astonished and terrified... to learn how the cannon roared, how its noise resounded, how it caused one to faint and grow deaf. The messengers told him 'A thing like a ball of stone comes out of its entrails: it comes out shooting sparks and raining fire. The smoke that comes out with it has a pestilent odour, like that of rotten mud. This odour penetrates even to the brain, and causes the greatest discomfort. If the cannon is aimed against a tree, it shatters the tree into splinters. This is a most unnatural sight, as if the tree had exploded from within'.

Aztec *Codex Florentino*

The messengers who brought this report to Montezuma had been systematically terrorised by Cortés; they brought the Aztec leader exactly the message that the Spanish Captain had wanted to send. Cortés had arranged for the cannon to be suddenly fired right next to the messengers, knowing that the shock of it would maximize their fear. The cannon, of course, would later do great damage to the tight formations of the Aztec army, slaughtering dozens with every blast. It is easy, however, to over-estimate its effectiveness in the campaign in the Americas. It gave the Spanish an advantage, but that advantage was not by itself, decisive.

The cannons, along with the early muskets that the Spanish brought, relied on gunpowder to wreak their havoc. In the humid climate of the Americas, this powder was prone to become damp and difficult to light. Powder was in short supply, and Cortés was often desperate for more. The cannons themselves had to be dragged across difficult terrain, slowing down the Spanish advance. The early muskets (*arquebuses*) were long and unwieldy and needed to be fired with a lighted match, itself lit from a flint and tinder, which could not be kept lit for long periods of time. There was often the danger that the arquebusiers would be overwhelmed before they could light their matches.

The crossbow, too, was only of limited use to the Spanish. It could fire at superior velocity when compared to the native bows, but that extra power was designed to penetrate metal armour on European battlefields. It was overkill when facing an army clad only in padded cotton armour. A crossbow bolt would certainly kill with a single shot any native that it hit, unlike a standard bow, but it took much longer to reload, and was prone to malfunctions. Of much greater use would have been a crossbow with less power but greater reliability. We know from several Conquistador accounts that many crossbows and arquebuses were no longer serviceable after several weeks in the field.

The Spanish, then, had superior weaponry, but it was fallible – and they were at a massive numerical disadvantage, had limited supplies, and were unfamiliar with the terrain. Their ultimate victory was by no means a foregone conclusion. They were able to triumph in part because of the fear their unfamiliar weapons instilled in the natives, and in part because of the manner in which the native people chose to fight. The New World's stone could have triumphed over the Old World's steel had they fought in a manner that minimised the advantages the Spanish possessed due to their superior technology. Instead, the natives fought in the way that had served them so well in the past. And though they ultimately succumbed to the invaders, they inflicted heavy losses on the Spanish, and came close to annihilating them on more than one occasion. The accounts that the Conquistadors left behind show that the Aztec and Inca armies were just as terrifying a sight to the Spanish as the Spanish troops were to the New World armies.

NEW WORLD STONE

The Indians wore armour made of cotton which reached down to their knees. They carried lances and shields, bows and arrows, slings, and many stones; and after the arrow-flights, with their feathered crests waving, they attacked us hand to hand. Wielding their lances in both hands, they did us great damage.

Wars were common in the New World, and indeed for the Aztecs warfare was more or less a necessity, for their gods required a steady supply of sacrifices. Most battles were relatively small scale affairs, however, and even the mighty Aztecs and Inca did not have large full-time standing armies. They relied on a class of seasoned warriors to fight their day to day battles – a full scale war involved mobilising a reservist army of peasant farmers who had only rudimentary training. Battles were generally fought in the open, with two armies facing one another en masse. Capturing enemy soldiers rather than killing them was often the chief objective, particularly for the Aztecs. Only the Maya relied extensively on guerrilla warfare – and their tactics proved remarkably successful against the Spanish for a long period.

Different clans from the Aztec empire formed themselves into fighting units called *calpulli*, which were then organised into divisions, commanded by blood relatives of the emperor. Mexican chronicles speak of armies of up to two hundred thousand warriors lying under the supreme command of Tenochtitlan, but many believe this to be an exaggeration, and armies of twenty thousand or so were certainly far more common. The Inca formed units of warriors based around a decimal system – from a squad of ten soldiers up to a 'corps' of ten thousand. Again, overall control of battles was assumed by a commander who was related to the 'Sapa Inca' (Supreme Inca). Things were slightly less formal in the patchwork lands of the Maya, but the essence of the military structure remained the same: a relatively small number of highly trained warriors, with a supporting multitude of armed peasants.

Aztec and Inca armour generally consisted of a tight-fitting quilted cotton suit which came down to the knees. Soaked in brine to toughen it, the armour was capable of protecting the wearer against many arrow-strikes. It was of almost no use against the Spanish crossbow bolts, arquebuses or cannon, however, and was no match either for thrusts or slashes from the razor sharp Spanish swords. Shields made of wood and hide were also carried by each warrior, with larger shields that could protect a man from head to foot being deployed by the Aztecs when under bombardment. Some Inca warriors wore helmets made from platted wood.

Captains and those of the higher warrior classes dressed more elaborately, carrying banners in wickerwork harnesses that were strapped to their backs. The Spanish describe the Aztec and Inca armies as a riot of colour, with feathers and jewels being used to distinguish men of rank from commoners. The elite Aztec 'Jaguar Knights' wore jaguar skins on their bodies, with their faces protruding from the open jaws of the dead beast; certain elite Mayan warriors wore similar garb. Trumpets, drums and whistles signalled the start of any attack, and the Conquistadors describe the sound as truly terrifying – the native armies were masters at intimidating their enemies.

It is worth noting that the Aztecs did not launch surprise attacks on their enemies; to do so would not have been considered chivalrous. They sent special cloaks and shields to the leaders of their enemies to inform them in advance that they would shortly be attacked. They expected their enemies to observe similar rituals, and were astonished when the Spanish armies attacked them without warning – 'before the bell', as it were. The Aztecs generally began their offensives with a hail of missiles from their bows, javelins and slings. The bows were around 1.5 metres (4–5 ft) in length and fired arrows tipped with obsidian or fire-hardened wood. Javelins and darts, both tipped with obsidian (a type of volcanic glass), were thrown with *atl-atls*; short staffs that could launch a missile at greater velocity and over greater distances than if it were simply thrown by hand. Some javelins were double-headed and were used in hand to hand fighting as well as being thrown.

The Inca tended to favour shorter bows, and spears with copper or bone points. The vast area of the Inca empire provided different units with different skills, depending on their local conditions. For example, the archers tended to come from the jungle forest areas where the springy wood for the bows could be found.

The Maya used *atl-atls* too, and also wielded a type of trident made from sharpened shells. They favoured bone and obsidian for their blades and arrow heads. Many of the Mayan weapons were almost identical to the weapons used by the Aztecs, but they had less highly-trained warriors at their disposal and a much higher percentage of the fighters were farmers first and foremost. The humble sling was a surprisingly effective weapon against the Conquistadors, as the stones it hurled could stun a soldier even if he was wearing a helmet. Once incapacitated, the unfortunate victim was dragged off to have his heart cut out, or simply hacked to ribbons where he fell. Rocks the size of chicken's eggs rained down on the Spanish army, thrown with great venom and accuracy by warriors specialising in sling warfare. In some cases women joined their menfolk in firing stones at the invaders – and were reported to be just as accurate. Rocks provided an almost limitless supply of ammunition, and the wooden and stone arrows and javelins could also be manufactured in great numbers.

The Inca used a weapon which consisted of two or three stone balls tied together with cord – the *bolas*. Thrown accurately enough, they could entangle themselves around the legs of a horse and bring it to the ground, and thus the weapon proved especially useful against the Spanish cavalry. Slings were also used to great effect, with the Inca hurling flaming hot stones covered in burning bitumen at the Spanish during the siege of Cuzco – a type of early napalm.

Lances tipped with sharp flakes of obsidian were used in hand-to-hand combat and had the advantage of keeping the Aztec warriors out of range of the deadly Spanish swords. For closer combat, the Aztecs used two different types of swords or clubs, the 'maquahuitl' and the 'macana'. The maquahuitl was a wooden sword about 1 metre long (3 ft) which had blades of obsidian embedded throughout its length. The razor sharp obsidian could slice through cotton armour – indeed when freshly knapped, obsidian could be sharper even than the Toledo steel of the Spanish swords. It did not hold its edge for long, however, which is why, in a prolonged battle, the Conquistadors had a significant advantage.

The macana was a wooden club with a thick round end. Even soldiers wearing plate armour and helmets were not immune to its effects. Many had their skulls fractured, or were knocked unconscious. In order to wield the weapon, however, the Aztec warrior had to leave himself open to attack by a thrust from a sword. Hundreds were sliced through before they could reach the enemy, and many others lost arms and hands immediately after delivering their attack.

Very similar weapons were used by the Inca warriors, although they favoured bronze cutting edges for their swords. They also wielded short hand axes called *champis*. Though the weapons were undoubtedly lethal in the right conditions, they had the same fundamental drawbacks as the other New World weapons mentioned above: they simply were not designed to take on a modern European army.

Battles in the New World tended to end when the

opposing captain was taken prisoner or killed, or the temple of one tribe was overwhelmed and burnt to the ground. No glory was associated with killing, but rather with capturing opponents. An enemy that had been routed was not pursued – once one side ran away, the battle was considered over. Though the fighting was fierce, there were relatively few fatalities when compared to European battles. The Spanish aimed to inflict as many casualties as possible on their opponents, and in time the New World armies were forced to adjust to account for this. In time, they may have adapted further, and perhaps their numerical supremacy would have led to the defeat of the Spanish. But the Conquistadors moved through the empires of the New World with astonishing speed, and simply did not give the natives the time they needed to work out how to defeat the utterly unfamiliar enemy they faced.

Early Contact

FRANCISCO HERNÁNDEZ DE CÓRDOBA

The Spanish experience of colonising Hispaniola and the other nearby islands had proved largely disappointing. Those that had settled in the new lands had found life there to be hard, and many were anxious either to return home or seek newer, more profitable lands. Although the coast of Brazil had already been sighted by 1500, the Spanish still believed that the lands they had found were islands. It was only after a voyage by Juan Ponce de León in 1513 that it became clear that a large landmass lay between themselves and Asia. In the same year Vasco Núñez de Balboa sighted the Pacific Ocean, after cutting through the tropical forests of Panama. Even then, there was still nothing to lead the Spanish to believe that these lands were inhabited by anything other than scattered primitive tribes. All of that was to change when the Spanish captain Francisco Hernández de Córdoba sailed from Cuba in 1517 and encountered for the first time the nation of Mexico, and her people. Aside from a handful of shipwrecked sailors who had been washed up in Mayan territory, it was the first time any European had come face-to-face with the people of the Americas.

Things went fine. At first. Ten large canoes full of Mayan Indians paddled out to meet Córdoba's ships. They were welcomed aboard, and the two cultures exchanged beads and clothes in a mutually friendly fashion. Córdoba was invited ashore with cries of *cones catoche* or 'come to our houses', and so the Spaniards named the area Cape Catoche. Clearly able to make out the Mayan pyramids dotted along the coastline, the Spanish named the settlement *El Gran Cairo* (Great Cairo). Although the Mayan empire had been in decline for centuries, it was clear to the Spanish that this was an advanced civilisation, very different to the New World settlements they had encountered previously.

The goodwill between the two worlds was not to last. The Spaniards went ashore and received more friendly welcomes. But as they followed the smiling Maya to their settlement, Córdoba and his men were ambushed and ferociously attacked by a large force of local warriors. Perhaps word had reached them of the atrocities carried out by the Spaniards on Hispaniola and elsewhere, or perhaps they were simply suspicious of strangers. Either way, the assault left over fifty of Córdoba's men dead, and many more wounded. One eyewitness to the events was Bernal Díaz, a Conquistador who later sailed with Cortés and wrote a detailed account of his adventures in a famous work entitled *The Conquest of New Spain*. Diaz is one of the most important sources of information about the life of a Conquistador, and scholars believe his accounts are largely trustworthy. He describes how the *Cacique*, or military chief, of the indigenous people suddenly shouted to his hidden warriors and ordered them to attack:

In response to the Cacique's call these bands quickly

fell on us with great fury, and began to shoot with such accuracy that the first flight of arrows wounded thirteen soldiers... Wielding their lances in both hands, they did us great damage. But, thanks be to God, when they felt the sharp edge of our swords and the effect of our crossbows and muskets, they quickly took to their heels, leaving fifteen dead on the field.

The Spanish retreated, looting some gold from a prayer house as they fled. But this skirmish was merely a taste of what was to come. Without any truly water-tight containers on board, the Spanish explorers were forced to land again further up the coast. At a settlement named Champoton, they were attacked once more, this time by an even larger force:

...dawn broke, and we saw that we were out-numbered by two hundred to one. So wishing one another a stout heart for the fight, we commended ourselves to God and did our best to save our lives... Then they attacked us hand to hand, some with lances and some shooting arrows, and others with

their two-handed cutting swords. Though we fought back with swords and muskets and crossbows they brought us to a bad pass.... Our captain saw that good fighting did not help us, since so many bands surrounded us and so many more were coming up fresh from the town... All our soldiers had received two or three arrows, three of them had their throats pierced by lance-thrusts, and our captain was bleeding from many wounds. Already fifty of our men had been killed, and we knew that we had no more strength to resist.

Córdoba retreated, and only narrowly avoided the total annihilation of his expeditionary party, who were cut down as they fled to the boats. Further hardships had to be endured on the way back to Cuba, with the lack of fresh water bringing the explorers to the very brink of death. But Córdoba finally made it back to the safety of the Spanish settlement at Cuba. And he brought with him small pieces of finely worked gold that the Maya said they had traded with a land far to the north, which went by the name of Mexico. Two captured Maya

Indians (christened 'Melchior' and 'Julian') told their interrogators that their land had gold mines. It is said that the Spanish asked them what the name of their land was, and when they replied 'Tectetan' – meaning 'I don't understand you' – the Spanish took this to be the country's name, which they then corrupted to Yucatán. We will probably never know if the region truly did take its name from such a fundamental misunderstanding, but it does epitomize the gulf that existed between the two cultures right from the very start.

Córdoba died of his wounds. His party had been decimated, and the fact that there were any survivors at all was largely a matter of good luck. The first encounter between the two worlds had been a disaster for the Spanish. Nonetheless, the message Córdoba brought back to the settlers on Cuba could not have been clearer – somewhere on the mainland, there was a major, as yet undiscovered, civilisation. And it had gold.

JUAN DE GRIJALVA

Finding volunteers willing to risk their lives on a return mission to the new land of Yucatán in 1518 was not a problem, and one of those who volunteered was Bernal Díaz:

> *As the report had spread that these lands were very rich, and the Indian Julian said there was gold, those settlers and soldiers in the island who possessed no Indians were eager and greedy to go. So we quickly collected two hundred and forty companions.*

The new expedition was to be led by Juan de Grijalva, the nephew of Diego Velázquez, the then Governor of Cuba. Grijalva landed first on the island of Cozumel – blown there accidentally by strong currents – before returning to the scene of the earlier bloody battle with native forces, Champoton. Grijalva must have been expecting trouble – and trouble is exactly what he got according to Diaz:

The Indian inhabitants and others from the district at once assembled, as they had done before when they killed fifty-six or more of our men and wounded all the rest... very proud of their recent victory, they were drawn up to the shore, ready to fall on us if we landed. But we had gained some experience from our earlier expedition, and had brought with us in our boats some small cannon and a good supply of crossbows and muskets.

The formidable weapons the Spanish brought with them made all the difference. Although Grijalva lost seven men in the vicious skirmish, the result of the battle was never in doubt, and the natives were soon routed. They had experienced for the first time the carnage that the Spanish military machine could inflict. After the invading force had rested and resupplied, the Spanish sailed on to Tabasco, where a wary native army greeted them peaceably, and they exchanged gifts. The natives of Tabasco brought the Spanish food and clothes, and a small amount of gold, telling them that there was much more gold in the place they called Mexico. The

Spanish sailed on around the coast, until they reached the mouth of the river *Rio de las Banderas*, named after the large white cotton flags that hung from the lances of the native warriors who met them there. It was here that the empire of Spain first encountered the empire of the Aztecs. For the warriors holding the white flags of peace were doing so under direct instruction from the mighty Aztec leader, Montezuma II.

PEACE AND GOLD

According to Diaz, Montezuma had been kept informed of the Spanish expeditions. He was aware of the battles Córdoba and Grijalva had fought and knew that, despite being few in number, the Spanish had ultimately prevailed. Montezuma had also been told of the Spanish love of gold, and so he decided to barter with the newcomers, and find out more about them, rather than fight:

> *Then the Indian Governor sent messages to all the neighbouring towns that gold jewels must be brought*

and bartered; and during the six days that we stayed there they brought more than sixteen thousand pesos' worth of jewellery of low-grade gold, worked into a variety of shapes.

Grijalva soon returned to Cuba with the gold, and with his reports of a great civilisation, ruled over by a mighty prince. The news delighted his uncle, Diego Velázquez. But Grijalva did not inspire trust in Velázquez, and despite his successful journey he was not chosen to lead the follow-up force that was assembled almost as soon as word of the new lands spread. Instead, the main Spanish expedition to the land of Mexico would depart under the leadership of an ambitious lawyer who had already made a fortune from Indian slaves and gold, and who by marriage had become Velázquez's stepson. His name was Hernán Cortés.

THE RISE OF HERNÁN CORTÉS

'Pale, sickly, restless, haughty and mischievous' – these are the words that the biographer Hernán Cortés used to describe his childhood and teenage years. Born into Spanish nobility in 1485, Cortés was sent from his home in Medellin to the University of Salamanca at the age of fourteen, where he studied law for two years. Then the restlessness in his character showed itself, and he returned home two years later, not yet fully qualified. Nonetheless, he carved out a career as a notary, whilst dreaming of following in Columbus's footsteps and making a fortune in the New World he had heard so much about.

One popular story relates that Cortés' journey to the Indies was delayed after he injured himself hurriedly escaping from the bedroom of a married woman. Whatever the truth of this tale, we know that Cortés did finally sail for Hispaniola in 1504, and in 1506 took part in the conquest of Cuba, receiving in return for his efforts an estate of land and a number of Indian slaves. Over the next few years he consolidated his position in the New World territories, helping in several expeditions and gaining a reputation as a daring soldier. He rose to the position of secretary to the Governor of Cuba, Diego Velázquez de Cuéllar.

Though undoubtedly a man of prestige and influence, Cortés was nonetheless an unusual choice for the Captain of such an important expedition. There were others in Cuba at the time who would appear, on the face of it, to have been safer choices. But Cortés had learned from an early age the importance of befriending those in high places, and he used his contacts to persuade Velázquez that he was the man for the job. He struck secret deals to divide the spoils of his conquests with his backers, secured the role as Velázquez's captain, and assembled a fleet. Velázquez soon grew alarmed at the size of the force that Cortés raised – within a fortnight he had three ships, three hundred men and twenty horses ready to depart. In addition, rivals for command of the force had been telling Velázquez that Cortés would double-cross him, and Velázquez had started to believe them. Deciding he had made a mistake, Velázquez stripped Cortés of his role as Captain and forbade him from purchasing any more supplies.

Cortés simply ignored him, and set sail. Legend has it that Velázquez came running down to the quayside as Cortés rowed out to his fleet. Velázquez beseeched Cortés not to leave in such a fashion, and Cortés replied with words to the effect that he was doing as Velázquez had ordered him to, and that it was too late now to turn back. 'What are your orders now?' he called out. But Velázquez was too stunned to reply.

Cortés must have known that he was now gambling all on the success of his expedition. He had sunk his own fortune into it, and by disobeying orders had now made some very powerful enemies in positions of high authority. From here on it was, quite literally, do or die.

THE
CONQUESTS

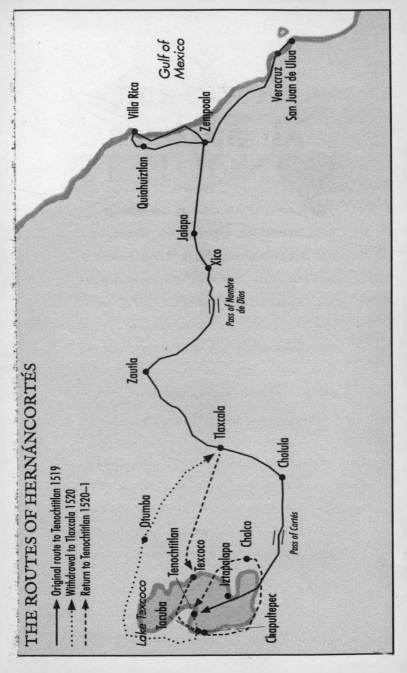

THE ROUTES OF HERNÁN CORTÉS

→ Original route to Tenochtitlan 1519
⋯ Withdrawal to Tlaxcala 1520
⇢ Return to Tenochtitlan 1520—1

Gulf of Mexico

Villa Rica
Zempoala
Veracruz
San Juan de Ulua
Quiahuiztlan
Jalapa
Xico
Pass of Nombre de Dios
Zautla
Tlaxcala
Cholula
Otumba
Lake Texcoco
Tenochtitlan
Texcoco
Iztapalapa
Chalco
Tacuba
Chapultepec
Pass of Cortés

Cortés and Montezuma

I shall not be able to relate an hundredth part of what could be told respecting these matters; but I will endeavour to describe, in the best manner in my power, what I have myself seen; and imperfectly as I may succeed in the attempt, I am fully aware that the account will appear so wonderful as to be deemed scarcely worthy of credit; since even we who have seen these things with our own eyes, are yet so amazed as to be unable to comprehend their reality.

Hernán Cortés' Second Letter to Charles V, 1520

It is perhaps the most extraordinary of all of the Conquistador stories. Cortés' conquest of the Aztec empire of Montezuma seems, even now, to defy belief. When he left Cuba, Cortés had just five hundred men, thirteen horses and a small number of cannons.

The Aztecs were said to be able to muster an army of seven hundred thousand warriors, many of whom were well trained, experienced and battle-hardened. They were used to the climate and terrain, and had built dozens of heavily fortified cities throughout their Kingdom. Their spies watched the Spaniards' every move. And their capital city, Tenochtitlan, surrounded by water and accessible only along narrow causeways that the Aztecs could raise whenever they wished, was considered impregnable.

On paper Spanish success appeared impossible. And indeed it may well have been, had it not been for certain peculiarities of the Aztec culture. In order to understand the incredible story that unfolded in Mexico between 1519 and 1521, we must understand first what was in the minds of the two main protagonists, Hernán Cortés and Montezuma II. We have seen how the Spain of Isabella and Ferdinand helped to mould the minds of the Conquistadors. Now we must turn to the New World that they first encountered, the strange and dark world of the Aztec empire ruled by Montezuma, for it was a clash of beliefs, as well as swords, that resulted in the fall of Montezuma's empire.

AZTEC GODS AND PROPHESIES

The Aztecs were magpies with regards to their religious beliefs. They were happy to adopt gods from different cultures and absorb them into their pantheon (Xipe Totec, a fertility god, for example, was originally a god of the Tlapanec people). Sometimes a foreign god would become assimilated through being identified with an existing Aztec god. Some Aztec deities were worshipped by other cultures too (though often under different names). Occasionally, two distinct gods were merged into one, or deities were transformed into different figures within a single story. For Christians used to 'one true God', Aztec religion looked like an unholy and demonic mess.

Religious practice was ultimately controlled by the Tlatoani (state leaders) and the high priests of the Aztec capital Tenochtitlan. The priests were responsible for ensuring the correct festival was held at the correct time. Although there were smaller ceremonies held on an almost daily basis, it was the ceremonies presided over by the high priests that held most significance, and these rituals involved the sacrifice of humans on a grand and terrifying scale.

The most spectacular ritual of all was the 'New Fire' ceremony which only took place every fifty-two years and which every citizen of the Aztec empire was expected to partake in. The Aztecs believed that if the New Fire ceremony was not held, the world would end. It is hardly surprising, therefore, that they took this ceremony particularly seriously. After the hearts of the human sacrifices had been torn out and offered up to the gods, a bonfire was lit on a Huixachtlan mountain (on the eastern bank of Lake Texcoco) and fire was taken from this single source out to every settlement in the empire. It is thought the last such festival was held in 1507.

The Conquistadors never saw this festival take place, but were horrified by the Aztec ceremonies they did witness.

They were repulsed at the brutality of the bloody sacrifices at the centre of many Aztec ceremonies, and their disgust was magnified by the absence of any context for the rituals. The clash of cultures can be vividly seen in the Aztec accounts of what happened when Montezuma ordered prisoners to be taken to Cortés and sacrificed in front of him as a sign of respect:

> *Montezuma.... sent captives to be sacrificed, because the strangers might wish to drink their blood. The envoys sacrificed these captives in the presence of the strangers, but when the white men saw this done, they were filled with disgust and loathing. They spat on the ground, or wiped away their tears, or closed their eyes and shook their heads in abhorrence. They refused to eat the food that was sprinkled with blood, because it reeked of it; it sickened them, as if the blood had rotted.*

As far as the Conquistadors were concerned, the Aztec were simply depraved savages. In fact, however, the belief system of the Aztecs was complex, and their actions were driven not by primitive blood-lust, but by the need to placate certain capricious and powerful gods. The most important of these, god of both the sun and of war, was Huitzilopochtli.

HUITZILOPOCHTLI

Huitzilopochtli was the god who led the Mexica tribe out of exile and pointed them towards the capital of their new empire, and so no god was closer to the hearts of the Aztecs. According to their creation myth, Huitzilopochtli told the Mexica to travel until they saw an eagle feeding on top of a cactus tree, and to build their new settlement at that location. Other later sources suggest the prophesy related to an eagle eating a snake on the cactus. At least one source relates that the cactus tree grew from the heart of Huitzilopochtli's nephew, whom Huitzilopochtli killed. At any rate, the Mexica believed that they had been led to a blessed and sacred place by their god – and the good fortune they enjoyed since founding Tenochtitlan seemed to confirm this view.

Huitzilopochtli's only equal in terms of power was Tlaloc, the god of rain, fertility and water. The two mighty gods were worshipped at the Great Temple in Tenochtitlan, where each had a separate shrine. It is thought that Huitzilopochtli's status as a solar god was first established after the burning of the earlier Mexica/Aztec legends texts; and that originally he was a high priest, deified in order to provide a compelling creation myth for the Mexica. Huitzilopochtli was responsible for keeping the sun moving across the sky, and it was believed that this movement was in permanent jeopardy.

Should the sun ever lose its constant battle with the darkness, the world would end, and so it was imperative for the Aztecs to help Huitzilopochtli. They saw it as their duty to provide him with nourishment in order to keep up his strength. The nourishment he required was blood. And the most nourishing blood of all was human blood.

HUMAN SACRIFICE

For the Aztecs, then, the end of the world was a very

real and ever present danger. They believed it had happened before, to earlier worlds. The world that they currently lived in was, they thought, the fifth such world, with the previous four all having been destroyed by the gods. The world had itself been brought into existence by self-sacrifice on the part of the god Nanahuatzin, and it was up to the Aztecs to continually revive that world, through sacrifices of their own. Death had created life, and only death could sustain life. The Aztec priests defended their practices to the Franciscans who challenged them as follows:

> *Life is because of the gods; with their sacrifice they gave us life… They produce our sustenance… which nourishes life.*

Not all of their sacrifices involved humans – dogs, eagles, jaguars, deer and rabbits were all bred for sacrifice, and even treasured possessions and effigies were sometimes ritually broken and offered up to the gods. But it was believed that there was great power in the sacrifice of human blood. The 'fire' of a human being lay in the heart, and so this was the preferred offering, held up, still beating, still warm, so that the fire of the sun could be provided with new strength.

For lesser matters, the blood of animals might suffice – or if the ceremony was of greater significance an Aztec might offer up their own blood, by cutting their arms, legs, ears or genitals. But for the hugely important business of preventing the end of the world, it was considered necessary to offer up fresh human hearts. Much of the Aztec military apparatus was therefore geared towards acquiring a regular supply of sacrificial victims. The appetite of the gods for human blood was insatiable; you simply could not have too many sacrifices. When victims were found, they were often kept in cages for many months, to be fattened up in preparation for the day of their slaughter.

THE SCALE OF HUMAN SACRIFICE IN THE AZTEC EMPIRE

Aztec codices tell us that the Great Pyramid at

Tenochtitlan, with its twin temples dedicated to the gods of the sun and the rain, Huitzilopochtli and Tlaloc, was reconsecrated in 1487. If the Aztecs are to be believed, the ceremony was unparalleled in terms of the amount of human blood spilt. They report that they sacrificed over eighty thousand prisoners over the course of four days. That equates to a sacrifice every fourteen minutes, or four an hour, every hour, if the blood letting went on all through the day and all through the night.

There is widespread scepticism that the figure of eighty thousand victims is accurate, however. The Aztecs glorified human sacrifice, and also used it to intimidate their opponents, so there is every reason to suppose that they may have exaggerated the scale of the slaughter. When later missionaries spoke to Aztec elders about the ceremony, they told of significantly lower numbers of victims – around four thousand or so. Still an extraordinarily high figure, but perhaps more credible than the massacre mentioned in the Aztec codices.

Experts in Aztec culture have tried to estimate, from collated records, what the average annual number of sacrifices might have been, but have come up with figures that range from twenty thousand per year to over two hundred and fifty thousand per year. It is simply impossible to say with any real accuracy just how many ended their days at the top of those vast pyramids in Tenochtitlan. What we can state with certainty is that human sacrifice was widespread, and that this was not casual butchery – the Aztecs were incredibly precise in their sacrificial rituals. The fate of the victim depended on their status and the god that they were sacrificed to. Many gods demanded blood from the Aztecs, but they required it served to them in different ways.

METHODS OF SACRIFICE

The majority of these sacrifices were made to Huitzilopochtli. The victim to be sacrificed was dragged up the temple stairs, then laid on a stone slab, with his hands and feet held down by four high priests. A fifth high priest made an incision through the victim's abdomen with a ceremonial knife made of obsidian or flint. A single cut sliced through the victim's diaphragm, allowing the priest to access the heart, which was torn out and held up to the sun, before being placed in a special ceremonial bowl. The heart was then burnt, and the body of the victim thrown down the pyramid's steep stairs. The body was often dismembered, with the arms and legs being eaten in an act of ritualistic cannibalism. If the victim was a captured enemy, then the warrior who captured him was given the body to dispose of. By capturing an enemy warrior, an Aztec warrior would ascend one step further up the hierarchy of the Aztec social system. Other parts of the victim's body would be fed to animals, and the head would be placed on display in a *tzompantli*, or skull rack, along with the many hundreds of those who had been sacrificed previously.

GLADIATORIAL SACRIFICES

Tezcatlipoca was a capricious god, known to the Aztecs as 'the Enemy Of Both Sides', and his power to bring about sudden reversals of fortune was greatly feared by all Aztecs. They believed he created war to provide food for the gods. In honour of this, victims were often sacrificed to him after a period of mock gladiatorial combat. The victim was tied to a post and given a useless weapon of some kind (for example a sword with the blades replaced by feathers), then forced to fight against several fully armed elite Aztec warriors ('jaguar knights' or 'eagle warriors'). Death was inevitable, of course, and the victim's remains were then offered up to Tezcatlipoca.

Once a year the Aztecs held a feast in honour of Tezcatlipoca, and naturally it too involved human sacrifice. A young man was chosen by the priests to stand in for Tezcatlipoca for a year. During this time he lived like a god, with four young wives and a host of attendants. During the week leading up to the feast he was worshipped as if he were the deity himself, until at the appointed time he was taken up to the temple and sacrificed. Even as his body was being eaten, a new victim was being chosen for the next year's feast.

ALTERNATIVE SACRIFICIAL OFFERINGS

The Aztec had two gods of fire, though many consider the two to be manifestations of the same entity, hence his name is usually written as Xiuhtecuhtli-Huehueteotl. It was believed that he had the power to bring a plague of fire upon the Aztecs if he was not appeased, and so victims were burnt in order to prevent such a disaster. Shortly before the victim died, his heart was torn out. Sacrifices of this nature usually took place at the end of a great festival of feasting and dancing.

Sacrifices were also made to the god of rain, Tláloc. However Tláloc, it was believed, required children to be sacrificed to him. The unfortunate victims were made to cry en route to their sacrifice as it was considered a good omen to provide Tláloc with a child's tears – one favoured method of obtaining the precious tears was to pull out the child's fingernails. Child sacrifices often happened on sacred mountain tops rather than in the Aztec temples. Although the

Spanish had come from a land in which the Spanish Inquisition had terrorised thousands with calculated and sustained barbarity, the actions of the Aztecs filled them with horror and disgust.

When the tales of such practices filtered back to Spain, it helped to popularize the notion that the people of the Americas were less than human. This in turn would justify countless acts of cruelty to come – including genocide and slavery. For the Aztecs, however, sacrifice was simply an act of duty – a repayment for what the gods had sacrificed for them. The gulf in understanding between the two cultures would prove disastrous, particularly for the Aztecs. Perhaps even more disastrous for them, at least according to Cortés, was their belief in the deity of Quetzalcoatl. For Cortés claims that the Aztecs believed that he himself was the god Quetzalcoatl, returning to claim the Kingdom of Mexico, just as they had always prophesied he would.

THE QUETZALCOATL PROPHESY

Montezuma… immediately sent out messengers. It was as if he thought the new arrival was our prince Quetzalcoatl. This is what he felt in his heart: He has appeared! He has come back! He will come here, to the place of his throne and canopy, for that is what he promised when he departed!…Then Montezuma gave the messengers his final orders. He said to them 'Go now, without delay. Do reverence to our lord the god. Say to him 'Your deputy, Montezuma, has sent us to you…. he welcomes you home to Mexico'.

Codex Florentino

The most controversial and hotly debated topic in the entire story of the Conquistadors is the role of the Aztec *Quetzalcoatl Prophesy* in their own downfall. Cortés maintained consistently that the Aztecs believed that he was a returning god, who it had been prophesied would return from the East to reclaim his Kingdom of Mexico from the Aztecs. The logic that follows from this is that the Aztecs thought that his victory was predestined from the start. Although they fought, they knew in their hearts that they would end up on the losing side. But is it true?

Certainly the Aztecs believed that Quetzalcoatl, the deity who had led them to Mexico, would one day return. Quetzalcoatl was also undoubtedly a hugely important figure in Aztec culture. But Quetzalcoatl was not just the feathered serpent god of the ancient Mexica tribe, he was also a man of flesh and blood, named after that god – and this man was only later deified for leading them out of the wilderness to Tenochtitlan. The name Quetzalcoatl was also a priestly title, reserved for the two most important priests at the great temple in Tenochtitlan. The Aztecs referred to the Conquistadors as 'Teotl', which has been widely translated as 'gods', but which might more accurately be understood as 'mysterious' or 'inexplicable'. To give a modern day English equivalent, a 'UFO' refers to an unidentified object, which may or may not be extraterrestrial – it is most certainly not the same as an angel. There is plenty of room for confusion between the two cultures, then, with regards to who or what the Aztecs perceived the Conquistadors to be. In addition there is the problem that many of the Aztec accounts that have been left to us were written after the invasion, rather than before, and thus may have been attempting to make sense of the fall of the great empire. Some argue that the story of Cortés as the returning Quetzalcoatl allowed the Aztecs to explain away how their armies of tens of thousands were defeated by a few hundred invaders. The vast majority of the material relating to the story comes from the *Florentine Codex*, which was written fifty years or so after the events. The idea of a returning god also chimed with the religious beliefs of the Catholic Spanish victors, so it is easy to see how the tale might have been eagerly seized upon by both sides.

The story, then, should be treated with extreme caution; it could well be one of the many myths that sprang out of the amazing tale of Cortés' conquest of Mexico. Yet there is no doubt that the sudden arrival of the Spanish caused panic amongst the native people, and as a highly religious culture they would surely have looked to their gods for an explanation, and for protection.

CORTÉS THE GAMBLER

Cortés had already ridden his luck by the time he was spotted by Montezuma's spies off the coast of Mictlancuauhtla. Just by setting sail he had defied his patron, and by extension the man that his patron represented, the King of Spain. He had left so hurriedly that he did not even know how many forces he had with him until a head count was taken at the first main landing site, the island of Cozumel. Five hundred or so had followed him, it transpired – a force large enough to establish trade with the natives, perhaps, but surely too small for what Cortés secretly had in mind: the conquest and settlement of the New World.

He made his intentions clear at Tabasco where, after defeating a band of local warriors in a short but bloody skirmish, he claimed the land for Spain in the name of the King. By placing himself directly under the King's authority he was cutting out the man who had arranged the expedition in the first place, Diego Velázquez de Cuéllar. He must have known that this would cause great consternation to a large number of his men, who had sworn allegiance to the aforementioned governor of Cuba, not Cortés.

The complaints soon grew in number as Cortés led them straight into battle with a native Mayan army that outnumbered them by three hundred to one. Although the Conquistadors triumphed, they suffered numerous casualties and several fatalities. Short of food, weakened by illness and plagued by mosquitoes, the men began to openly question the wisdom of continuing the expedition. Montezuma had sent messengers to Cortés bearing gifts of gold and silver, but also making it clear that Cortés was not welcome, and should return to his ships. Had Cortés done so, he could have returned to Cuba, paid off his debts, made peace with his patron and been lauded for conquering new territory and proving that the new land of Mexico was rich in gold. Not bad, given his inauspicious start. Many men would have quit while they were ahead – but not Cortés. Cortés wanted more. For him it was all or nothing.

He bought off those planning insurrection by giving them pieces of the gold Montezuma had sent. He assured his men that he would force nobody to accompany him – but he also put the chief troublemakers in irons for their insolence. And with that he marched his men towards the nearest major native settlement, the town of Cempoala. His men and his women, now, too – for the chief of Tabasco had given Cortés twenty slave women as a peace offering after Cortés had defeated him in battle. Cortés did not know it yet, but the gift that the chief of Tabasco had handed to him was more valuable than all of Montezuma's gold.

LA MALINCHE

The gambler had enjoyed one stroke of unbelievable good luck on his adventure thus far: at Cozumel he rescued a Spaniard captured after an earlier expedition led by the Conquistador Valdivia had been shipwrecked off the coast of Jamaica. The man in question, Gerónimo de Aguilar, had been living with the native people and had learned their Mayan tongue. He would play a vital role in translating between Cortés and the people of the New World during some of their earliest encounters in the Mayan territories of the north. But even more important was his role in teaching Spanish to one of the young slave women given to Cortés after his victory at Tabasco. Her name was Malinche.

Malinche, or La Malinche; or sometimes Malintzin; or Dona Marina − as the Conquistadors swept through the New World she would be given many names. She was probably born 'Malinalli', and took the name of Marina when she converted to Christianity after being presented to the Spanish. The native people would later add '-tzin' to her name as a mark of reverence, and the Spanish would act similarly by calling her 'Dona', or 'Lady'. It is not surprising that she earned such respect from both the native people and the Spanish troops, for she was always at Cortés' side, and would in time become so closely associated with him that native people would see the two of them almost as a single entity, calling both by the same name of 'Malintzin'. She is there in the Aztec codices, painted as prominently as Cortés himself; for every promise and threat that Cortés made was passed on to Montezuma's people through her voice. It is impossible to overstate her importance in the story of the conquest of the New World. Without her, Cortés had only his sword. But with Malinche at his side he could deploy his most deadly weapon: his words.

She was strikingly beautiful and Cortés took her as his lover (or mistress, as he was a married man). There seems little doubt that there was genuine love between them; she stayed at his side even when his cause seemed lost, and he cohabited with her long after she had outlived her usefulness as a translator. But Malinche was more than just a pretty face; she learned Spanish fluently and swiftly, and spoke with great forcefulness to a range of powerful chiefs in the most dangerous of situations. The fact that her native tongue was Nahuatl, the same language that the Aztecs and many of their allies spoke, allowed her to convey Cortés' messages using idioms and references to local culture that the natives could easily comprehend. Crucially she also spoke the language of the Maya, which allowed her to converse with Gerónimo de Aguilar, the Mayan-speaking Spaniard that Cortés had rescued from Cozumel. He could then teach her Spanish, making communication possible with all of the tribes that the Conquistadors encountered.

Bernal Díaz tells us that she was born to important lords of a town called Paynala, but that her father died when she was very young. Her mother remarried and had a son with her new husband, whereupon the step-daughter Malinche became a cause of friction in the household. And so she was secretly given away to another tribe, whilst her parents spread the word that she had died (the body of a dead slave girl being presented as evidence of the tragedy). Whilst we know where she came from, and what her vital role in the fall of the Aztec empire was, we know little of what became of Malinche after Cortés' ultimate victory in the New World. It is reported that he took her with him during a campaign in Honduras from 1524–1526. It is thought she died sometime around 1551. The rest is a mystery. Her name in modern day Mexico is symbolic with treachery and victimhood, yet she is also considered by many to be the mother of the modern Mexican nation. Her sexual relationship with Cortés has given her yet another new name, that of 'La Chingada' – or in English, 'the fucked one'.

Reviled or respected, her importance to the story of the Conquistadors is not in question. Cortés himself said that, after God, the main reason for his success was La Malinche.

REVOLUTION IN CEMPOALA

En route to Cempoala, the Spanish passed through several abandoned villages, for the local natives were terrified by the sight of the approaching army, and it became clear that the population had fled towards the fortified town of Quiahuiztlan for safety. In Quiahuiztlan, Cortés made another crucial throw of the dice. He befriended the locals, treated them kindly, and assured them he was a man of peace. He listened to their reports of the great chief Montezuma, and of how they were forced to pay tribute to the Aztec Kingdom. Upon hearing that Montezuma's tax collectors had, in the past, abducted and raped the wives of the Totonac-speaking locals and demanded their sons and daughters be given up for sacrifice, Cortés ordered the tax collectors to be arrested. He also decreed that the people of Cempoala must stop paying tribute to the Aztecs.

It was an incredibly audacious move. They locals were terrified by the prospect of disobeying Montezuma's men – to arrest them seemed to be tantamount to declaring war. But Cortés, somehow, managed to persuade them to follow his orders. Word of what had happened spread to all the local towns. And then, in a masterstroke of duplicity, Cortés took personal charge of the imprisoned tax collectors and went to speak to them. He gave the impression he knew nothing about the reasons for their arrest, and made sure that they returned to Montezuma carrying the message that Cortés had intervened to free them. Cortés even provided boats to the grateful tax collectors to ensure they could travel home without passing through hostile territory (it was only hostile, of course, because of the insurrection that Cortés had just engineered). They went home to tell Montezuma about the revolt of the Totonac speaking tribes, and that the Spanish Captain Cortés had rescued them from certain death, as a gesture of kindness to Montezuma.

When they discovered that their former captives were gone, the Totonacs were even more terrified than before. They knew the Aztec emperor would take revenge on them for their actions, and begged Cortés for advice on what they should do next. Cortés cheerfully replied that he and his men would stand by their new found friends and protect them, as long as they pledged allegiance to Spain. The Totonacs were left with little choice, and agreed. Cortés had begun to loosen Montezuma's iron grip on Mexico. He had entered a heavily fortified town without having to fire a single shot, had secured the allegiance of its people, and given Montezuma the impression that he had just done him a favour. The gambler was on a roll: in full control of the situation, and executing his plan with brilliant cunning. In contrast the man who stood between Cortés and glory, the great prince Montezuma, was in turmoil. He knew that the entire future of his Kingdom would be determined by what he decided to do about the army of strangers now advancing remorselessly towards him.

THE TWO MINDS OF MONTEZUMA

The great Aztec chief was trying to stall for time. He was desperate to know more about the unprecedented threat he now faced. The initial reports that reached him, of the arrival of a mysterious people from the East, filled him with fear and despair. He was told that floating castles had been sighted off the coast, and that men of iron had come ashore and defeated an army that vastly outnumbered them.

What the Spanish could not know was that this was not, in Montezuma's mind, an isolated event – it came on the back of a whole series of bad omens. The Aztec codices tell us that these omens began some ten years before the arrival of the Spanish, with a 'flaming ear of corn' in the sky, which burnt brightly from midnight until daybreak. More omens followed – the temple of Huitzilopochtli burnt down and the temple of Xiuhtecuhtli was damaged after being struck by lighting. More fiery lights were seen in the sky, and then the Lake of Mexico 'boiled', with the resulting flood destroying many houses. A ghostly woman was heard wailing in the middle of the night, and then the Aztec fishermen caught a strange creature in their fishing nets. It was a bird, a little like a crane, but had a mirror in the crown of its head. It was brought straight to Montezuma, and according to witnesses:

... when he looked at the mirror a second time, he saw a distant plain. People were moving across it, spread out in ranks and coming forward in great haste. They made war against each other and rode on the backs of animals resembling deer.

Finally, deformed humans appeared – two men melded into one, and then a man with two heads. But when they were brought before Montezuma, they disappeared into thin air. The net effect of this series of omens was to cause widespread fear across the Aztec empire:

To the natives, these marvels augured their death and ruin, signifying that the end of the world was coming, and that other peoples would be created to inhabit the earth. They were so frightened and grief-stricken that they could form no judgement about these things, so new and strange and never before seen or reported.

It would appear that Montezuma could 'form no judgement', either. He sent presents to the visitors, but also threats. He considered fleeing but changed his mind and stayed. He spoke of peace but organised ambushes. As the Conquistadors marched across Mexico towards him, Montezuma paced and agonised over what to do. His indecisiveness was to prove fatal.

THE FOUNDATION OF VERACRUZ

Cortés moved swiftly to consolidate his gains by founding his first settlement in the New World on a plain about a mile and a half from the fortified Totonac town of Quiahuiztlan. He had no authority to do so from his patron; his mission was supposed to be one of trade, not settlement. Instead he again went over Velázquez's head and acted in the name of the King. Cortés himself helped dig the foundations of Villa Rica de la Veracruz, and he and his men worked so swiftly that the town was almost built by the time Montezuma's tax collectors had brought him news of how they had been imprisoned by the Totonacs, before Cortés arranged their release.

Montezuma's spies had already told him of the insurrection in the south, and he had become enraged by the insolence of the Totonac tribes, ordering a large army to gather in preparation for an overwhelming assault. The news that Cortés and the Spanish had assisted his tax collectors caused him to have second thoughts – just as Cortés had planned. Montezuma decided to send messengers to Cortés to remonstrate with him for assisting a people that he considered to be traitors, but also to thank him for releasing his servants. Cortés responded with words of friendship, claiming that he worked as Montezuma's vassal. He sent the messengers back to Montezuma in good spirits, having been well treated.

No sooner were the messengers gone than the first test of the new alliance between the Totonacs and the Spanish arrived. A neighbouring tribe, the Culuan, were reported to be attacking the town of Cingapacinga, destroying fields and looting property. Cortés honoured his pledge to help the Totonacs, and marched an army some 40 km (25 miles) to

Cingapacinga. He was met outside the town by a deputation of Culuan chiefs, who asked Cortés why he was marching against them and siding with their ancient enemy, the Cempoalans. Cortés used his diplomatic skills to arrange a peace pact between the Cempoalans and the Culuan, uniting them under the flag of Spain; and just as significantly, uniting them in their hatred of Montezuma and the Aztecs. For all of the tribes shared a long list of grievances against their Mexican rulers, and Cortés was quick to exploit the fact.

The Spanish returned to Cempoala, where they were greeted as heroes. Rather than bathe in the locals' new-found affection for him, however, Cortés responded by ordering his men to destroy the sacred idols of the Cempoalans' temples. The Conquistadors hurled the idols down the steps of the temples, smashing them to pieces, as the horrified Cempoalan chief ordered his men to take up arms in order to stop them. Cortés promptly took the chief hostage, burnt what remained of the idols, and turned the temple into a Catholic church. A mass was said there, attended by all of the important Cempoalan dignitaries. Cortés assured them that as long as they gave up their practices of sacrifice and sodomy, and worshipped his Catholic god instead, he would protect them from Montezuma's wrath. If they did not do so, he warned, the Cempoalans and the Spanish would become mortal enemies.

The Cempoalans had been played by a master of duplicity. They found themselves having to choose between facing the wrath of their gods, or the wrath of Cortés and Montezuma combined. Either one seemed to spell certain death for them. Their gods seemed powerless against Cortés, and without his protection they would surely be slaughtered by Montezuma's Aztec army. And so they had no choice but to agree to Cortés' terms. Once again, Cortés had managed to succeed in all of his objectives without a drop of blood being spilt. He marched his men back to the new Spanish settlement at Veracruz in absolute triumph. He did not know it, but he was about to face another major challenge; one that threatened his entire expedition. It came not from the mighty Montezuma and his armies, but from his own men.

NO GOING BACK: THE MUTINY AT VERACRUZ

Discontent had been spreading amongst certain sections of the troops for some time, and whilst Cortés had managed to contain it up until this point, he had not fully quashed it. Many of his men were becoming increasingly alarmed at his reckless behaviour and his apparent disregard for the orders he had been given by his patron Velázquez. It was clear to them that Cortés was intent on building settlements, in the name of the King, rather than establishing trade with the natives, as instructed by Velázquez. The final straw came when, upon arriving back at Veracruz, the Conquistadors were greeted by new ships from Cuba, commanded by Francisco de Saucedo. Saucedo brought news from Spain that Velázquez had received a decree empowering him not only to trade but to found settlements, too. This prompted Cortés to shore up his own position with the King. He was aware that his actions thus far might well lead to accusations of treachery from Velázquez, and he needed to persuade the King that he was indeed acting with the King's best interests at heart. So he decided to send to the King all the gold that he had acquired on the expedition thus far, along with a letter giving his side of the story. There was a major problem with this plan, however: he had been obliged to give much of the gold to his troops in order to keep them on his side.

Rather than taking the gold back by force, Cortés signed away his own share of the spoils and invited others to do the same, in the hope that the King might bestow favours upon the expedition. Appealing to the men's fervent patriotism worked, and all signed over their own share of the gold. Many remained deeply unhappy about their situation though: they had suffered months of hardship and risked their lives for Cortés, and now had nothing to show for it. They were also nervous about being seen to side with Cortés over Velázquez, especially now that the latter appeared to have the King's blessing.

A plot was hatched to sail a ship to Cuba in order to send a message to Velázquez, informing him that he could intercept the gold and Cortés' letter to the King if he sent a fleet to Havana to seize Saucedo's ship. The plotters readied a ship and loaded with it supplies and, just after midnight, were about to set sail when Cortés got wind of the plan.

As usual, he acted swiftly and decisively. He ordered that the sails, compass and rudder should immediately be removed from the mutineers' ship, and he had the conspirators arrested. They freely confessed to the plot, and implicated many others in the company. Cortés was wise enough to ignore the men they named, however – too many were involved for him to punish them all. Instead he sentenced the lead conspirator to be hanged, and another to have his feet cut off (though it is not entirely clear if this sentence was ever actually carried out). And then came an act that typified the man: he ordered all that was useful to be taken off his fleet of ships, and for all of the ships themselves to be destroyed. Each and every one of them was duly scuttled off the coast of Veracruz. Now no man left on shore had any hope of returning to Cuba, or to Spain. The debate was at an end: they had to go on.

Bernal Díaz, the Spanish chronicler, was there to witness the destruction of the fleet, and he tells us:

> ...Cortés made a speech to the effect that we now understood what work lay before us, and with the help of our lord Jesus Christ must conquer in all battles and engagements. We must be properly prepared, he said, for each one of them, because if we were at any time defeated, which God forbid, we should not be able to raise our heads again, being so few. He added that we could look for no help or assistance except from God, for now we had no ships in which to return to Cuba. Therefore we must rely on our own good swords and stout hearts.

Even as he gave this speech, a Spanish ship was silently pulling into a harbour further along the coast from Veracruz. It brought a dark new threat to Cortés and his expedition.

SPAIN'S SECOND WAVE

Word of the New World spread rapidly in Spain, and Cortés was not the only one who sensed the opportunities therein. Francisco de Garay, the governor of Jamaica, had used his connections at the court to petition for a commission granting him the rights to any land discovered north of the Rio San Pedro y San Pablo. Upon being granted his request, de Garay immediately dispatched a fleet of ships and some two hundred and seventy men to claim the new territories. One of Cortés' deputies spotted a ship from Garay's fleet and signalled to it, but was ignored. When Cortés learned of the arrival of the newcomers from Spain, he rode as quickly as he could to intercept them. Cortés and a small band of his men came across a party of four Spaniards who had come ashore to claim possession of the land in the area. They told him why they were there, and who they were working for. Cortés resolved to try and capture the ship and thwart their attempts to take possession of the lands. He ordered the four men to signal to their captain and try and make him come ashore. When this failed, he dressed four of his own men in the clothes of the newcomers, and led the rest of his men away, so that those on the ship might believe he had left the area. It nearly worked: some members of the ship's crew did begin to row towards shore, but the rest became suspicious when their four supposed fellow crew members failed to respond to their calls. So in the end, Cortés had to admit defeat and watch the ship sail on around the coast. He was left with the four men that he had captured plus two more who had come ashore to investigate. Cortés must have known that further ships from Spain would soon follow, now that word of the treasures of the New World had spread. The clock was ticking for him. He had to push on at once if he wanted to be the first to gaze upon the fabled Aztec city of Tenochtitlan.

Cortés would learn much about the great capital city on his march through Mexico. Everywhere he stopped, the locals told him of the great fortress, with its houses built on water and bridges that could be raised to prevent invaders entering. The Conquistadors seemed to take these descriptions as a challenge – Bernal Díaz says, after hearing one chief by the name of Olintecle wax lyrical about Tenochtitlan:

> *Such is the nature of us Spaniards that the more he told us about the fortress and bridges, the more we longed to try our fortune, although to judge from Olintecle's description the capture of Mexico would be an impossible enterprise.*

The Conquistadors were also told, by Olintecle and others, of the great hatred that the neighbouring Tlaxcalan people felt towards the Aztecs. Cortés would have to pass through Tlaxcalan territory on the way to Mexico. Given their enmity towards Montezuma, and their reputation for being a peaceable people, Cortés was probably not expecting trouble from the Tlaxcalans on the morning that he marched his men towards the town of Tlaxcala. Yet trouble is exactly what he got. On previous journeys he had managed to avoid bloodshed, but this time even he could not talk his way out of a battle. The 'good swords and stout hearts' of his men were about to be tested in earnest.

WAR WITH THE TLAXCALANS

Cortés sent messengers to the Tlaxcalans, bearing gifts and messages of friendship, stressing that he was not the servant of Montezuma – for he knew that in this part of the country Montezuma was hated. But the Tlaxcalans had been tricked many times before, and they were in no mood to receive the strangers kindly. They knew full well that the Spanish had befriended the Cempoalans, who paid tribute to Montezuma, and they had readied their army at the first sign of the Conquistadors' approach. The messengers were taken prisoner, and only narrowly escaped with their lives when their guards became distracted. The messengers told the Conquistadors that the Tlaxcalans had made it clear what fate lay in store for them and their Spanish allies:

According to their story, when they were in prison the Tlaxcalans had threatened them, saying: 'Now we are going to kill those whom you call Teules [gods] and eat their flesh. Then we shall see whether they are as brave as you proclaim. And we shall eat your flesh too, since you come here with treasons and lies from that traitor Montezuma'.

The messengers could hardly speak through fear, but the Conquistadors were less easily intimidated, and pushed on into Tlaxcalan territory. When they spotted thirty or so Tlaxcalan scouts, the Spanish sent their horsemen to capture them. The Conquistadors were charging directly into an ambush, however, and a force that Bernal Díaz describes as 'more than three thousand strong' began to shower them with arrows and sling shot. Ferocious hand-to-hand fighting followed, which was only brought to an end by the arrival of Spanish artillery. The Tlaxcalans sustained heavy losses and began to fall back – but the Conquistadors had been given a taste of what was to come, and Diaz expressed admiration for the bravery and skill of their opponents:

...they had kept their ranks and fought well for a considerable time. In this skirmish four of our men were wounded, and I think one of them died of his wounds a few days later.

After dressing their wounds, and eating Tlaxcalan dogs to keep up their strength, the Conquistadors slept in their full armour, posting numerous sentries for fear of a night attack. It did not come, but the following morning they found themselves face to face with two armies of warriors, estimated to be around six thousand strong. Cortés tried once more to negotiate for peace, sending three captured Tlaxcalans to tell the armies that he wanted the Spanish and Tlaxcalans to be brothers. The response was swift: 'On being addressed by the three prisoners, the Indians became much more savage and attacked us so violently that we could not endure it'. But with no way of turning back, endure it they must.

The Conquistadors rushed the native armies, and drove them back towards some nearby woods – or so they thought. In reality it was a trap and forty thousand Tlaxcalan warriors were waiting in ambush to counter-attack. The Spanish had been drawn into terrain that did not suit their cavalry or artillery, and they quickly realised their mistake. Withdrawing back onto the level ground of the initial battle, they used their assets to greater effect, but they soon found themselves surrounded on all sides by the vast Tlaxcalan army.

Bernal Díaz describes the ensuing battle as one of the most difficult he fought in the entire campaign. The Spanish kept together in a tight formation, as any single soldier stepping out into the multitude of obsidian blades and lances would surely be doomed – 'For they were so numerous that they could have blinded us with clods of earth if God, of His great mercy, had not aided and protected us.'

The ferocious struggle continued for an hour, with the Spanish mowing down large numbers of the tightly packed Tlaxcalan fighters with their cannons. In return the Tlaxcalans rained forth arrows and sling shot, and slashed the Spaniards with their two handed obsidian swords and lances. At times the small band of Conquistadors came close to being overwhelmed, but in the end their discipline, fighting prowess and superior technology told. The Tlaxcalans, having lost several of their leading captains, fell back. The Conquistadors felt relief rather than exhilaration when they saw their opponents retire:

> *We were not sorry, and made no attempt to follow them. Being so tired that we could hardly stand, we stayed where we were, in that little town... When we saw that the victory was ours we thanked God for delivering us from great danger.*

The exhausted Spaniards retreated to the Tlaxcalan temples to dress their wounds with fat taken from their opponents' corpses. They repaired their weapons, dined on fowl and native dogs, and rested. Cortés knew, however, that though he had won an important battle, the war was not yet over.

His opposite number was the Tlaxcalan captain

Xicotenga, who was a brave and cunning general, and prepared to fight to the death to protect his people. When Cortés sent him a message proposing peace, Xicotenga replied that 'they would make peace with us by filling themselves with our flesh and honouring their gods with our hearts and blood'. With armies numbering fifty thousand men under his command, Xicotenga could afford to sound confident.

Another battle was inevitable, and it proved to be just as bloody and ferocious as the first. Bernal Díaz describes how the Conquistadors found themselves standing upon 'a plain six miles long, and perhaps as broad, swarming with Indian warriors'. With a force of just 'four hundred, of whom many were sick and wounded', the invaders were hopelessly outnumbered. Despite the heroics of their cavalry and swordsmen, and the terrible damage done to the attacking force by their cannons and muskets, the Spanish came within an inch of defeat because of the seemingly endless swarm of Tlaxcalan warriors attacking them:

...I saw our company in such confusion that despite the shouts of Cortés and the other captains they could not hold together. The Indians were charging us in such numbers that only by a miracle of swordplay were we able to drive them back and re-form our ranks.

The Spanish ranks held; the Tlaxcalan ranks did not, and eventually the native army retreated. Xicotenga was expecting to be reinforced by two further armies but they did not arrive due to a dispute between Xicotenga and another Tlaxcalan general over the lack of bravery displayed in the earlier battle. Divisions and in-fighting between the tribal armies may well have cost them a famous victory.

Xicotenga was determined to continue the fight, despite his two defeats and the catastrophic losses inflicted upon his forces. His next attack came at night, after he had consulted soothsayers who had advised him that the Spaniards' strength disappeared when the sun went down. The Conquistadors had received word of the attack from captured Tlaxcalan spies however, and were ready and waiting. It was a disaster for Xicotenga, whose already depleted forces were hacked down in droves. With the light of a full moon to assist them, the Spanish cavalry pursued the routed Tlaxcalan army and inflicted further carnage upon them as they fled.

Cortés again sent messages of peace. Although he had now won three decisive battles, he was aware that his position was precarious and the expedition was in crisis. His troops were exhausted, his supplies were limited, and morale was low. Many of his men considered their mission suicidal:

> ... *on waking next morning we realized our sad plight. We were all weary and wounded, some with two or three wounds, many of us were ragged and sick, and Xicotenga was still on our heels... it is not surprising that we wondered how these battles would end, and what we should do and where we should go when they were done. We thought it would be*

a tough business to march into Mexico, which had great armies, and wondered what would happen to us when we had to fight Montezuma if we were reduced to such straits by the Tlaxcalans, whom our Cempoalan allies described as a peaceful people.

Seven representatives met Cortés to urge him to accept defeat and retreat:

… the most eloquent of them… spoke for the rest… and… said, as though by way of advice, that Cortés ought to consider the condition we were in, wounded, thin, and harassed… and in continuous fighting both by day and night. According to their argument, we had lost more than fifty-five of our company since leaving Cuba, and we knew nothing of the settlers we had left at Villa Rica.… They accused him of preparing his own death and that of all his followers, and begged him to preserve us all by leading us back to Villa Rica.… the Tlaxcalans… had no such reputation as the Mexicans. Yet we had been in great danger of our lives, and if they were

to attack us on the morrow in another battle like
those of the past, we should be too weary to hold
our own. But even if they did not attack us again
the march to Mexico seemed to them a very terrible
undertaking…

Cortés didn't listen and vowed to fight on. Shortly
afterwards, messengers from the Tlaxcalans arrived to
tell the Spanish that they had decided to make peace.
Xicotenga wanted to continue the fight, but he had
been overruled by his chiefs. Instead of retreating,
Cortés marched his men in triumph into the city of
Tlaxcala on 23 September 1519. There he forged an
alliance with the Tlaxcalan forces against their hated
tyrant neighbour Montezuma, and the Aztecs. Cortés
was now just three days march from the fabled capital
city of Mexico.

THE MASSACRE AT CHOLULA

Montezuma had heard of Cortés' triumph over, and
new alliance with, the Tlaxcalans. The news both

angered and terrified him. His Aztec empire had been at war with the neighbouring state for over one hundred years. It must have been clear to him, finally, that Cortés would never turn back now, and that he must choose once and for all whether to welcome or fight him. We cannot know for sure what was in his mind, for the surviving accounts differ as regards what happened next. All agree that Montezuma sent messengers to Tlaxcala inviting Cortés to visit him. But were these invitations genuine, or sweet words designed to lure Cortés into a trap? Montezuma's ambassadors urged Cortés to take the road to Mexico that led through the town of Cholula, since that town was friendly to the Aztecs and he would be assured safe passage. The Tlaxcalans, however, warned Cortés that he should take an alternative route, as the Cholulans were notoriously treacherous and war-like, and he would almost certainly be walking into an ambush.

Cortés decided to ignore the Tlaxcalan advice and take the road to Cholula. He took one thousand Tlaxcalan warriors with him, later ordering them to stay on the outskirts of the town when the residents of Cholula objected to their presence. So it was only the small band of Conquistadors who marched into the centre of Cholula – and into infamy. For the events that followed were some of the most bloody and controversial of the entire campaign.

CORTÉS THE KILLER

According to Tlaxcalan chronicles, the Cholulans were secretly scheming to slaughter the Spanish as soon as they exited the city on the road to Mexico. Other accounts claim that the Cholulans had no such plot; it was invented by the Tlaxcalans in order to persuade the Spanish to turn on the Cholulans and slaughter their sworn enemies. There are even suggestions that Cortés had no reason at all for his actions against the Cholulans – he simply wanted to terrify the Aztecs and send a clear message to Montezuma ahead of his arrival in his city. Whether he intended that message to be sent to Montezuma or not, it was certainly the message that reached him. His messengers told him that the Spanish had entered Cholula and had been made welcome there. They had asked the Cholulan chiefs to provide two thousand soldiers to escort them on the road to Mexico the next day. The troops assembled in a courtyard, where the chiefs presented them to Cortés. Cortés ordered that all exits to the courtyard be blocked, and then gave the command that all of those trapped inside should be slaughtered. The Spanish cannons, muskets and swords cut down the helpless Cholulans, leaving the streets of Cholula awash with blood. It was a massacre without parallel in the long history of the Americas.

Perhaps Montezuma had indeed laid a trap for Cortés on the road to Mexico outside Cholula. If so, his plan very badly backfired. If he had not, then the actions of the Conquistadors in slaughtering so many people just a short distance from Mexico must have seemed incredible to him. News of the terrible carnage sent shock waves through a country well used to bloodshed. The merciless nature of the slaughter is what seems to have horrified the Aztecs – for their culture prized the taking of prisoners above all else, and such whole scale killings were unknown to them, except as offerings to their gods.

> *And when this had taken place, word of it was brought to Montezuma....The common people were terrified by the news; they could do nothing but tremble with fright. It was as if the earth trembled beneath them, or as if the world were spinning before their eyes, as it spins during a fit of vertigo...*

MONTEZUMA'S DESPAIR

Brutal, but as an act of intimidation and terrorism, utterly effective, the massacre at Cholula seems to have confirmed in Montezuma a sense that resistance was futile. His actions from here on seem increasingly desperate as the Conquistadors marched to the gates of his city. He sent a chief by the name of Tzihuacpopocatzin to meet Cortés, instructing him to pose as Montezuma himself. Tzihuacpopocatzin carried many gifts, which Montezuma hoped would satisfy the Spanish thirst for gold, for it was already well-known that this above all seemed to delight the strangers. His messengers begged Cortés to turn back from Mexico, with the promise that if they did so, Montezuma would send far more gold to the ports for them to take back to Spain. The sight of such fine treasure merely spurred the Spanish on towards Tenochtitlan, however:

> ...*when they were given these presents, the Spaniards burst into smiles; their eyes shone with pleasure; they were delighted by them. They picked up the gold and fingered it like monkeys; they seemed to be transported by joy, as if their hearts were illuminated and made new. The truth is that they longed and lusted for gold. Their bodies swelled with greed, and their hunger was ravenous; they hungered like pigs for that gold. They snatched at the gold ensigns, waved them from side to side and examined every inch of them...*

They asked Tzihuacpopocatzin if he was the great prince Montezuma, and he replied that he was, and that he was at Cortés' service. The Tlaxcalan and Cempoalan allies accompanying the Spanish, however, knew Montezuma, and the deception was quickly exposed. The chronicles record that the Spanish responded with contempt when they discovered that Montezuma had attempted to deceive them:

> *'You are not Montezuma: he is there in his city. He cannot hide from us. Where can he go? can he fly away like a bird?...We are coming to see him, to meet him face to face. We are coming to hear his words from his own lips.' They taunted and threatened the envoys in this fashion, and the gifts of welcome and the greetings were another failure. Therefore the envoys hastened back to the city.*

Montezuma, in a last desperate throw of the dice, sent his magicians to see if they could stop Cortés with their spells. They turned back after meeting a drunkard who foretold the destruction of Mexico, and showed them portents of doom. When the drunkard pointed back to Tenochtitlan, the magicians seemed to see it in flames, and when they attempted to speak with the mysterious stranger they found their words would not come out, as if they were drunk themselves. They decided that the drunken stranger was the god Tezcatlipoca, and they turned back to the city to report the events to Montezuma.

And if the native accounts are to be believed, Montezuma now just gave up, resigned to whatever was about to come. Even at this late stage he could have raised the bridges of his mighty fortified city, raised his enormous army and opposed the Spanish and their allies. But the bridges remained open, the warriors kicked their heels in their houses. Bernal Díaz, in his account of the expedition, states that Montezuma had previously planned to attack the Conquistadors and had cut away part of a hillside above the road to Tenochtitlan in order to facilitate a deadly ambush upon them. But at the last moment the warriors had been ordered home, and the barricades had been cleared, after the gods told him to let Cortés pass. In truth, the great leader of the Aztecs had been utterly terrorised by the approaching army, just as Cortés had hoped:

> *When the envoys arrived in the city, they told Montezuma what had happened and what they had seen. Montezuma listened to their report and then bowed his head without speaking a word. For a long time he remained thus, with his head bent down. And when he spoke at last it was only to say 'What help is there now, my friends?... We will be judged and punished. And however it may be, and whenever it may be, we can do nothing but wait.'*

They would not have to wait long. Cortés and his men were already at Iztapalapa, the settlement beside the causeway that led to the Mexican capital. They were gazing for the first time upon the mesmerising city of Tenochtitlan.

FACE TO FACE WITH MONTEZUMA

Even after all they had been told about the wonders of

Montezuma's city, the Conquistadors could scarcely believe their eyes:

> '...when we saw all those cities and villages built in the water, and other great towns on dry land... we were astounded. These great towns and 'cues' [temples] and buildings rising from the water, all made of stone, seemed like an enchanted vision... Indeed some of our soldiers asked whether it was not all a dream... It was all so wonderful that I do not know how to describe this first glimpse of things never heard of, seen or dreamed of before.

As they approached the main city along a broad causeway, thousands of inhabitants came out to gaze upon the newcomers. It is difficult to imagine who was more astonished, or terrified, as the two worlds finally came face to face with each other for the first time:

> ...we... followed the causeway... it was so crowded with people that there was hardly room for them all...For the towers and the 'cues' were full,

and they came in canoes from all parts of the lake. No wonder, since they had never seen horses or men like us before! With such wonderful sights to gaze on we did not know what to say, or if this was real that we saw before our eyes.... we were scarcely four hundred strong, and we well remembered the words and warnings... we had received to beware of entering the city of Mexico.... What men in all the world have shown such daring?

If the sight of the city and its people was intoxicating, the arrival of Montezuma must have left the visitors dumbstruck. He was carried aloft in a litter on the shoulders of other great Aztec chiefs. A rich canopy of bright green feathers, decorated with gold, silver and pearls shielded the prince from the sun. He was clad in rich garments decorated with gold and precious stones, and approached the Conquistadors walking on the cloaks of his chiefs so that his feet did not have to touch the earth. Cortés dismounted from his horse, walked towards Montezuma, and bowed to him. Montezuma bowed back. The leaders of the

New World and the Old World were face to face with one another for the very first time. The date was the 8 November 1519.

Cortés attempted to embrace Montezuma, but was prevented from doing so by his chiefs, who grabbed his arm. No one was allowed to even look upon Montezuma's face, let alone touch him. The two men exchanged warm greetings, and Montezuma instructed his chiefs to show Cortés and his men to their lodgings – which were, they soon discovered, magnificent. The Spanish made themselves at home and rested, as Montezuma had urged them to. They also, however, posted sentries and placed their artillery where it would best protect them should they have cause to need it.

Over the course of the next few days, the two leaders spoke frequently about their different worlds, and different beliefs, with Cortés stressing that his King had sent him to convert the Aztecs to the one true faith of Christianity, and Montezuma countering politely that his gods had served his people well for many generations. The Spanish were treated to lavish banquets and had luxurious quarters in which to sleep. Montezuma gave Cortés a great deal of gold and other gifts, and showed him around the vast city complex of Tenochtitlan. The Spanish were shown the Aztec's armoury, stacked with lethal obsidian-bladed weapons; the aviary stocked with eagles, exotic parrots and hundreds of other types of birds; the zoo, where tigers, lions, wolves, dogs and venomous snakes were fed on human sacrifices; and of course the great temples where those sacrifices took place. Though they did not know it, many of the Spaniards would later be fed to them by their hosts. For now, the two sides were at peace. But that peace was not to last.

THE RIGHTEOUS BACKLASH

Tensions began to build after Cortés asked for permission to place a cross on one of the Aztec temples. Montezuma refused; but he did allow the Spanish to build a church in their own quarters. As they sought out the best place to build, they discovered a door that had been plastered over and painted. Deciding to open the door, they found behind it a hidden room that was full of gold and treasure. The sight of such riches bewitched the Conquistadors, but they knew they were in no position to seize it – yet. So the door was blocked up again and plastered over, while the Spanish decided what to do.

The Aztecs who brought the Conquistadors food each day had become increasingly insolent, the Spanish perceived. Mindful of earlier warnings from their allies that Montezuma intended to let them into his city and then kill them all there, the small band of warriors grew increasingly nervous. Then, two Tlaxcalan messengers arrived in secret to inform Cortés of a surprise attack by the Aztecs on the town of Almeria, which had sparked unrest across Cempoala and other territories previously pacified by the Spaniards. The troops stationed there could not control the natives, and the situation was threatening to spiral out of control. Fearing this may be the start of the Aztec counter-attack he had feared all along, Cortés once again acted decisively and with astonishing audacity.

He marched into Montezuma's own palace, and there took him hostage. The most powerful man in the New World was suddenly a prisoner in his own city.

Why did Montezuma agree to go with Cortés and his men? It is a mystery. At first he argued with them, and even offered his sons and daughter as hostages if they would spare him the disgrace of being taken prisoner. It may be that Cortés somehow persuaded him that no-one would be hurt if he did as he was told, or it may be that the gods decreed that he should offer himself up as a captive. Certainly, had he called for his guards and instructed them to slaughter the Spanish, the Conquistadors would not have stood a chance. But Montezuma went quietly, assuring his officials that he was visiting the Spanish quarters of his own free will. For several days he continued to inform all who asked that he was happily lodging with his visitors, and that they should not be alarmed.

Cortés attempted to rule through Montezuma, using him as a proxy for his own commands. He began by cajoling Montezuma into summoning the chiefs responsible for the uprising in the south. Upon their arrival, Cortés made a very public example of them by having them burnt alive in front of the Aztec leader and his horrified citizens. It was another example of psychological warfare by Cortés, a further attempt to crush Aztec resistance through the use of terror. Cortés had gambled everything on such audacious moves from the very outset, and this was merely the latest incredible throw of the dice, as Bernal Díaz records:

> ... *readers... must wonder at the great deeds we did in those days: first in destroying our ships; then in daring to enter that strong city despite many warnings that they would kill us once they had us inside: then in having the temerity to seize the great Montezuma, King of that country, in his own city and inside his very palace, and to throw him in chains while the execution was carried out... what soldiers in the world, numbering only four hundred — and we were even fewer — would have dared to enter a city as strong as Mexico.... and, having seized so great a prince, execute his captains before his eyes?*

MONTEZUMA'S FALL FROM GRACE

But this time Cortés had misjudged his situation. Since the arrival of the Spanish, Montezuma had become fatally weakened in the eyes of his people. The god-like figure who no-one could even look in the eye clearly did not command the respect of the Spanish, who not only looked upon him whenever they wished, but also touched him and even put him in chains. Cortés had misunderstood the Aztec social structure: their leader did not have absolute power as Cortés thought. Leaders who failed to command respect could – and usually were – overthrown. In the following days, as Montezuma enjoyed pleasure cruises on the lake, and chuckled at the antics of his jugglers, his chiefs discussed how to restore the pride of the Aztec people and rid themselves of the invaders. Through his fatalistic acceptance of Spanish rule, Montezuma had sidelined himself. If he could not, or would not defend the capital city, there were others who could, and would.

For a man in such a precarious military position, Cortés was acting with almost breathtaking boldness. He was, as his generals often reminded him, the commander of a small force of men, effectively marooned on an island surrounded by bridges that could be raised to prevent his escape at any time. He was surrounded by a vast population that included tens of thousands of highly trained and experienced Aztec warriors. And yet he relentlessly demanded more gold, continually pressed Montezuma to replace the temples to their gods with churches and destroy the idols his people held to be so sacred, and so powerful. Montezuma agreed to allow an altar and image of the Virgin Mary to be set up in one of the temples and, with tears streaming down his cheeks, finally pledged allegiance to the Spanish King.

Cortés' daring had served him well thus far, but now he was beginning to overplay his hand. To the Aztec population, his actions were utterly intolerable, and no matter how much Montezuma attempted to soothe them, it was only a matter of time before their burning anger exploded into violent resistance. Montezuma had reached breaking point, and could indulge the invading force no more. He informed Cortés that the gods had instructed the Aztecs to attack and kill the Spanish, in retaliation for desecrating their temples. Cortés knew instantly that his forces faced annihilation if the populace turned against them, and he pleaded with Montezuma to give him a period of grace in order to build some ships to transport his men away from the city. Montezuma agreed, on the condition that the Spanish left as soon as the ships were built. Word spread across the city that the Spanish were on the verge of leaving, and an uneasy truce formed as the carpenters set about their work.

What happened next is an astonishing twist of fate. Word reached Cortés of a potentially disastrous new development for him; the arrival of a fleet of Spanish ships laden with troops, sent to arrest and return him to Cuba in chains. Or, if he chose to resist, to kill him. The patron of his expedition, Diego Velázquez, had not forgotten that Cortés had ignored his orders and now it was payback time. Just as Cortés seemed so close to his dream of capturing Mexico, Velázquez was about to take it all away from him.

WITH GOD ON HIS SIDE

Cortés had barely enough troops to defend the Spanish quarters in the city, let alone pacify the rest of its vast and increasingly hostile population. He now faced an advancing army of his fellow countrymen — an army as well armed and as well trained as his own. They were led by Pánfilo de Narváez, a capable captain and a man that Cortés knew personally. He had nineteen ships and around 1,400 soldiers under his command — a force vastly superior to Cortés' own depleted army. Montezuma was delighted with the news — after all it removed Cortés' last excuse for staying in Tenochtitlan. He now had the ships he said he needed in order to remove his men from the city, and the Spanish were free to leave at once.

The situation for Cortés seemed utterly hopeless. He was surrounded by tens of thousands of natives who wanted to see his heart cut out should he stay, and if he somehow managed to escape that threat he would have to face the rough justice meted out to traitors by his own countrymen. Yet once more, the desperado rolled the dice and went for broke. He decided to try and hold the city whilst also defeating the army sent to capture him. Leaving behind a skeleton force of just one hundred and twenty men in Tenochtitlan, he led his Conquistadors towards an opposing army, not of New World natives, but of Spanish troops.

Cortés, although outnumbered, had some significant advantages over his opponents, and he sought to maximize those advantages in order to gain an improbable victory. Firstly, his men were now used to fighting in the hostile terrain of the New World, whereas the forces of Narváez were not. Secondly, Cortés knew the fighting style of his opponents and could deploy both his own and the natives' weapons to counter their offensive weaponry. He bought long copper-tipped lances from the Chinantec people to tackle Navarez's cavalry, and made the capture of the newcomers' artillery a priority for his own men. Thirdly, and decisively, he had the element of surprise on his side. Narváez could not in his wildest dreams have imagined that his quarry would ride out from a heavily fortified city in order to launch an attack on him before he had got any further than Cempoala. And yet that is exactly what Cortés chose to do, attacking at night and scattering Narváez's bewildered troops. Narváez himself lost an eye in the battle, and five of his men were killed, with many more injured. The rest agreed to join Cortés. Once more he had turned disaster into triumph: instead of being killed or captured, he now suddenly had fresh reinforcements with which to protect his position in Tenochtitlan. It must have seemed to him further evidence that God was indeed on his side.

He did not have long to savour his extraordinary achievement however. At the very moment of his victory came word from the men he had left in Tenochtitlan. The Spanish were being besieged in their quarters and seven of them had already been killed. By the time the Conquistadors rushed back to Tenochtitlan, the Aztec capital was ablaze.

THE NIGHT OF SORROWS

Pedro de Alvarado, the man Cortés had left in charge of Tenochtitlan, was a veteran of Juan de Grijalva's earlier expedition, and would later become infamous for his cruelty towards the native people of Guatemala and El Salvador – hanging, burning and feeding to dogs those who displeased him. His contempt for the Aztec people of Mexico was no less intense. Though accounts of the events leading up to the insurrection vary, all seem to agree that Alvarado launched a merciless attack on unarmed citizens celebrating the festival of Toxcatl in the holiest temple of the Aztec capital. Cortés had granted permission for the festivities, knowing that it was one of the most important in the Aztec calendar. Montezuma had persuaded the revellers not to carry arms, believing Cortés' deputy would honour his word to allow the celebrations. After the massacre Alvarado claimed that he had received information that the Aztecs intended to attack the Spanish garrison as soon as the festival was over, and so he launched a pre-emptive strike to try and thwart the Aztec plot. The Aztecs, however, maintained that no such plan existed, and that Alvarado simply attacked them without any justification or warning:

> *...the songs had hardly begun when the Christians came out of the palace. They entered the patio and stationed four guards at each entrance. Then they attacked the captain who was guiding the dance. One of the Spaniards struck the idol in his face, and others attacked the three men who were playing the drums. After that there was a general slaughter until the patio was heaped with corpses... The Mexicans could only fight back with sticks of wood; they were cut to pieces by the swords. Finally the Spaniards retired to the palace where they were lodged.*

Codex Aubin

Cortés tried to repair the damage his captain had done, but it was far too late. The true face of Spanish cruelty had been revealed to the Aztecs, and they would neither forgive nor forget. Cortés railed furiously at Alvarado that 'it was a bad thing and a great mistake'. He was right on both counts, and the Spanish would pay dearly for it with their blood in the days that followed.

Having boasted to his new troops of the great respect that the Aztecs held him in, Cortés found that the atmosphere in the capital had changed dramatically by the time he returned. The great market was closed, no citizens turned out to greet him, and the Spanish were no longer brought food and other supplies.

Then news arrived that the road from nearby Tacuba was thronged with heavily armed warriors marching towards Tenochtitlan. Cortés dispatched a force to try and intercept them, but they were immediately attacked with such ferocity that fourteen were killed and the rest were forced to retreat back towards the Spanish quarters. So numerous were their assailants that they could barely get back inside, despite the cannons and crossbows used to cover their retreat. The native multitudes surrounded the Spanish and set fire to their quarters, whilst raining down arrows and javelins.

The attack lasted all of the rest of the day and well into the night. It was the ultimate nightmare for Cortés and his men: surrounded by tens of thousands of hostile warriors intent on preventing them from escaping. Not for the first time, it appeared certain that his expedition would end in disaster and the death of every Conquistador.

As soon as dawn broke, Cortés decided to try and blast his way out by using his cannons and cavalry to their full effect. He had achieved miraculous results with such tactics when heavily outnumbered in his war against the Tlaxcalans. Against the Aztecs, however, the method was of little use. The warriors he faced were the finest in the New World, and although his attacks did them great damage they retained their discipline and fought on. Drawbridges were raised to prevent the Conquistadors from moving in any direction without jumping into deep water, where they were more vulnerable to the avalanche of sling shots the Aztecs fired from their rooftops. Bernal Díaz describes how even veterans of Spain's previous wars were left astonished at the bravery and ferocity of the Aztec warriors:

> ...*three or four soldiers of our company who had served in Italy swore to God many times that they had never seen such fierce fighting, not even in Christian wars, or against the French King's artillery, or the Great Turk; nor had they ever seen men so courageous as those Indians at charging with closed ranks.*

The Spanish were getting nowhere. They retreated back to their quarters, almost all of them now bearing wounds from the battles, and a further twelve of their number having been hacked to death.

A second attempt to break out followed a day or two later, with the Spanish this time protecting themselves behind wooden towers which they hurriedly constructed to use as primitive armoured personnel carriers. They made for the great holy temples, hoping to find a more secure refuge there. Again they were fought every inch of the way by the Aztec army, and although they achieved their objective they were soon forced to turn back. If anything the assaults they faced were growing more ferocious, as the Aztecs lost their fear of the invincibility of the strangers. They goaded and taunted the Conquistadors, accusing them of running like cowards, and pledging that not a single one of them would escape with their lives. The horses — such a potent weapon for the Spaniards until now — slipped on the wet causeways and were next to useless.

The cannons cut down dozens of natives with every shot, but were nonetheless overwhelmed in moments by fresh bands of natives who rushed relentlessly into the line of fire to attack the gunners. The wooden towers were smashed into splinters, and a further sixteen Spaniards were killed before they could make it back to their quarters. There they found yet more Aztecs destroying their fortifications, and the heavily wounded Spanish forces had to fight to expel them and then hurriedly patch up the defences.

It was clear to Cortés that he could not fight his way out: the losses he had suffered thus far had been catastrophic, and his men were exhausted. The forces he had recruited from Narváez with promises of gold now cursed him for leading them to such a horrific fate. For all agreed that they would end up dead in the great lake surrounding the city of Mexico, or having their hearts torn out in the temples of the Aztecs. Cortés was desperate, and decided to beg the angry natives to make peace. He would use the last card available to him: Montezuma. When Cortés ordered him to stand before his people and beseech them to allow the Spanish to leave the city safely in return for a pledge they would never return, Montezuma replied:

> *I do not believe that I can do anything towards ending this war, because they have already chosen another lord, and made up their minds not to let you leave this place alive. I believe therefore that all of you will be killed.*

These are the words of a man who already knew

that it was all too late. They were perhaps not his last words, but as no other recorded words survive, they must serve as Montezuma's epitaph, for he was dead by the next day. One account suggests it was his own enraged people who killed him, hurling stones at him as he delivered Cortés' plea for peace. Another records that the Spanish stabbed him in the abdomen, and there are also accounts suggesting that Cortés garotted him once it was clear he had outlived his usefulness. In any event, by the time he was killed he had lost all authority, and his successor, Cuitláhuac of Iztapalapa was the man in charge of regaining control of Tenochtitlan for the Aztecs.

Though the crowds wept when the body of Montezuma was delivered to them, they also shouted to the Conquistadors that their new King would not be so faint-hearted as to believe their false promises. Cuitláhuac had advocated resistance to the invading force from the outset, and he meant to avenge the deaths that the Spanish had been responsible for. After Montezuma's death, Cortés tried once more to attack the armies besieging him, this time hoping not to escape but simply to inflict as much carnage as possible on the Aztecs, in the hope that this would force them to negotiate a peace. But in Cuitláhuac he faced an opponent with implacable resolve: the Aztecs would suffer any amount of losses in order to annihilate the Spanish army.

Short of gunpowder, food and water, Cortés was forced to concoct one final do-or-die plan to escape from the fortified city. He ordered the construction of walkways to cross the gaps in the causeways where the bridges had been raised. Then he led his men out at night, when he hoped the Aztecs would be off-guard. The chaotic and blood-soaked midnight charge from Tenochtitlan would later be known as *La Noche Triste* or 'The Night Of Sorrows'. It was a disaster for the Conquistadors, but given their position it was perhaps always likely to be. What is astonishing is that any survived, given the number of warriors who assaulted them as they desperately scrambled across the dark causeways to freedom. Most experts believe that around four hundred and fifty of the Spanish were killed as they made their escape; some put the number as high as 1,150. Almost none of those left alive were unwounded. Many of those who died drowned, weighed down by the Aztec gold they carried with them. Even after making it out of Tenochtitlan, the survivors were pursued through neighbouring towns and relentlessly attacked.

Cortés was one of the lucky few who made it out alive. His deputy, Pedro de Alvarado, whose actions had triggered the uprising, was another. Badly wounded, he had crossed a gap in the causeway that had been filled in with the bodies of the dead, later known as Alvarado's Leap. They and the rest of the survivors limped back through Mexico, with the remnants of the Tlaxcalan army who had shared their fate.

There was one more destructive battle to fight, on a plain a few days' march from the capital, when an army of several thousand Aztecs caught up with the exhausted Conquistadors. But somehow the Spaniards and their allies found new strength, and in the open their superior technology – and their few remaining horses – once more proved deadly. Although dozens more Conquistadors were cut down in the battle, the losses on the Aztec side were even greater, and eventually they retreated. Cuitláhuac had missed his best chance of totally destroying the Spanish force, and henceforth the Conquistadors would fight to their strengths, in tight formations that made best use of their lethal Toledo swords.

Bernal Díaz records that after the flight from Mexico and the 'battle of Otumba', more than eight hundred and sixty of his fellow soldiers lay dead, along with at least one thousand Tlaxcalan warriors. Just four hundred and forty Conquistadors remained alive to stumble wearily into the relative safety of the Tlaxcalan capital Tlaxcala. All were wounded, and exhausted, and few had any gold of real value to show for their efforts. The Aztecs had shown that their army and fortified city was simply too strong for such a small force to defeat.

Even as the Conquistadors dressed their wounds and thanked god that they had escaped with their lives, however, Cortés was planning another attack on the Aztec empire.

SIEGE AND SMALLPOX

As far as the governor of Cuba was concerned, the traitor Cortés was dead or in chains. He sent fresh supplies and reinforcements to his captain Narváez, utterly unaware that they were being commandeered by Cortés, who was absolutely desperate for both. It is one of the great ironies of Cortés' story that if he had made fewer enemies his expedition may well have failed. Thanks to Velázquez's determination to destroy him, Cortés suddenly had one hundred and fifty more fresh soldiers and twenty horses, along with gunpowder, arms and ammunition. He managed to keep the rebellious troops of Narváez's company on his side, and began to train them so that they would show the same great discipline in battle displayed by his own men. For three weeks the Conquistadors rested, dressed their wounds and regained their strength. Then they moved to Tepeaca, where they found the locals hostile. Cortés brought forth a notary to witness a new decree from him: that any Mexicans who revolted after pledging their obedience to the King would be enslaved. Himself a trained lawyer, Cortés wanted everything to be seen to be above board. The decree outside Tepeaca ushered in a new terror that would plague the New World in the years to come: slavery.

Tepeaca was taken with relative ease after the locals and their Aztec allies chose to fight the Conquistadors among maize fields, allowing Cortés to deploy his cavalry to maximum effect. From their new base the Spanish were free to raid the locality and capture countless slaves, who were branded and put to work or sent back to Cuba. Cortés moved to shore up support at the settlement of Villa Rica and in the surrounding country, and again his forces easily crushed the local rebels who made the same mistake of fighting them in open country.

Meanwhile a fresh hell was descending on the Aztecs and their allies: disease. It is widely thought that the Spanish brought smallpox with them to the New World

– though there is some dispute about the exact nature of the disease that now swept across all of Mexico. There is no dispute about its lethal effects, however: those infected erupted in sores and boils, and rarely survived.

> *The illness was so dreadful that no-one could walk or move. The sick were so utterly helpless that they could only lie on their beds like corpses, unable to move their limbs or even their heads. They could not lie face down or roll from one side to the other. If they did move their bodies, they screamed with pain. A great many died from this plague, and many others died of hunger; they could not get up to search for food, and everyone else was too sick to care for them, so they starved to death in their beds.*
>
> *Codex Florentino*

One of the first casualties was the new Aztec leader Cuitláhuac, who died shortly after overseeing the expulsion of the Spanish from Tenochtitlan. He was replaced by Cuauhtémoc, the twenty-five-year-old husband of one of Montezuma's daughters. It thus fell to Cuauhtémoc to defend Mexico against Cortés' new attack, and he immediately sent reinforcements to his garrisons across the empire. These warriors repeated the mistakes of previous Aztec occupiers by raping and looting, which turned the local populations against the new leader. The Aztec empire had learned nothing from its encounter with the Conquistadors; Cortés, on the other hand, had learned a very valuable lesson concerning the capture of Tenochtitlan, the city that so beguiled him.

He ordered the construction of thirteen large ships which he hoped would allow him control of the great lake that surrounded the city. His plan was not to launch another direct attack on the city; he had tasted the wrath of its defenders and knew that a frontal assault would guarantee heavy losses. This time, he would lay siege to the city, and starve its people into submission.

The timber for the boats was cut to designs prescribed by the master carpenter Martin Lopez, to be transported by eight thousand Tlaxcalan natives to the Spanish forward base at Texcoco. Texcoco was one of the largest cities outside of Tenochtitlan, which Cortés had taken with the assistance of over ten thousand Tlaxcalan warriors who had now joined his invading army. The locals, already devastated by smallpox and all too aware of the Spaniard's reputation for cruelty, sued for peace, and were soon followed by neighbouring towns. Only at Iztapalapa did the Conquistadors encounter any real resistance – here they were forced back after the town was deliberately flooded by its defenders, soaking the gunpowder of the Spanish army.

Cuauhtémoc himself remained defiant and refused Cortés' offers of peace, pledging to destroy the Spanish if they dared attack his city. As negotiations continued, the ships were constructed and ditches dug out into canals to allow Cortés' forces to sail into the great lake surrounding Tenochtitlan. Major skirmishes followed, with both the Spanish and Aztec armies attacking surrounding areas to try to subjugate the local populations. The Spanish took control of most of the important territory around Tenochtitlan, making allies of some populations and enslaving others. Cortés survived a plot to assassinate him, hatched by soldiers close to the governor of Cuba, and asserted his authority over his forces, ordering the people of Tlaxcala, Huexotzinco and Cholula to send him twenty thousand warriors. Fifty thousand arrows tipped with copper were also demanded, and duly sent. There would be no more talk of peace, for the time being. Cortés marched his army towards Chapultepec, the source of Tenochtitlan's water supply. There he defeated the Aztec garrison charged with defending the town, and broke the pipes that pumped fresh water to the tens of thousands of Aztecs living in the capital. The siege of Mexico had begun.

THE LAST BRUTAL STRUGGLE

The value of the Spanish sloops was demonstrated in the very first battle on the lake. Cortés sailed to the rescue of a company under attack from a large Aztec force, and soon found himself surrounded by over a thousand Aztec war canoes. Using a favourable wind and a sudden spurt from his oarsmen, however, he was able to smash through the canoes and inflict great losses on his enemy. The sloops allowed the Spanish to sail to whichever part of the city they chose, and gradually they began to fill in the gaps in the causeways to allow troops to enter the city. The Aztecs knew that the relative narrowness of the causeways would create problems for any advancing army and so they sought to break apart the Spanish repairs whenever they could. They had changed tactics, too – leaping into the water whenever the cavalry charged them. A lethal game of cat and mouse ensued, but time was on Cortés' side as the Aztecs became increasingly short of food and fresh drinking water.

The battles became increasingly desperate and savage, with each side suffering heavy losses. Bernal Díaz describes it from the Conquistadors' point of view:

*Wounded and bandaged with rags, we had to fight
from morning till night, for if the wounded had not
fought but stayed behind in camp, there would not
have been twenty sound men in each company to
go out.*

The Spanish pulled down and burnt every house that
they came across, to prevent the Aztecs from using
them as cover in any counter-attack. They knew that
in open battle they had a significant advantage, and
the canals between the houses were gradually filled
in to ensure the cavalry could charge freely into the
native army ranks. By night the Aztecs attempted to
clear them again. Day after day the brutal struggle
between the two sides continued. But one by one, the
lakeside towns that had fought with the Aztecs began
to want peace and ally themselves with Cortés. They
kept his army supplied, whilst the Aztecs gradually
starved. Yet Cortés sensed that his army was getting
bogged down and that their failure to make progress
into the centre of Tenochtitlan was giving heart to
those defending the city. He resolved to gather all of

his forces together and attempt to make a decisive strike deep into the city, by occupying the great market place at Tlatelolco. It was a huge gamble: by pushing so far into the city he knew that the Aztecs could circle around and cut off all escape routes, trapping the Conquistadors inside the city. They had already experienced what it was like to try and fight their way out under such circumstances. Nonetheless, Cortés ordered his men to strike forth and seize as much of the capital as they could.

The gamble did not pay off – indeed it was a gamble which very nearly cost Cortés his life. Ambushed at one of the gaps in the causeways, he found his forces outnumbered and such was the scale of the slaughter that the discipline of his men finally deserted them. Many turned and fled, despite Cortés' cries to hold firm. More than sixty Conquistadors were captured alive and taken off to be sacrificed, and Cortés very nearly suffered the same fate. He was rescued from the clutches of six or seven Aztec captains and hauled back to safety by his men. The Aztecs threw down the severed heads of the men they killed as the Conquistadors beat a disorganised retreat back along the causeways. The other companies fared no better, and were also driven back to their quarters having suffered catastrophic losses.

It was a humiliating defeat, and many of the lakeside towns who witnessed the slaughter refused from then on to send any forces to help the Spanish, believing they were doomed. That night, as the small Spanish force nursed their wounds, they were forced to watch in horror as their captured compatriots where led up the steps of the great temples to be sacrificed. Cuauhtémoc sent their hands, feet and the skin of their faces to all the towns that had allied themselves with the Spaniards, warning them that unless they changed sides and sent their warriors to help the Aztecs they too would suffer the same fate.

Attacking the Aztec capital head on was clearly suicidal, even with experienced and disciplined troops. Cortés was in no doubt that the numbers facing him were simply too vast to overcome. But this huge army, he now realised, might easily become a problem for Cuauhtémoc. It needed to be fed, and drinking water was already in short supply. Cortés elected to remain inside the heavily fortified garrisons along the shores of the lake, and step up patrols to prevent any re-supply of the Aztec capital. His ships sailed back and forth along the lake by day and night to intercept the canoes that sought to bring food and water to the capital. The Aztec army was so numerous that it needed huge amounts of food every day to keep up its warriors' strength. It would prove to be a fatal weakness.

Cortés reverted to the earlier tactic of bridging the gaps in the causeways to allow his troops and horses to move freely. This time he did his best to hold each new position gained. Inch by bloody inch, the Spanish moved along the causeways and into the city, pushing back the Aztecs with cavalry charges and cannon fire. Although they fought with incredible bravery and resilience, the New World army simply could not halt let alone reverse the advance.

After thirteen more days of struggle, Cortés was reinforced by warriors from Tlaxcala and Texcoco. The Aztecs' gods had promised them victory within ten days, and there is some suggestion that once this period had passed they began to lose heart, no longer believing that their victory was preordained. More battles followed, resulting in the Conquistadors taking control of the last source of drinking water within the city. From this moment on, Cuauhtémoc was doomed. Though he fought on for several weeks, rejecting every offer of peace from Cortés, by the time the Conquistadors reached the market place at Tlatelolco, right in the heart of the city, he must have known his empire was lost. The Aztec codices describe the scene:

> *During this time the Aztecs took refuge in the Tlatelolco quarter. They deserted the Tenochtitlan quarters all in one day, weeping and lamenting like women. Husbands searched for their wives, and fathers carried their small children on their shoulders. Tears of grief and despair streamed down their cheeks.*

The Aztecs had defended their city with incredible tenacity, but the end had come for them. Cuauhtémoc was paddled out in a canoe to meet Cortés and surrender to him. He begged Cortés to kill him, but Cortés refused, telling the Aztec King that he respected the way that he had fought to save his people. The Spanish fired their cannons to celebrate their victory, as thousands of Aztecs fled what was left of the great city. The war was over. Cortés had achieved the glory he had always lusted after.

Now what he wanted was gold.

THE LUST FOR GOLD

At first Cortés treated Cuauhtémoc with great respect, lodging him in fine quarters and bringing him the very best food. He agreed to Cuauhtémoc's request that those natives remaining in the city be allowed to leave; there were so many bodies lying in the streets that the city was no longer habitable. It is thought one hundred thousand were killed in the siege, the battle, and its aftermath. The proud Aztec people streamed out from the capital into the surrounding towns and villages, each one searched by the Spanish for anything of value before they were allowed to leave. Cortés ordered the dead to be buried and the causeways rebuilt, and marked on a map the areas he intended to claim for Spanish settlers, as well as those that would be left for the indigenous people.

It was inevitable that sooner or later Cortés would want to know what the Aztec King had done with the vast reserves of gold that the Conquistadors had seen when they were last in the city. Already the Spanish troops were ransacking the houses and temples of Tenochtitlan in search of treasure. Those in the boats did best, having had ample opportunity to eye up the houses that they knew contained valuable objects. Others searched in reed beds surrounding the lake, having seen the locals hiding their treasures there. But Cortés was after gold on a much grander scale. He believed that Cuauhtémoc held the key to enormous reserves of precious stones and gold artifacts, and he demanded to know where they were. When Cuauhtémoc replied that he had already given Cortés all the gold he had, Cortés refused to believe him. In order to get him to talk, he had Cuauhtémoc tortured, by holding his feet over a fire. After four agonising days, Cuauhtémoc confessed that he had thrown a great deal of treasure into the lake, and several hugely valuable objects were retrieved by the Conquistadors. Still, it did not satisfy their lust for gold, and they continued to believe that the Aztec empire had more than he was letting on. If that was true, the rest was never found.

Cortés had Cuauhtémoc executed several years later, in Honduras – as he feared the Aztec leader might lead an insurrection against him. Though Cortés became a very wealthy man from his expedition, many of his followers did not: some received so little gold that it did not even cover the debts they had accrued while fighting the countless bloody battles of the Mexican campaign.

Cortés had the shattered city of Tenochtitlan largely

rebuilt, with churches replacing the ancient temples and the palaces of the Aztec elite commandeered for use by the Spanish. The remnants of the Aztec people were at first allowed to share their ancestral home, but it soon became necessary to reward the Spanish Conquistadors with land, and the natives were rapidly squeezed out, forced to work land they no longer owned under the 'encomienda' system devised by the Spanish. This system involved the natives paying tribute to their Spanish masters in produce or labour – in truth only one step removed from slavery.

The city was prone to flooding, and Lake Texcoco was later drained. Over the course of the next centuries almost all of the fabled ancient city was transformed into what is now Mexico City. Spanish settlers poured into the newly conquered empire of Mexico, in search of wealth and land. But by the time they arrived, many of the Conquistadors had already left for new adventures. For although Mexico and the Aztecs had fallen, it was known that other amazing lands existed further south in the New World. One of these was said to be full of gold – its name was Peru.

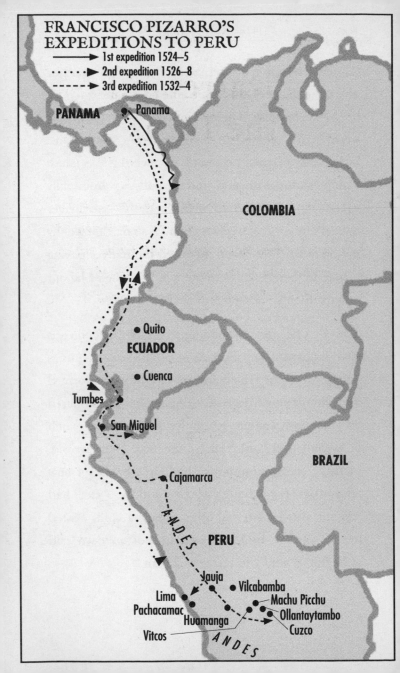

FRANCISCO PIZARRO'S
EXPEDITIONS TO PERU

→ 1st expedition 1524–5
····▶ 2nd expedition 1526–8
- -▶ 3rd expedition 1532–4

PANAMA • Panama

COLOMBIA

• Quito

ECUADOR

• Cuenca

Tumbes

San Miguel

BRAZIL

• Cajamarca

ANDES

PERU

Jauja

Lima • • Vilcabamba

Pachacamac • Machu Picchu

Huamanga • • Ollantaytambo

Vitcos • Cuzco

ANDES

Pizarro and
the Incas

Floating rumours had reached the Spaniards, from time to time, of countries in the far west, teeming with the metal they so much coveted; but the first distinct notice of Peru was about the year 1511, when Vasco Núñez de Balboa, the discoverer of the Southern Sea, was weighing some gold which he had collected from the natives. A young barbarian chieftain, who was present, struck the scales with his fist, and, scattering the glittering metal around the apartment, exclaimed, 'If this is what you prize so much that you are willing to leave your distant homes, and risk even life itself for it, I can tell you of a land where they eat and drink out of golden vessels, and gold is as cheap as iron is with you.'

William Hickling Prescott,
A History of the Conquest of Peru (1847)

Even before Cortés had marched so triumphantly across Mexico and seized its treasures, the Spanish had known of another land that lay further to the south, the land we now know as Peru. One of those accompanying Balboa on his trek through Panama in 1511, was Francisco Pizarro, the man who would later conquer Peru. He was at Balboa's side when the fabled country of gold was first mentioned, and beside him again when they finally hacked through the jungle and became two of the first Europeans ever to gaze upon the Pacific Ocean. Balboa would never live to see the land of the Incas: he was executed in Panama eight years later, for allegedly attempting to usurp the authority of a rival. The man who arrested him and handed him over to his executors was Francisco Pizarro, who would not only live to see Peru; in time, he would rule it, too. The story of how the illiterate bastard child of a Spanish captain led fewer than two hundred Conquistadors to victory over the largest army in South America is breathtaking, brutal and bloody, even by the extraordinary standards of that most extraordinary time.

PIZARRO'S CHANCE

He was in his early fifties; he had missed his moment, it seemed. In truth Pizarro had rarely been seen as an exceptional individual, but rather as a dependable Captain with a cool head and a steely determination. He was talented, yes, and had made a modest income from his business endeavours in Panama and elsewhere in the New World. He had accompanied Balboa on a largely successful mission to explore the land West of Panama. For a former pig herder from Trujillo who left Spain sometime around 1502, he had done reasonably well. Unlike some of the more squeamish Spanish settlers, he had no qualms about using extreme force to put down any rebellion from the indigenous people, and indeed had personally tortured natives in Panama to extract information from them. When left in charge of a settlement in Hispaniola in 1510, Pizarro displayed the kind of savage pragmatism that summed up the man: he had only one boat, and so deliberately waited until the colony was reduced by starvation to just a handful before he embarked for home.

His ruthless streak was an asset in turning a profit in the inhospitable environment of Panama. But he was also stubborn and difficult, and his cruelty led others to question whether he was capable of taking sole charge of an army whose long-term respect and loyalty could only be earned with the sort of charisma and charm shown by the likes of Hernán Cortés. At the time, common soldiers tended to respect Captains of noble birth: the illegitimate Pizarro was not in that league, and there were even rumours that he had been forsaken by his parents as a child, and would have died if he had not been nursed by a sow.

However, Pizarro's keen nose for a profitable alliance had seen him rise to the position of mayor of the newly founded Panama City – a role bestowed upon him partly as a reward for his loyalty to Pedrarias Dávila, the governor of the Spanish settlements around Panama. Dávila's long running feud with his rival Balboa was brought to an end when Pizarro seized his fellow Conquistator and delivered him to the governor for trial – and ultimately execution. Pizarro's new position of authority allowed him to make influential contacts, and one of these was with Deigo de Almagro, a fellow bastard who had joined Dávila's armada in order to flee Spain after stabbing a servant. Pizarro and Almagro both dreamed of seeking their fortunes in the fabled land of gold, Peru, and they managed to persuade a Spanish priest, Hernando de Luque, to back their proposed expedition. Luque controlled the funds of the community he was a vicar too in Panama, which was enough to get the show on the road. It was agreed that Francisco Pizarro would head the fleet, while Almagro stayed behind to recruit more men and gather supplies. At last, Pizarro had been given his chance at glory.

But the expedition that he so proudly led in September 1524 turned out to be a disaster.

PIZARRO'S FIRST EXPEDITION

Pizarro's first fleet consisted of just two ships, the largest of which was originally built for Balboa, who had intended to make the same journey. A motley crew of around one hundred desperate men was all that could be assembled; previous expeditions south along the coast had all led to great hardship and ultimate failure, so troops were wary of signing up. They set off from Panama in November 1524 – the very worst time of year to begin an expedition. It was the rainy season, when navigation to the south became doubly difficult. Still, Pizarro's little fleet made it south as far as the Biru river, and there dropped anchor to disembark and search for the legendary hordes of gold.

They had landed at the edge of a vast swamp. The rains made conditions even worse than they might have been, and every step taken by the band of Conquistadors was treacherous and exhausting. When not squelching through swamps the men were hacking through tangled woods or climbing barren rock faces. In searing heat, they hauled their armour-clad bodies through the inhospitable terrain until completely exhausted and desperate for water and food. It became clear to everyone except Pizarro that there was nothing to find in the region, and in the end even Pizarro had to admit that the landing site had been a poor choice. They returned to their vessel and sailed further south – straight into a series of violent storms.

For ten long days they battled against the ferocious elements, bailing out their ships and trying desperately to prevent themselves being shipwrecked. Their supplies were soon consumed or smashed to pieces, and they decided to make for a landing site they had visited earlier to take on water and food. It was dry land, but that was all that could be said for it. A dense, almost impenetrable forest lay in all directions. The rain was incessant, the biting insects ferocious. The men were utterly forlorn, and pleaded to be allowed to return to the safety of Panama. But Pizarro persuaded them to stay, and sent a small party back to the Isle of Pearls (off the coast of Panama) to bring fresh supplies while he and his men looked for native settlements.

He searched in vain for weeks. There was still no sign of the promised supplies, and twenty of his men had by now starved to death. But eventually Pizarro stumbled across a small village, upon which his famished men descended for desperately needed food. It prevented the whole scale disaster that, until now, his expedition had threatened to become, and perhaps almost as importantly it provided new evidence for a land of gold. The natives of the village, having fled at the sight of the strangers, warily returned and communicated with them. Around their necks they wore roughly-worked gold necklaces, and they told the Conquistadors of a mighty land across the mountains where they said there was more of the precious metal. Much more.

Supplies finally arrived from the Isle of Pearls – held up by more ferocious storms that had almost cost the rescue party their lives. The Conquistadors forgot their hardships and struck out south once more. Spying a native settlement they went ashore, only to find it abandoned. In their haste to flee, the inhabitants had left their dinner cooking on the fire: it was human flesh. Returning to their ships in horror, the band sailed south once more, to a spot where paths seemed to lead through the mangrove trees, suggesting possible inhabitation. There they disembarked once more, and Pizarro sent his battered ship back to Panama to have the storm damage it had suffered repaired. Finding a native settlement deserted, Pizarro decided to send his deputy, Montenegro, to scout the area and attempt to make contact with the locals.

The locals had decided to make contact, too. They greeted Montenegro with a hail of arrows followed by a frontal assault that killed three of his men and wounded several others. They then turned on Pizarro's company. Pizarro himself was wounded in seven places and had to be rescued from certain death by his men. The native attack was finally repelled, but at the cost of a further two Spanish lives. The Conquistadors had neither the heart nor the supplies to pursue an offensive campaign against such ferocious native armies, and decided to cut their losses and return to Panama.

On the way back, unbeknown to them, they passed

Pizarro's partner Almagro, heading in the opposite direction to assist him. Almagro reached the same spot where Pizarro had lost ten of his men, and explored the interior with not dissimilar results: Almagro lost an eye in a ferocious skirmish with the natives. His remaining good eye led him further south than Pizarro, to the mouth of the Rio de San Juan, where he found native settlements of a more sophisticated construction than he had previously seen. And crucially, here and elsewhere on the coast, he found natives who had gold. By the time he sailed back to Panama to look for Pizarro, Almagro had on board a considerable booty. It may have cost him the sight of one eye, but at least he had something to show for an expedition that might otherwise have been deemed a fiasco. Despite the high death toll and long list of hardships, as long as there was the promise of gold, the dream was still alive.

PIZARRO'S SECOND CHANCE

Pedrarias, the governor of Panama, was not a man

much given to dreaming. Upon hearing of the catastrophic losses the pair had suffered for such paltry returns, he flatly refused to grant permission for any future expeditions. There the story might have ended, had it not been for the intervention of the priest Hernando de Luque. It was he that changed Pedrarias' mind, no doubt stressing that along with the high risk of such an enterprise came the potential for high rewards. Pedrarias reluctantly agreed to sanction a second expedition, but so unimpressed was he with Pizarro's leadership that he insisted that from that point onwards Almagro must be Pizarro's equal in command. This turn of events led to friction between Almagro and Pizarro, as the latter suspected Almagro's promotion was the result of his former deputy blaming him for the mission's failures.

Still, Pizarro had been given a second chance at glory, and this time he was determined to succeed. He and Almagro pooled the knowledge they had each gleaned of the fabled land of Peru from their expedition. It did not amount to much. They knew that the land was ruled by a mighty king, who had recently expanded his empire, ruthlessly taking control of territory formerly ruled by other tribal leaders. It was clear to them that this man was a force to be reckoned with, as they each had first-hand experience of the ferocity of the local militias. They would need better arms, and better men, in order to launch a successful expedition into the territory of such a powerful overlord. They had barely begun to explore the interior of the land in their first expedition, yet had suffered huge losses through hunger, disease and battles with the natives. The scale of their task must have seemed formidable; yet everywhere they landed the tales of gold were confirmed, and these tales beckoned them on to explore the mysterious land whatever the cost in blood may be.

They knew little, then, of the land they were about to leave for, or the kind of people who might live there. And far to the south, in his great palace at Cuzco, the legendary Inca leader Huayna Capac knew even less about the strangers who dared to invade his extraordinary kingdom.

THE CHILDREN OF THE SUN

Born around 1464, the 'Sapa Inca' Huayna Capac had been on the throne since 1498. He was by all accounts a popular king, revered by his army and his people. One description of his rule, provided by the half-Inca and half-Spanish chronicler Felipe Guaman Poma de Alaya, states:

> *Having read accounts of the various kings and emperors of the world, I am sure none of them had the majesty or power of Huayna Capac Inca. The monarchs of Turkey and China, the Roman emperors, Christian and Jewish rulers, the kings of Africa: none of them enjoyed such esteem or wore so lofty a crown.*

Under his leadership the Inca empire had expanded to take in the entire known world – for before the Spanish arrived, the Inca believed only small bands of barbarians lived in the tangled groves beyond their lands. 'Tawantinsuyu', or 'the Land of the Four

Quarters', embraced parts of modern Ecuador in the north and modern Chile in the south, with the Andes forming a natural barrier to the east. In European terms, the land mass would stretch from Moscow to the Conquistadors' homeland of Spain.

A patchwork of provinces made up the Land of the Four Quarters, all ruled by local chiefs but all paying tribute to the one great leader, the Sapa Inca. Rebellions were ruthlessly crushed and Inca law zealously enforced. The vast distances between settlements, along with the hostile mountainous terrain, made governance difficult at times, but the Inca devised a network of roads to allow messengers to run in two mile relays, carrying the royal commands. A sophisticated system of warehouses connected up with the roads to ensure surpluses of food could be stored in preparation for the frequent times of famine. Although not all the people subject to Inca tribute welcomed their rule, they knew that the mighty empire at least provided protection against hunger and invasion from even more aggressive tribes. And there was little point in resisting, anyway: the Inca army was enormous, well trained and famed for its bravery.

The total population under Inca control at this time has been estimated at sixteen million. They were all, now, 'children of the sun': worshipping the Inca sun god Inti and the creator god Viracocha. The Inca believed that Viracocha had emerged from Lake Titicaca and brought all things to life, including mankind, before disappearing from the earth by walking west across the Pacific Ocean. Inca legends told that Viracocha would return from the same direction in times of trouble. One account describes Viracocha as a white man, carrying a staff: as with the Spanish invasion of Mexico, there are persistent reports that the natives may have mistaken the Conquistadors for returning gods.

The single most important figure in the history of the Inca nation was Manco Cápac, the first Sapa Inca. He was said to be the son of the sun god Inti, and it was he who founded the city of Cuzco on his father's orders, sometime around the year 1200. The Sapa Inca claimed direct descent from Manco Cápac and thus from his father Inti, and in turn the Sapa Inca acted as a father to all the Inca people – they were almost literally 'the children of the sun'. The annual ceremony of Inti Raymi gave thanks to Inti, and many sacrifices were made to ensure the resurrection of the sun. There then followed nine days of feasting, drinking and dancing. Inti was considered a largely benevolent deity: in times of war the god of thunder and lightning, Catequil, became of greater significance. Idols of Catequil were often carried into battles by Inca armies. Catequil was also believed to prophesy the future, and force the other gods to talk. His opinion on the wisdom of fighting battles at particular times and in particular places was thus of enormous importance to the Inca priests and generals. The Inca would very shortly be asking for his advice on the subject of the white men who came from the sea.

HUMAN SACRIFICE AND CANNIBALISM IN INCA CULTURE

Like the Aztecs, the Inca practised human sacrifice, albeit on a much reduced scale. The majority of their sacrifices were of animals, and only the most significant occasions would require them to offer human flesh and blood to their gods. The Inca seemed to favour the sacrifice of children rather than adults in a practice known as Capacocha. Ice mummies found at the top of the Llullaillaco volcano (on the border between present day Chile and Argentina) suggest that children were fattened up on special diets of llama meat and maize before sacrifice. The Inca believed that if sacrifices were offered at high altitudes they would be closer to the gods. The sacrificed children may have been drugged with coca leaves before being suffocated, struck on the head, or left to die of exposure.

Major events, such as the death of a Sapa Inca, were marked with more widescale human sacrifices. As many as four thousand individuals could be sacrificed on such occasions. A deceased Sapa Inca would be mummified, and left in their palace, which would then be abandoned by the living, with a new palace being constructed for the next Sapa Inca. At key festivals the mummified bodies of important deceased Inca figures would be carried through the streets, and the Conquistadors report seeing such practices during their conquests. However the religious practices of the Inca did not inspire the same revulsion and fear in the Spanish as the staggeringly bloody rites of the Aztecs had on earlier expeditions. There was only one great taboo in which the Inca may have indulged that left the Conquistadors utterly horrified – cannibalism.

Pizarro had witnessed the cannibalism practised by the natives of the coasts when he visited their settlements during his first expedition. Although many scholars do not believe that cannibalism was widespread within the Inca culture itself, several chroniclers do mention cannibalistic practices. It may be that the notion of endemic cannibalism was used by the Spanish to justify their actions in 'civilising' Peru: if it did exist at all it was almost certainly exaggerated. Garcilasso de la Vega's famous work *History Of The Inca Kings* suggests that the people of the Andes had 'butcher's shops for human flesh, where sausages are prepared, in order for nothing to be wasted', but there is scant evidence for such institutionalised cannibalism. Vega, although born of an Incan mother, was writing for a European audience, and tended to stress the glory of both the Spanish and the Inca empires at the expense of those they conquered. Cannibalism was a popular charge because it painted the people of the New World as primitive and bloodthirsty. When smallpox later ravaged Peru, it was said that it first took hold after the Sapa Inca Huayna Capac ate the flesh of two infected Spaniards – although there is every chance that this story has no basis in fact, but was disseminated by the Spanish to imply that the disease was spread as a result of the savage behaviour of the Inca people.

In truth, at around the time that Pizarro set out on his second expedition in 1526, the Inca empire was a relatively stable confederation with most of its major battles behind it. Huayna Capac was an experienced and wise ruler, and he had managed to successfully hold together all the disparate cultures that paid tribute to him, despite the huge logistical problems inherent in such a vast empire. Things were calm in Peru, at least by the turbulent standards of the day. In marked contrast, Pizarro, at around this time, was presiding over an expedition that was in total chaos, and which threatened to go down in history as the most disastrous mission in the history of the New World.

PIZARRO AND THE ISLE OF GORGONS

In March 1528, Pizarro was marooned on an insect-infested island, gradually starving to death. Just thirteen of his men remained to share the hell with him. They had been living as castaways for seven months, awaiting a rescue ship. The majority of Pizarro's party had eagerly seized an earlier opportunity to desert the man they now considered a lunatic and return to the safety of Panama. On the nearby Isle of Gallos ('Roosters'), Pizarro had tried in vain to persuade his troops not to abandon the mission when the governor of Panama's rescue ship arrived. He drew a line in the sand with his sword, stating:

Comrades and friends, on that side lies the part
which represents death, hardship, hunger, nakedness
and abandonment; this side here represents comfort.
Here you return to Panama – to be poor! There you
may go on to Peru – to be rich. You choose which
best becomes you as brave Spaniards.

Sixty-seven of the brave Spaniards in question chose to go home. The fact that so few of the men present responded to Pizarro's words says much about the hardships they had endured, and the lack of faith they now had in their leader's dreams. They boarded the boat 'weeping with joy', delighted to escape with their lives, for Pizarro's second expedition had floundered in a similar fashion to his first.

Pizarro and Almagro had sailed directly from Panama to Rio de San Juan, where they surprised a native settlement and made off with reasonably large quantities of gold and jewels. It had been a promising start to their enterprise. Their earlier attempts at drumming up support for the expedition had been received with only lukewarm enthusiasm, and because of this they had departed with a rag-tag army, few horses, and inadequate supplies. It was agreed that Almagro should return with the early spoils of adventure to see if the sight of gold could persuade more followers to join them in Peru. Pizarro would remain at the settlement, while his deputy Ruiz continued to explore the land further south – crossing the equator for the first time.

While Almagro and Ruiz were away, Pizarro's fortunes took a turn for the worse. He marched his men into the interior, through thick woodland and up high hills, in search of a benign spot he could establish a settlement at. Poisonous snakes and alligators accounted for several of his men, and the natives who harassed them with arrows at every turn accounted for several others. The Conquistadors found almost nothing to eat in the unfamiliar forests of South America, and hunger and thirst were a constant problem. Mosquitoes and other insects persecuted the men incessantly. Worst of all, they were getting nowhere: the promised lands of gold were a distant dream to Pizarro's men by now, and they longed to return to Panama. Utterly dejected, they headed back to their coastal base, to find Almagro and Ruiz waiting for them. Almagro had brought reinforcements of around eighty men, and Ruiz told more tales of a kingdom of fabulous wealth lying across the mountains. Ruiz had also captured two natives to serve as translators, and they had told him of the Inca palaces, where gold was as common as wood. All thoughts of turning back were now banished, and the three vessels immediately sailed south to the promised lands that Ruiz had scouted.

But the winds had changed since Ruiz was last in the area. Now they blew north, and great tempests battered the small Spanish ships. They were forced to make land at the Isle of Gallos, in order to repair their vessels and find food and shelter. When the winds had died down they sailed on to the port of Tacamez, passing signs of advanced civilisation all along the coast. This was Quito, not Peru, but at Tacamez the Conquistadors gazed in delight at the gold and jewels worn by many of the local people. Pizarro went ashore with a small band of his men to negotiate trade with them. It did not go well. An army of around 10,000 attacked them, and might well have slaughtered every last man were it not for a moment of farce that appears to have saved many Spanish lives. A nobleman of the cavalry fell from his horse, and the sight of him getting to his feet so astounded the native army that they fell back momentarily in confusion. They had assumed that the man and the horse were one single creature, and the division of the two appeared to them so remarkable that they were paralysed with incredulity. It gave the Spanish time to retreat hastily back to their boats.

Clearly, the Conquistadors could not take on the vast army with their scant armaments – but they also had creditors to pay, and to return home now would spell financial ruin for Pizarro and the rest. Almagro suggested that he should return once more to Panama in order to bring back more men and better arms, while Pizarro once more waited for him at a suitable spot on the coast. But Pizarro had had quite enough of starving in thick forests, and a violent argument ensued. As the two men reached for their swords to settle their dispute, Ruiz intervened and calmed the situation. In the end, Almagro's plan was adopted – perhaps because no-one could think of a better one.

Once more, then, Pizarro was left to try and eke out an existence on some of the most inhospitable terrain on earth while Almagro returned to Panama. To make matters worse, all along the coast heavily armed natives waited with hostile cries when they attempted to land. Running short of supplies, the only place Pizarro could find to land was the barren Isle of Gallos. His men were outraged at being marooned once more at such a desolate spot, and smuggled letters back to Panama begging the governor to send a ship to rescue them from the madman Pizarro. The ship was duly sent, and only the thirteen who chose to stay with Pizarro remained determined to continue, somehow, to Peru. They were dropped at the nearby Isle of Gorgons to await a new ship from Almagro. They had hoped that the island would be more hospitable than the Isle of

Gallos. It wasn't. They scanned the horizon every day for signs of a rescue ship, but in vain.

Finally, after seven long months, with all of the men at the very brink of death, Almagro's ship arrived, piloted by Ruiz. The luck of Pizarro and his Conquistadors had finally turned. And at almost exactly the same time, across the sea in the land of the Incas, the luck of Huayna Capac and his empire was turning too.

DEATH OF HUAYNA CAPAC

It may have been smallpox: others suspect measles, or some indigenous plague. The jury is still out on what exactly killed Huayna Capac, but whichever disease struck the Inca king, its effects were sudden and lethal. Worse still for the Incas, the king's chosen heir, Ninan Cuyuchi, died beside him. Huayna Capac perished before he could nominate a new heir, robbing the kingdom of any chance of a peaceful and smooth succession. Instead the Inca were plunged into a savage civil war. Some of Huayna Capac's attendants stated that he had nominated his twenty-five-year-old son Atahuallpa to govern, others said Huáscar, Atahuallpa's brother by a different queen, was the chosen one. Huáscar was in Cuzco at the time, and most accounts agree that he took the throne there, backed by the Inca nobility. Atahuallpa was far away in what is now Ecuador, but he had the most experienced divisions of the Inca army on his side. When Huayna Capac's funeral cortege arrived at Cuzco, carrying the mummified remains of the great king, Huáscar was alarmed to discover that his half-brother was not present to welcome it, nor to welcome him as the new king. The spectre of war hung over the funeral ceremony, at which hundreds of Inca were sacrificed in order to help Huayna Capac win favour with the gods in the afterlife. The messengers that Atahuallpa sent to bring Huáscar good wishes were returned home to him having been tortured and maimed. It was clear that the brothers could only settle their differences on the battlefield. It is estimated that up to sixteen thousand men were killed in the first battle alone. Atahuallpa won that encounter, and it was said that for years afterwards he drank from a gilded cup that had been fashioned from the skull of the commander of Huáscar's forces. Another report suggests that Atahuallpa was initially captured but escaped from his prison by breaking its walls with a copper bar smuggled in to him by a local woman.

Huáscar set out to avenge the defeat by assembling an army that vastly outnumbered Atahuallpa's, and marched north to face down his brother's rebellion. As the Inca empire tore itself apart, Pizarro and his small band of explorers were landing on the northern fringes of modern day Peru.

FIRST CONTACTS

Seven months of starving misery on one of the bleakest islands on the planet had not dulled Pizarro's enthusiasm for his mission. Aside from anything else, he knew that this was his last chance at wealth and glory. So when Ruiz's rescue ship arrived at the Isle of Gorgons, he had immediately pressed on rather than asking to be taken home. The new fleet sailed to the Inca port of Tumbes, led there by the two native prisoners. It was April 1528 when Francisco Pizarro finally set foot in the fabled land of Peru.

The reception from the natives was in marked contrast to his earlier encounters: here he was greeted warmly by the astonished local population. They 'sailed out to the ship on balsa rafts without any guile or menace but rather with joy and pleasure to meet such new people'. Bringing them Spanish food and gifts, they welcomed them ashore, where the local chief assured the Conquistadors that they need not fear any attack. For their part, the Conquistadors appear to have been just as astonished and transfixed as the natives, and had no qualms about trusting people they immediately recognised as rational and cultured. Each side questioned the other with intelligence, openness and genuine curiosity. An African servant who had sailed with the Spanish was asked to wash his face to prove that his skin colour was real; the almost seven foot tall Pedro de Candia was mobbed by natives who took him to be from a race of giants. The Spanish, too, marvelled at the sights before them: all around there were buildings of a finer construction than ever seen before in the New World, and there were miles of roads, irrigation canals and planted fields that groaned with agricultural produce. There in Tumbes they also became the first Europeans to gaze upon a Peruvian temple, so heavily decorated with gold and silver that it dazzled their eyes as it shone in the sun. Several of the Conquistadors were so overwhelmed that they begged to stay in this incredible new world rather than return to Panama. At least one fell in love with a local woman.

It is one of the more poignant moments in the blood-soaked story of the Conquistadors. When the two worlds came face to face with one another for the first time, it resulted in something approaching ecstatic joy on both sides. We know, of course, that this brief moment of peace, of tolerance and understanding, was not to last. Indeed it would turn out to be the prelude for one of history's most tragic and bloody events. Leaving two of his men behind to learn the language and culture of the wondrous new world he had found, Pizarro sailed for home. He fully intended to return.

And return he did, in 1532. This time he was in the land of the Inca not to explore, but to conquer.

PIZARRO'S THIRD EXPEDITION

It had taken time for Pizarro to acquire the necessary permissions from the Spanish crown and to raise the funds to pay for another expedition. By the time he sailed once more from Panama the civil war in Peru was reaching its murderous conclusion. Atahuallpa had won a hard-fought victory over the forces commanded by his brother, and although the exact chronology of events is unclear it appears he finally captured and imprisoned Huáscar just as the Spaniards were returning to Peru.

Despite his tales of the fabulous new land that was waiting to be conquered, Pizarro had failed to raise a force that might, on paper, be seen as any kind of threat to an Inca superpower of at least five million. Indeed the Spaniard had been forced to set sail hurriedly to avoid an inspection of his fleet by officers of the Council of the Indies, who he feared would realise he had not gathered nearly enough men, horses, provisions or ships to satisfy his part of the agreement with them. He left his brother Hernando behind to face the inspectors, who assured them that the vast majority of the forces had already sailed with Francisco. The deception worked, and the expedition was allowed to proceed – though more men deserted when they were told tales of the alligators, venomous snakes and endless jungles that awaited them in the land they were headed for.

And one other sticky problem remained: Pizarro had been placed in sole charge of the mission, and he had to explain this new situation to his partner Almagro, who was by now used to being his equal in standing. The tensions between them were exacerbated by Pizarro's brother Hernando, who from their very first meeting treated the veteran Almagro with contempt.

Almagro was so enraged that he attempted to acquire his own ships in order to lead a separate expedition to Peru, but the rift was smoothed over by Father Luque when it was agreed in writing that all proceeds of the expedition would be split equally between the original three instigators of the adventure – Pizarro, Almagro and himself. This prevented a disastrous split between the parties, but the tensions remained bubbling just beneath the surface, and in due course they would explode back into the open with devastating effect.

The total size of the force that landed once more in Peru was around one hundrd and eighty men and twenty-seven cavalry. Better armed than before, and in better spirits, but far fewer boots on the ground than Pizarro had estimated he needed, and far fewer than he had promised his backers he would provide. They disembarked not at Tumbes, as intended, but further up the coast in the Bay of St. Matthew, due to strong currents and high winds. The journey south was agonising for the Conquistadors as they struggled to swim and cross rivers swollen by heavy rain. Their hardship was soon forgotten, however, when they came across a native settlement, which they duly ransacked for much needed supplies, and for a large cache of gold and jewels. They shattered giant emeralds of incalculable value and, believing true examples would prove unbreakable, dismissed them as mere coloured glass. Some of the gold was sent back to Panama to try and persuade new recruits to join them – a policy which appears to have worked. The natives, however, had now been alerted to the true nature of the Spanish invasion, and never again would the newcomers receive the kind of welcome that they had experienced a few years earlier at Tumbes. Instead they found each settlement they came to deserted, and devoid of any treasure. The Conquistadors rapidly lost heart as their torturous progress through the hostile terrain brought them no new compensation, no new gold.

Pizarro reached Tumbes expecting to find the same majestic city that had so beguiled him on his earlier visit. Instead his weary men slumped down amidst the scattered rocks that traced out on the scorched earth –

all that remained of Tumbes. The savage brutality of the recent civil war was evident from the sheer scale of the destruction: no building remained unscathed, and the entire population had either been slaughtered or had fled. Yet for Pizarro the sight was more beautiful than all the palaces and spires of the Tumbes he had known from four years earlier. For in the charred ruins he saw a new vision, a new opportunity. The mighty Inca empire was clearly deeply divided, and he knew that such a situation would make his attempt at conquest far easier. His timing was perfect: any earlier and he would have had to face the experienced king Huayna Capac; just a few years later and the new king Atahuallpa would have had a chance to assert his authority. As it was he faced a leader who was still quashing pockets of resistance and whose right to rule was questioned by many of his people. If he could somehow remove Atahuallpa from the throne the Inca empire might well crumble from within. With renewed belief in the success of his mission, Pizarro pushed on south to Atahuallpa's stronghold at Cajamarca.

THE CONQUEST OF CAJAMARCA

Atahuallpa, for his part, was watching the progress of the Spanish force closely. He may well have been distracted by events elsewhere in his empire, since it seems that his brother's forces were not yet entirely defeated. Perhaps the arrival of such a small force seemed of little importance to a man who led an army of fifty thousand seasoned warriors. Certainly he made no attempt to intercept Pizarro as the Spaniard marched his Conquistadors through the Andes mountains towards Cajamarca. He sent word to the strangers that they could camp in the town, and that he would visit them there the next day. Pizarro feared a trap, and ordered his men to stay on watch for the entire night. Gazing out at the countless camp fires of the Inca army blazing in the darkness, even the most seasoned Conquistator was terrified at the prospect of what lay in store, as Pizarro himself later admitted:

> *The Indians' spies were letting the Inca know that we were all inside the hall, full of fear... And it was*

> *true what they were saying, because I saw myself*
> *many of us who without noticing pissed ourselves*
> *out of sheer terror.*

However, no attack came. Instead, late on the following afternoon, Atahuallpa arrived just as he had promised, carried by his officers on a golden throne. With him were several thousand Incas who crammed into Cajamarca's plaza to get a sight of the men who had come from the other side of the world. None of them were armed. It can only be assumed that Atahuallpa did not believe that he was putting himself in danger by meeting with such a small band of invaders, deep inside his own territory. One account by Agustin de Zarate certainly suggests that Atahuallpa and his men had a low opinion of the Conquistadors:

> *They thought so little of the Christian army that*
> *they expected to capture it with their bare hands. For*
> *an Indian governor had sent to inform Atahuallpa*
> *that the Spaniards were very few and so despicably*
> *lazy that they could not walk without getting tired,*

*for which reason they rode on a sort of large sheep
that they called horses.*

Other sources state that Atahuallpa had planned
an ambush, and that heavily armed warriors had
surrounded Cajamarca ready to fall upon the Spanish
when their leader gave them the signal. Whatever the
truth, Atahuallpa's decision to enter the town without
an armed escort proved to be a catastrophic error of
judgment. He was met by Friar Vicente, who held a
crucifix in one hand and a book of prayers in the other
(though some state it was a Bible). After being more or
less ordered by Vicente to renounce all the Inca gods
and embrace the Christian faith, a bemused Atahuallpa
enquired of the friar what authority he had to make such
a demand. When Vicente replied that it was all told to
him by the book that he was carrying, Atahuallpa asked
the friar to hand the book to him so that he could examine
it. Agustin de Zarate tells us what happened next:

*The bishop gave it to him, and Atahuallpa turned
over the leaves from end to end, saying that it said*

The charismatic leader Hernán Cortés conquered the Aztec capital of Mexico in 1521, claiming the country as New Spain.

The Aztecs were well-known for performing human sacrifices, including removing the heart or skinning the victim.

Hernán Cortés meets Montezuma c.1518. The king of the Aztecs is protected by warriors in plumed hats and skirts.

The last independent Aztec ruler, Montezuma II, ruled most of what is now Mexico on the eve of the Spanish conquest.

The last Inca Emperor of Peru, Atahuallpa, was captured and imprisoned by Francisco Pizarro.

Atahuallpa is executed by the Spanish Conquistadors by garrote having been charged with heresy in 1533.

Native slaves building Mexico City on the ruins of Tenochtitlan under the direction of the Conquistadors.

Francisco Pizarro was a captain with a cool head and a steely determination. He was known for being stubborn, difficult and cruel, and his casual use of extreme force struck fear into those he commanded.

After three arduous expeditions spanning a decade, the ruthless and determined Francisco Pizarro leads his army to victory and conquers the Inca Empire.

Machu Picchu was built around 1450, at the height of the Inca Empire, and abandoned just over 100 years later as a result of the Spanish Conquest.

The ancient Aztec ruins at Teotihuacan. Teotihuacanos practised human sacrifice, evidence of which was found during excavations of the pyramids.

nothing to him. In fact it did not speak at all. And
he threw it on the ground.

The Inca leader's disrespect for the holy book outraged
Vicente and gave Pizarro a pretext for attacking
Atahuallpa. He had already told his men to prepare for
action should he give them a signal, and this he then
gave by ordering a gun to be fired. The Conquistadors
then launched a ferocious attack upon Atahuallpa and
his people from all sides, massacring as many of the
bewildered and terrified Incas as they could:

They killed the Indians like ants. At the sound of
the explosions and the jingle of bells on the horses'
harness, the shock of arms and the whole amazing
novelty of their attackers' appearance, the Indians
were terror stricken. The pressure of their numbers
caused the walls of the square to crumble and fall.
Desperate to escape from being trampled under the
hooves of the horses, in their headlong flight so many
were crushed to death. So many Indians were killed
it was impracticable to count them.

Atahuallpa was seized by Pizarro and dragged away by the hair. The fleeing natives were ruthlessly pursued back to Atahuallpa's camp, where even more were cut down or taken captive. It is estimated that between two thousand and ten thousand died in just a few horrific hours of sustained violence. When the Spaniards ransacked the camp they discovered a treasure trove of gold, silver and precious jewels, which they brought back to Cajamarca and divided amongst themselves. The size of the bounty that every man received was enough to allow him to live comfortably for the rest of his life. They could hardly believe what had happened. The terror they had felt the night before was replaced with jubilation at their overwhelming victory and astonishingly lucrative rewards. Unbelievable as it may have seemed to them, however, the treasure they fingered so delightedly that night was merely a foretaste of what was to come. The Conquistadors would soon be rich beyond their wildest dreams. For all of the incredible tales they'd heard about this land being full of gold were true.

ATAHUALLPA AND THE
RANSOM ROOM

The Inca king rapidly recovered his composure after the disaster at Cajamarca. He knew that what the Spanish really lusted after was gold, and he knew that he could provide that for them in vast quantities. So as soon as Pizarro visited him in the prison in which he was now being held, Atahuallpa attempted to strike a deal. The offer he made to the Conquistadors to secure his freedom left them dumbstruck:

> *...Atahuallpa said that being the Governor's prisoner he hoped to be well treated, and promised, as ransom, to fill a certain room... with gold vessels and pieces and more silver than could be carried away. When this offer was interpreted to him the Governor was amazed and quite incredulous. Atahuallpa repeated it, however, and said that he would give even more. The Governor promised to treat him very well, and Atahuallpa expressed great gratitude. He then sent messengers to all parts of*

*the country, and to Cuzco in particular, to collect
the gold and silver he had promised as his ransom.
The promise was so great that its fulfillment seemed
impossible. For he had undertaken to fill a very large
room in the royal apartments of Cajamarca with
gold vessels to the height his hand could reach when
he stood upright...*

The room Atahuallpa offered to fill with gold still stands today, if the folk-tales of the people of Cajamarca are to be believed. As early as the seventeenth century tourists were being shown around it to marvel at the scale of the ransom that Atahuallpa pledged to Pizarro. A faint line cut in the wall shows the high tide mark of the sea of gold that flowed into Cajamarca from across the Inca kingdom. Perhaps the chronicles exaggerate when they speak of a room 5 metres wide and 6.7 metres long (17 ft by 22 ft long) that was to be filled to a height of 2.7 metres (9 ft). Whatever the exact dimensions, it is clear that the Conquistadors did not believe that it was possible for Atahuallpa to deliver on his incredible promise. Pizarro may well have thought that it was a desperate ruse by Atahuallpa to stall for time while his forces massed to rescue him – and perhaps that was indeed what was planned. It seems more likely, however, that Atahuallpa genuinely believed that if he delivered enough gold to the Spanish they would be satisfied, and would leave. He did not realise that the Conquistadors' thirst for gold was unquenchable.

As the room filled with treasure brought from all across Peru, Pizarro and Atahuallpa conversed about their different worlds and different gods. Atahuallpa rapidly learned Spanish, and the game of chess, which seems to have delighted him. Another game of chess was being played out by the two leaders, as each attempted to cover his weaknesses and move himself into a more favourable position. Pizarro, for his part, was acutely aware that he was still highly exposed so deep in Inca territory and with such a small force. Reports swirled around him of armies secretly gathering in the lands around Cajamarca, ready to avenge the recent massacre of their people. He sent messengers back to San Miguel to find out if reinforcements had arrived from Panama. Ideally he would have liked to push on towards Cuzco, as he knew that without control of the capital city his hold on the Inca was weak. However he simply did not have the men to both hold Atahuallpa and march against the massive armies he might yet encounter on any offensive in the south. And, of course, every day that he waited in Cajamarca brought him and his men vast new quantities of gold.

Atahuallpa saw that his life now depended on pleasing the Spanish, but he also knew that he had to try and wrest some control back after the calamity of his capture. He reasoned that he still had considerable power, commanding many tens of thousands of warriors. If he could deliver such a vast amount of gold to Pizarro, the Spaniard would surely realise the kind of iron grip that Atahuallpa had over his kingdom. Pizarro would naturally fear that if any harm came to such a great and beloved leader, the people would rise up and destroy the invaders. Entirely confident of his ability to raise the ransom, the Inca leader's main concern now was that the Spanish might decide to make some sort of deal with his brother, Huáscar, who remained Atahuallpa's prisoner. Huáscar had ruled over Cuzco during the civil war, and many of the city's inhabitants still believed he was their true leader. That was suddenly a major problem for Atahuallpa, as Cuzco was the main source of Inca gold. In order to remove any potential problems, Atahuallpa quietly passed a death sentence on his brother, who was drowned in the river Andamarca. Other members of his family were put to death too – Atahuallpa was determined to make sure the Spanish knew he was the undisputed leader of Peru. But with his dying breath Huáscar is said to have prophesied that his brother's rule as Sapa Inca would be even shorter than his own.

When Atahuallpa later feigned grief to the Spanish regarding his brother's demise, Pizarro commiserated. The two men continued to feast together and cordially discuss the merits of their different gods. The Spanish built a church, chess games resumed, and all the while Atahuallpa's ransom room filled with gold.

There was no doubt now that Atahuallpa was indeed capable of raising the agreed ransom. The question of what to do once that was achieved began to play on Pizarro's mind. He still suspected a plot of some kind was being hatched, and he dispatched his brother Hernando to the sacred city of Pachacamac to test the lie of the land and see if the arrival of gold could be hastened. Hernando guided a party of men through the freezing Andes mountains and across precarious bridges of willow to the city of the Inca creation god. There he was greeted peaceably and found no evidence of a revolt. He looted the temples, desecrated the Inca idols and returned to tell his brother of the news. Peru was so rich in precious metals that it is said Hernando had his horses shod with silver for the journey back to Cajamarca.

And similar reports came back from Cuzco too: the people were obeying Atahuallpa's instructions and dutifully bringing gold rather than planning war. The walls of the great temple of the sun had been stripped of their golden panels, and were deposited in the ransom room with all of the other treasures. If Atahuallpa thought that the Spanish would now be satisfied, however, he was horribly mistaken. In the middle of February 1533, he watched from his prison a fresh wave of Spanish troops march into Cajamarca. Almagro had arrived from Panama to reinforce Pizarro, and the second stage of the conquest of Peru was about to begin.

THE MURDER OF ATAHUALLPA

There was still a great deal of tension between Pizarro and his partner Almagro, and some reports state that when Almagro landed in Peru he did not intend to join Pizarro but instead hoped to claim all of the lands outside of the area granted to Pizarro by the king. If that was the case, he rapidly changed his mind upon hearing of the staggering amounts of gold now in Pizarro's possession. That treasure, however, would not be divided between Almagro's men as they had played no part in its capture. Resentment rapidly grew as the newcomers had to watch more and more gold being piled up in front of them, knowing that none of it would ever be theirs. They wanted to push on and grab some gold for themselves, and Pizarro now also felt he had the troops necessary to move to Cuzco. He reasoned that since most of the gold for Atahuallpa's ransom came from there, he could take it for himself rather than waiting for it to be brought to him. The treasure already won had to be divided between the men before they departed, and so it was melted down into ingots that could be weighed and measured. Thousands of beautiful Inca artworks were lost as a result. The haul was so huge that it took a month before the devastation was complete. When the goblets, vases, plates and statues had all reduced to blank blocks of metal in the Spanish furnaces they were left with seven tons of gold and thirteen tons of silver. A fifth of the booty was sent back to the king in Spain, in the custody of Hernando Pizarro. Atahuallpa was especially sorry to see him leave, as he believed that Hernando had been protecting him from certain parties in the Spanish camp who would wish to see him harmed. He was right to be worried.

Atahuallpa was simply too dangerous to be allowed to live. If they released him he would undoubtedly raise an army against the Conquistadors, and if they held on to him then it would be clear to all that the Spanish had not kept their word. It is not certain exactly who came up with the plan to put Atahuallpa on trial for treason, but it seems pretty clear that both Almagro and Pizarro sanctioned it once it had been proposed. The story was put around that Atahuallpa had been secretly mustering an army that was about to attack at any moment. It was nonsense, and everybody knew it, but that didn't matter to anybody but Atahuallpa. He was sentenced to be burnt to death – a punishment favoured by the Inquisition back in Spain for the crime of treason. As Atahuallpa wept and pleaded for his life, he was told that if he converted to Christianity he would be strangled rather than burnt. Given that Inca belief held that a mummified body was needed in order to reach the afterlife, Atahuallpa had little choice but to agree. The sentence was carried out with unseemly haste, and the Sapa Inca's body was left hanging in the square until the following morning.

Pizarro feigned sadness at the events and rapidly sought to disassociate himself from them, blaming others for the decision to try and then execute Atahuallpa. Many of the Spanish themselves felt revulsion at what had happened, and argued that Pizarro did not have the authority to put a sovereign leader to death. It was an ugly episode, and the injustice of it was highlighted when the accusations of an imminent assault were later proved to be entirely groundless. Even the battle-hardened soldier Cieza de León later wrote that the murder of the Inca leader was, 'the most despicable thing we Spanish ever did in the Indes'.

THE CONQUISTADORS IN CUZCO

Pizarro marched from Cajamarca to Cuzco with relative ease. There had been minor skirmishes en route, including one in which a Spaniard had his head cleaved in two by an Inca battle axe, but no great army had opposed him. The great walled capital city itself did not resist either, and the thousands of inhabitants who thronged the streets came only to gaze at the strangers, not to wage war against them. The Spanish were astounded at the skill of the masons who constructed Cuzco; conceding that the walls were better built than anything they had seen before, even back in Spain. Their hopes of finding at Cuzco a real-life 'El Dorado' where gold was as common as wood were largely realised: although a vast amount of treasure had already been sent to them at Cajamarca, huge reserves remained. The Spanish looted everything, including life-size men, women and llamas made of gold and silver. And once more the artifacts were thrown into a furnace that roared night and day to melt the precious relics into ingots.

News of Atahuallpa's death at Pizarro's hands had by now spread to all corners of the kingdom, and he decided that it would be prudent to place a puppet king on the throne in order to avoid a dangerous power vacuum. Manco, a young son of Huayna Capac, was chosen for the job. He was duly crowned in the traditional Inca fashion, and as the mummified remains of earlier dead kings were paraded through the streets, a month long celebration began. As he drank the local 'chicha' beer, Pizarro must have watched the events with a mixture of astonishment, pride and unbridled joy. He was sitting in the capital city of what he now firmly believed was the wealthiest country on earth, and it was a land that he controlled. The man who had been given one last chance at glory in his mid-fifties had grabbed that chance with both hands.

It was to be Pizarro's finest moment, however, and in truth the seeds of the coming disaster had already been sown. From the beginning, it seems Manco and Pizarro had misunderstood one another: Manco believed the Inca were now allies with Spain, however, as far as Pizarro was concerned Peru was now a vassal state. At first the different interpretations did not seem to matter – but tensions between the two leaders would rapidly grow. And another, perhaps even deeper fault line also threatened to wreck Pizarro's dreams of governing the fabled land of Peru: his partner Almagro shared the same dream as he did.

THE DIVISION OF PERU

Magnificent as Cuzco undoubtedly was, it was impractical as a capital city for the Spanish. They needed a port to send home the great wealth that they had accumulated, and to welcome reinforcements and settlers. Pizarro decided to build a new coastal settlement at Lima, which would become his power base in the new Spanish colony. It was while he was constructing the city that word first reached him of the king's decision to divide Peru between the conquering captains. Pizarro was granted the northern part of the kingdom, and Almagro the south. It was a decision that enraged two of Pizarro's younger brothers, Juan and Gonzalo, who had been left in charge of Cuzco and now treated it as their own personal fiefdom. The magnificent ancient capital would henceforth be ruled by Almagro. Not only that, but all of the lands south of Cuzco, which were yet to be explored, were part of Almagro's new kingdom too. It was believed that those lands, in what is now Chile, might be even richer than the territory already conquered. Almagro's supporters believed it was their right to explore to the south, since they had missed out on much of the earlier campaign and still felt cheated at being given no part of the treasure seized at Cajamarca.

The two factions were openly hostile to one another by the time Pizarro arrived back in Cuzco in 1535 to try and negotiate a settlement. The deal struck was that Juan and Gonzalo Pizarro would remain temporarily in charge at Cuzco while Almagro explored in the south. The deal was a fudge, and may well have fallen apart upon the return of Almagro when the Pizarro brothers would have had to hand back control of the city, had it not been rendered irrelevant by the events that were to follow. For while Almagro was away, the Inca rose up and took back their city from 'the bearded ones' who by then were making their lives unbearable.

THE INCA REVOLT

This, as I know from experience, was the most fearful and cruel war in the world; for between

> *Christians and Moors there is some fellow-feeling,*
> *and both sides, acting in their own interests, spare*
> *their prisoners for the sake of the ransom. But in*
> *this Indian war there is no such feeling on either*
> *side; both kill as savagely as they can.*

Agustin de Zarate

By the time Hernando Pizarro joined his brothers at Cuzco, Manco Inca's plot was already maturing. He had secretly ordered that vast fields of crops be planted so that he could feed a large army. Weapons were being made and ammunition gathered in preparation for a massive surprise assault. Manco Inca first needed to escape from prison in Cuzco, however – for he had already made one unsuccessful bid for freedom and was now in chains and kept under constant guard. He used the return of Hernando to effect his escape. Initially he was freed from prison so that he could greet Hernando (though some accounts state that Hernando actually freed Manco when he arrived), and he then used the Spaniard's ever-present lust for gold to trick him. Claiming he knew the location of a life size replica of his father Huayna Capac made from solid gold, Manco asked permission to attend a festival at Yucaya, promising he would return with the statue as a gift to show his gratitude. From Hernando's perspective it was too good a deal to miss out on, and he agreed to let the Inca leader go. With Manco now free, the long-planned insurrection could finally begin.

The revolt was born from the terrible injustices that the people of Cuzco in particular, and the Inca more generally, had suffered since the arrival of the Spanish. The 'bearded ones' had looted every sacred Inca temple and melted down the holiest relics of the Inca culture in front of the eyes of the disbelieving people. Despite the great wealth they had taken, they were always greedy for more. As Manco Inca once memorably said, 'Even if all the snow in the Andes turned to gold, still they would not be satisfied'. They had also mistreated the Inca nobility, including the Sapa Inca himself. Juan and Gonzalo Pizarro constantly abused and insulted Manco Inca, and are even reported to have urinated on him, as well as threatening to burn him alive. This was no idle threat, either – the Spanish had already burnt one Inca general at the stake, and routinely tortured Incas with fire if they thought that information about the location of gold could be obtained.

The grievance that wounded the Inca most deeply was the Spanish treatment of their women. They raped and abused the women with a casual disregard for either the women themselves or their families – indeed the mistreatment often happened in front of the children and husbands of the women concerned. The final straw for Manco Inca came when Gonzalo Pizarro decided that he wanted to sleep with the Sapa Inca's wife, Coya Ocllo. When Manco and Coya protested, Gonzalo raped her anyway. It was too much for Manco to bear. As he faced a secret gathering of Inca nobles and generals, Manco catalogued the injustices the Inca people had endured at the hands of the Spanish:

> *I have sent for you in order to tell you in the presence*
> *of our kinsmen and followers what I think about*

what these foreigners are trying to do with us, so that before it is too late, and before more join them, we can devise a plan of action which will be to everyone's good. Remember the Incas my ancestors ruled from Chile to Quito, treating their vassals so well they might have been their own children. They did not steal and killed only when it served justice.... Now the bearded ones have entered our land, their own country being so far away. They preach one thing and do another. They have no fear of God, and no shame; they treat us like dogs, calling us no other names. Their greed is such that there is no temple or palace left that they have not plundered... They keep the daughters of my father and other women, your sisters and kin, as their concubines, behaving in this like animals. They want to divide up, as they have already begun to, all the provinces, giving one to each so that they can loot them. Their goal is to see us so down-trodden and enslaved that all we will be fit for is to find them precious metals and give them our women... I believe it would not be just or honest for us to accept this. Rather we should attempt with every determination either to die or to kill these cruel enemies.

All were in agreement that the Inca must rise up and attempt to overthrow their tyrannical new rulers: the only disagreement related to how and when the attack should be launched. Some urged that they should begin the uprising as soon as possible in order to retain the element of surprise, but Manco argued that they should wait until reinforcements could arrive from distant parts of the kingdom. In the end Manco won the day, and a plan was hatched to launch a coordinated attack on both Lima and Cuzco on the same day. Manco's forces would gather at Calca, around 24 kilometres (15 miles) from Cuzco, where his father had built a summer palace. It took almost two weeks for all of the warriors to arrive there, brought from every distant corner of the empire's 'land of four quarters'. Finally, early in May 1536, an Inca fury that had been building for three years was suddenly unleashed upon the unsuspecting Spanish.

THE ASSAULT ON CUZCO

*One morning the Indians broke into Cuzco at more
than seven points, burning as they advanced and
fighting so fiercely that they gained half the city; and
there was little that did not burn since the houses
were thatched with straw.*

Alonso de Guzmán

The Inca army, numbering at least 50,000 (some
estimate 200,000), swarmed into Cuzco and overwhelmed the 170 Spanish defenders and their 1,000
or so native allies, driving them back into their
compound. There they struggled desperately to
hold back Manco's forces, hurling pails of water at
the fires that raged all around them. Manco cut the
water supplies to Cuzco, but the Spanish managed to
survive the initial devastating onslaught – a miracle
they would later attribute to Saint James, for it seemed
certain that they would all be killed.

In the days that followed the Spanish cleared away the

debris of the fire in order to allow their cavalry a clear charge at the Inca ranks. The horse once more proved to be a deadly weapon, inflicting carnage upon the native army, but the Inca had a secret weapon that the Spanish had not encountered before. The *bolas* was a type of lasso made from rocks strung together, and when thrown at the cavalry it was capable of bringing down a horse. The Inca had some success with it, and they also ambushed the flanks of the Conquistadors whenever they attempted to break out of their quarters. Toledo steel and gunpowder still trumped the stone and copper blades of the Old World, however, and the Inca suffered terrible losses during the battles that raged on almost every day, and through many of the nights. They took up a position in a fortress that overlooked the Spanish quarters, which allowed them to rain down arrows and stones without exposing themselves to the Conquistadors' fearsome weapons. The fortress in question, Sacsahuaman, allowed the Inca army to dominate Cuzco, and it became too clear to the three Pizarro brothers that they were doomed unless they could somehow manage to take it back.

Formidable as their objective was, they broke out and led a daring mission to scale the giant walls of Sacsahuaman, while thousands of Inca warriors attacked them from all sides. The resistance was led by the Inca nobleman Titu Cusi Gualpa, later revered as a true Peruvian hero for his bravery on that day. As the Conquistadors scaled the walls of Sacsahuaman on ladders, Titu charged up and down the ramparts, forcing them back with a captured Spanish sword. Any of his men who attempted to flee he hacked down, having ordered each of them to fight to the death. Despite being struck twice by arrows, he continued to foil every attempt at scaling the fortress. Even Pizarro would later admit that the Spanish were astonished at his fighting prowess and stamina.

Titu's heroics, and the countless other acts of bravery performed by the Inca warriors, were not enough. The savage struggle for the fortress ended when the Spanish attacked simultaneously at four separate points. Even Titu could not cover all of the gaps that the Conquistadors had hacked and blasted in his army's ranks. Hernando Pizarro ordered that Titu be taken alive, but true to his word he chose to die rather than be captured, throwing himself from a high tower after hurling his weapons at his attackers. Once he was dead resistance rapidly faded away and the Spanish began to massacre the weary Inca warriors. Many of them followed Titu's example and threw themselves from the high walls – some surviving the leap after landing on the great pile of bodies that now lay around the fortress. Sacsahuaman was soon under complete Spanish control, and Manco had lost a key position in Cuzco.

It is not known exactly how many Spaniards were killed in the brutal fighting for Sacsahuaman, but it is known that one of those who fell was Juan Pizarro, who led the charge. He was struck by a stone and died of his wounds a day later, whereupon he was buried in secret so that the Inca would not be encouraged by his death. The Inca had suffered catastrophic losses and could hardly believe that they had been defeated by such a small force. This was an army that was used to winning, and which had no previous experience of the savage effectiveness of the Spanish military machine. They now knew all too well how difficult it would be to retake Sacsahuaman. Further attacks were launched, and skirmishes continued, but from their new position of strength the Spanish managed to resist Manco's warriors and thus hold on to Cuzco.

Manco decided to retreat to an imposing fortress at Ollantaytambo, more than 48 kilometres (30 miles) from Cuzco, in the 'Sacred Valley' of the Incas. There he inflicted a rare defeat on the Spanish army, who were led by Hernando Pizarro. Manco flooded the narrow entrance to the valley as the Conquistadors entered it. Using captured Spanish weapons and horses, Manco and his army fought ferociously and the impressive fortifications of Ollantaytambo proved too strong for Pizarro and his men to overcome. Hernando was forced to retreat back to Cuzco. For the first time the Spanish had been defeated by a New World army in open battle. But Manco knew that he was now on the back foot – the initial attack on Cuzco had failed to bring him the swift and decisive victory he had dreamt of. It was much the same story in Lima, where Francisco Pizarro had been subject to a similarly vicious attack.

Upon hearing of the uprising in Cuzco, he sent seventy horsemen to the Inca capital in order to assist his brothers. Almost the entire force was wiped out after being ambushed in a narrow gorge. The Inca army hurled boulders down upon them: the few who survived were sent to Manco as slaves. Two more relief parties met a similar fate before they could get anywhere near Cuzco, as the Spanish learned to their cost the difficulty of moving through narrow mountain passes when facing a hostile and well disciplined army. Manco's general Quizo Yupanqui was by now confident of his ability to inflict massive losses on Pizarro's men, and he marched his army directly to Lima. A party of seventy horsemen sent by Pizarro to check Yupanqui's advance returned back to Lima bloodied and exhausted, with Pizarro's chosen captain for the mission having had his teeth knocked out in the brutal hand to hand fighting.

The Inca army then poured into the city and attacked its

defenders from all sides. The initial attack was repulsed, with cavalry once again proving crucial in breaking the native army's ranks, and Yupanqui retreated to the hills above Lima to regroup for another assault. Pizarro came to realise the apparent hopelessness of his position, and sent desperate messages to Cortés in Mexico and the Spanish authorities in Panama, begging for reinforcements. But he knew any help that did arrive would come too late to save him, and that his small band of Conquistadors would have to somehow triumph over Yupanqui's massive army if Peru was to remain in Spanish control.

Yupanqui decided on an all-out attack from three sides, hoping to overwhelm the Spanish through sheer force of numbers. Pizarro countered with a massive cavalry charge directed straight into the flank that was being led by Yupanqui himself. The horsemen smashed through Yupanqui's ranks and slaughtered many of his officers and warriors, and despite their vast numbers Yupanqui's men were soon on the back foot. When the great Inca general was himself mown down by the

Spanish war horses, his men began to lose heart. The attack faltered and the native army melted back into the hills. Pizarro had managed to hold Lima, just as his brothers had held Cuzco. The Inca insurrection would rumble on for several months, but Manco must have known that Spanish reinforcements would now pour into his country and that his best opportunity to overthrow the tyrannical rulers had passed.

He had one last hope, however. The Spanish had ruthlessly exploited divisions within the Inca people themselves, and he might yet be able to do the same to them. For at this point Manco learned that Pizarro's great rival Almagro had returned from his expedition in the south and was marching towards the besieged capital of Cuzco.

THE CONQUISTADORS VERSUS THE CONQUISTADORS

Almagro sent a message to Manco offering to take his side in the battle for Cuzco. He had hastened back to

Peru once word of the uprising had reached him, and hoped to take advantage of the war in order to claim the lands he believed were rightfully his and expel the Pizarro brothers once and for all. Manco agreed to meet with Almagro and may have seriously considered doing a deal with him. But the Pizarro brothers were also sending messages of their own to Almagro and it seems that Manco just did not trust any alliance with his enemies. He attacked Almagro with a force of fifteen thousand men, hoping to prevent him from entering Cuzco and reinforcing the Spanish there. Almagro had placed his men on high alert however, fearing just such an attack – though he may well have wondered if it would come from Manco or from the Pizarros. Either way, he was ready: the Inca army was slaughtered, and Manco began to doubt he could ever defeat the Spanish militarily.

Flushed with success, Almagro marched into Cuzco. Negotiations between the two parties of Conquistadors had failed to resolve the dispute over who should rule Cuzco, and though a tentative truce was agreed it soon

broke down amidst suspicion and acrimony. Almagro
attacked his fellow countrymen and with his greatly
superior army assumed control of Cuzco, throwing
Hernando and Gonzalo Pizarro in prison. Clearly he
judged that they represented a greater threat to him
than Manco did. Many of Almagro's followers urged
him to execute the brothers, to solve the problem of the
Pizarros once and for all, but Almagro decided not to. It
was a decision he may later have regretted as Gonzalo
escaped while Almagro was engaged in affairs outside
of Cuzco, and Hernando later had to be yielded up in
order to prevent an all out war starting between Almagro
and Francisco Pizarro. Both sides feared the slaughter
such a war would undoubtedly bring, and feared even
more the judgement of the king of Spain once he
became aware of such in-fighting in his new territories.
But though both men knew that a peaceful agreement
was in both of their interests, both were stubborn and
lusted after power. Despite numerous attempts to broker
a peace, neither man would relinquish his claim to rule
over the Inca capital. And so in April 1538 two Spanish
armies squared up to one another on a plain outside

Cuzco. Thousands of curious Incas watched from the mountains as the two forces battled to determine who would rule over their empire.

Hernando Pizarro had been entrusted with leading the Pizarro brothers' army, and had around seven hundred men under his command. Almagro had around five hundred, but about half of them were horsemen, which meant his cavalry was superior to Pizarro's. At the time of the battle, Almagro was unwell and his deputy Orgonez took charge of his forces. The site Orgonez chose for the battle was not well suited for horses, but he favoured it because a swamp protected access from one side. With fewer foot soldiers than his opponent, he did not want to find himself out-flanked. In addition a small stream cut across the battleground, which he hoped would slow down Pizarro's troops and leave them vulnerable to his cannons.

As the sun rose, mass was said and battle was joined. Gonzalo Pizarro led the infantry over the stream as the cannons of Orgonez roared, causing as much damage to the Spanish force as it had against so many native armies. Gonzalo herded his scattered troops back together and ordered his arquebusiers to fire directly at Orgonez's front line and cavalry. The musketeers had a deadly new type of shot which consisted of two bullets linked by an iron chain, and it caused carnage to Orgonez's army. Using the hail of fire as cover, Gonzalo's brother Hernando led a cavalry charge at his enemy, who immediately dispatched his own horsemen to meet him. For the first time in the New World that most feared weapon, the horse, would be used by both sides in the same battle. The clash of the cavalry was greeted with whoops of amazement from the watching natives as the previously almost untouchable horsemen fell in droves. With two such experienced and heavily armed forces on the field, the battle was always likely to be a bloody affair, and so it proved. Orgonez excelled himself, running through several of Hernando's men with his lance. Thinking one of them was Hernando himself he cried 'Victory!' to his men. But his shouts were premature – he was struck in the face by chain-shot from Pizarro's arquebusiers and, after falling from his horse, found himself surrounded. Following the strict rules of chivalry, he insisted on surrendering his sword only to a knight, but none were nearby. And so one of Pizarro's men posed as one, and when Orgonez had given up his sword, he stabbed him in the heart. Orgonez's head was cut off and placed on a pike so that his men could clearly see that their leader had been slain.

Without his charismatic leadership the troops began to lose their stomach for the fight. They streamed back into Cuzco to escape the bloodshed, pursued all the while by Hernando's army. Almagro, seeing the day was lost, followed their example and made it back to the capital, but there was no hiding place. Hernando took Cuzco without any further resistance and threw Almagro into the same prison that had once caged him and his brother. The battle had lasted just two hours, and on the field outside Cuzco around two hundred of the finest troops in Europe lay dead. Their bodies were soon looted by the Inca natives – a behaviour they had learned from their years under Spanish rule. Hundreds more men had been wounded on each side, and the cavalry was seriously depleted. The violence had been so ferocious that all of those who took part were exhausted, with many literally unable to stand.

Had the Inca attacked at this point, who can say what might have happened. Perhaps a massive war against the natives might have been one battle too far for the Conquistadors. Split now into two factions, they may have lacked the resolve and discipline that had thus far been key to their military successes. We will never know, because the attack never came. Manco had moved his forces deeper into the jungle, and was preoccupied only with defending his position, not with counter-attacking his enemy.

THE HUNT FOR MANCO INCA

Hernando Pizarro swiftly dealt with the remaining unrest in Cuzco. His first priority was to take care of Almagro, who had caused so many problems for the Pizarro brothers. When Almagro had taken Hernando and Gonzalo prisoner, he had resisted his followers' calls to have the brothers executed. Now that the tables were turned however, Hernando showed his captive no mercy: Almagro's crimes were listed in a document that was two thousand pages long; a trial has held; the death sentence that followed was a formality. Though the seventy-year-old Almagro begged Hernando to 'spare his grey hairs', he was garroted in his prison cell and then beheaded in a public square. The Pizarro brothers appeared as the chief mourners at his funeral, just as they had done at the funeral of Atahuallpa. The dead man's most loyal follower, Alvarado, stood next to the Pizarros during the service. It was Alvarado who had persuaded Almagro not to execute the two brothers – but though he tried desperately, he could not persuade Hernando to spare Almagro in return. Almagro's son Diego had been dispatched to Lima with assurances that his father would be spared. And so the great rival to the Pizarros now lay in his grave beside the tiny church in Cuzco: Our Lady of Mercy.

Francisco Pizarro duly rode south from Lima and on reaching Cuzco divided Peru between his brothers in order to reward them for their victory. With the spoils decided, the Pizarros turned their attention back to Manco and the Inca insurgency. In 1539, Gonzalo was sent into the Inca's 'Sacred Valley' in order to hunt down the Sapa Inca and end his people's resistance once and for all.

THE PLAIN OF GHOSTS

Having decided that his fortress stronghold at Ollantaytambo was too close to the main Spanish force at Cuzco, Manco retreated first to an ancient Inca summer palace at Vitcos and then to Vilcabamba, far into the remote mountainous jungles of Peru. Here he built a fortified settlement: the last remnant of the Inca empire in the very furthest corner of the 'Land of Four Quarters'. Today it is known as 'Espíritu Pampa', or The Plain Of Ghosts. It is so remote that it was only rediscovered in the 1960s, having been lost for almost four hundred years. In the same 'Sacred Valley' lies that most iconic of Inca settlements, Machu Picchu – itself only rediscovered in 1911. It was to this far-flung region of mountain hideouts and secret pathways that Gonzalo and his three hundred men travelled in search of the fugitive king.

Manco's sister-wife Coya Ocllo was forced to travel with Gonzalo's expedition, and his troops regularly attempted to assault or rape her – a fate she protected herself against by smearing herself with animal dung. The trek through the mountain passes of Peru was murderously difficult, and Manco had cut numerous rope bridges as he retreated so progress was slow. With little food to be found en route, the Conquistadors were in constant danger of starvation. But finally they found Manco, as they passed through a narrow valley beneath Chuquillusca. The Inca army ambushed the Spanish by throwing down great boulders from above and then attacking them in hand to hand combat. Pizarro was forced back, and the battle inflicted heavy losses on his army: thirty-six men are recorded as having been killed, along with six horses. A stunned Pizarro sent messages back to Cuzco asking for reinforcements, as it appeared the Inca chief might be a more formidable opponent than he had previously imagined. Manco's tactic, however, was to hit and run: he would strike suddenly at the Spanish and then disappear back into the dense undergrowth in The Plain of Ghosts. It was hugely frustrating for Gonzalo and his men, who trudged endlessly across mountains and through jungles in pursuit of Manco but never quite managed to catch up with him. Indeed, at one point it is said that Manco taunted the Conquistadors from the other side of a river bank, shouting, 'I am Manco Inca! I am Manco Inca!' and claiming that they would all perish and he would avenge his earlier defeats.

In the end Gonzalo reached the Inca king's stronghold at Vilcabamba and destroyed it, but once again Manco the Ghost eluded him. Perhaps by then he was at Machu Picchu, which it is thought the Conquistadors never managed to find. It is possible: there were thousands of hiding places in the mountains and the jungles, and Gonzalo must have by now realised the futility of his mission. Exhausted and critically short of supplies, he was forced to return to Cuzco while his quarry remained at large. Perhaps Manco watched Gonzalo's weary retreat from some high mountain hideout, delighted to have out-witted the Spaniard, and hoping that the Pizarro brothers would now give up their pursuit of him. If so, his hopes would soon be dashed.

Francisco Pizarro was furious, and executed several Inca noblemen to teach Manco the price of insolence. He also murdered the Sapa Inca's sister-wife, Coya Ocllo. It was the most brutal execution imaginable: the unfortunate woman was stripped naked, bound to a tree and flayed until there was barely a patch of skin left on her body. Her agony was then ended with a hail of arrows. She bore the torture with barely a groan and without ever asking for mercy. Even the Conquistadors were amazed at her courage; and at their commander's savage cruelty. Legend has it that her body was placed in a basket and allowed to float down the Urubamba river for Manco's men to find it. The Inca king wept when the news of her fate reached him. But such savagery betrayed the fundamental impotence and frustration that now consumed the Pizarros: they were forced to vent their anger on Manco's loved ones because they knew now that they may never capture the man himself. His new homeland was too distant and alien for even the rugged Conquistadors to take.

And as it turned out, the Inca king would out-live the Spaniard who took his empire from him. Pizarro was living on borrowed time.

THE DEATH OF FRANCISCO PIZARRO

All of the Pizarros had made enemies: none more so than Francisco. From the very start of the campaign in Peru he had displayed a ruthless streak that may have served him well in terms of rising to power, but which also left animosity and resentment in its wake. Although he sought to distance himself from the execution of Almagro – as he had done after the murder of Atahuallpa – everyone knew that nothing of importance was done without Francisco's consent. Almagro's followers, who now banded around Almagro's son in Lima, seethed with a sense of injustice. Not only had their leader been killed, but they themselves had received nothing in return for all their endeavours in the New World. Indeed many of them had been reduced to abject poverty. Pizarro and his men on the other hand were wealthy beyond measure, and paraded their good fortune in front of Almagro's men on a daily basis after returning in triumph from Cuzco. It was too much to bear for Almagro's son and his followers. They had hoped the king would look favourably upon their complaints, but when no arbitrator came from Spain they decided to take matters into their own hands. They hatched a plot to assassinate Pizarro as he left the Sunday church service in Lima.

The extraordinary thing about the plot that would kill Pizarro is that the victim knew of it from the outset. One of the conspirators had a change of heart – or perhaps became terrified at the consequences of such a grave act – and told Francisco exactly when, where and how Almagro's men planned to kill him. So sure was Pizarro of his own security, however, that he laughed it off, saying:

Let the poor fellows alone. They have enough to bear in their poverty, shame and defeat.

Talk was cheap in his book. The only precaution he took was to feign illness on the day in question and stay at home rather than attend church. He ate a large meal with some friends as the would-be assassins paced up and down near the church wondering why their intended victim did not show. They deduced he must have been told of the plot and, realising that they would hang for having dared to even plan such a deed, decided to storm Pizarro's home and kill him there. It could hardly be called a surprise attack: the conspirators ran through the streets shouting, 'Long live the king! Death to the tyrant!', and half of Lima came out to see what the commotion was about.

The reason for this noisy and public demonstration was, as they afterwards explained, that they wanted to persuade the rest of the city that they had many

supporters. For if they had not they would hardly
have dared to do the deed so openly.

An attack in broad daylight against such a powerful
man was indeed brazen, and perhaps Pizarro thought
it was too incredible to countenance. The huge gate
to his quarters, that could easily have prevented a
large army from entering, had been left open. One
of Pizarro's officers was told to block the door to the
house itself while he changed into his armour, but the
assassins killed the officer and set about Pizarro before
he had time to fully prepare. Nonetheless he defended
himself admirably for a sixty-five-year-old man, and
several of his followers leapt to his aid. Others had
gone to grab their weapons (or at least that is what
they claimed), but by the time they returned Pizarro
had been slashed in the throat and overwhelmed.
Staggering to his knees, he drew a cross on the floor
with the blood that poured from his wound, crying
out 'Jesu!'. Then as he bent his head to kiss the cross a
single blow from behind finished him. After surviving
all that the hostile lands of the Americas and her

people could throw at him, the legendary Spanish general died at the hands of his own countrymen on 6 June 1541.

He was mourned by few in Lima. Almagro's son was immediately instated as the new governor, and hundreds of men now flocked to his side to support him. Pizarro's followers barricaded themselves in their quarters, fearing they would be massacred, but the moderates in Almagro's party prevailed and only a handful were killed or arrested. As the air swirled with demands for Pizarro's head to be cut off and displayed on a pike, his body was hastily buried in the grounds of the cathedral later that night with little ceremony. There was no time to clothe him in the cloak of the order of Santiago, though no single knight ever won more wealth or territory for Spain than Francisco Pizarro. The man who just hours earlier had ruled a 4,828 kilometre-long (3,000 mile) empire was given the funeral service of an illegitimate pig herder from Trujillo.

THE BLOOD BATH AT CHUPAS

The twenty-two-year-old Almagro, nicknamed 'El Mozo' or 'The Lad', had little direct experience of battle and no experience of governing an empire. Given the circumstances of his sudden rise to power, it was inevitable that he would face fierce opposition. Word had reached the king of the bitter in-fighting between the Spaniards in Peru, and he sent one of his most trusted and experienced subjects, Cristóbal Vaca de Castro, to sort the matter out. Vaca de Castro was delayed by bad weather and illness and so arrived in Quito in September 1541 to find that Pizarro had been assassinated and Almagro had now claimed the governorship of Peru. Both sides talked to one another of their desire for a peaceful resolution, while raising as many men as possible for the battle they surely knew must come. It would finally take place on the plains of Chupas, near Cuzco, on 16 September 1542, and would become infamous as the most bloody battle ever to be fought between two Old World armies in the New World.

The fugitive Inca leader Manco had sided with Almagro, whose mother was an Inca princess. He sent Almagro arms captured from Cuzco – Spanish swords and armour, guns and ammunition – and pledged to send a detachment of Inca warriors to assist him when he launched his campaign. Almagro needed all the help he could get, and welcomed Manco's overtures of support. Although Almagro's force of five hundred men was relatively small, he brought many pieces of artillery to the field which he hoped would prove decisive in the battle. In the fading light of the late September afternoon, his cannons opened fire on the advancing troops of Vaca de Castro. The carnage Almagro had anticipated did not unfold, and he suspected his gunner of deliberately firing too high. Fearing the man in question had been bribed by his opponent, Almagro had him executed and replaced with a gunner who fired directly into Vaca de Castro's ranks. But soon the well disciplined forces of his opponent were upon him, and fierce hand to hand fighting ensued.

By the time it was over, between three hundred and five hundred Conquistadors lay dead, most of them followers of Almagro. The young general fled the field and made towards Manco's hideout at Vilcabamba, where he had been promised sanctuary. However he was overtaken by Vaca de Castro's men and captured, along with most of his key followers. They would be taken back to Cuzco, tried and executed. Only seven of his party made it to Vilcabamba, where they were welcomed warmly by Manco as allies:

> *He ordered that they should have houses in which to live. He had them with him for many days and years, treating them very well and giving them all they needed. He… took his meals with them, and treated them as if they were his own brothers.*

As Vaca de Castro celebrated his victory and thanked in turn each and every man that fought, the Inca king and the Spanish fugitives made the best of life in The Plain of Ghosts, building homes and rebuilding fortifications in case the thundering hooves of the

Conquistadors' horses ever threatened to find them hidden deep in the jungle. In Lima and Cuzco various Spanish factions fought for control of the country over the next few years, as Manco and his guests played quoits with horseshoes. For a time Gonzalo Pizarro ruled the empire, and it must have grieved Manco to learn that the brother of his most hated foe was in control of his land. Pizarro had not forgotten about the man he pursued through the jungle years earlier, and though Manco now no longer represented any real threat to him, he hated unfinished business. Word was sent to Almagro's fugitive band in the jungle that if they helped the Spanish capture Manco they would be pardoned for all their crimes. Bored from years in the wilds and tempted by the prospect of returning to civilisation – perhaps even one day to Spain – the seven plotted to murder their Inca host. Manco's son, Titu Cusi, was with him at Vitcos in 1544 when the assassination took place:

> *...just as my father was raising the quoit to throw, they all rushed upon him with knives, daggers*

and some swords. My father feeling himself to be
wounded, strove to defend himself, but he was alone,
and unarmed, and they were seven fully armed; he
fell to the ground covered with wounds, and they left
him for dead.

The seven would never see Spain again as they hoped. Indeed they never made it as far as Cuzco. They were hacked to death by the Inca army who pursued them as they ran desperately through the jungle. The heads of the seven were still being displayed on pikes in Vitcos when a Spanish priest visited there some thirty years later. Gonzalo Pizarro had finally got his man, however. Final defeat for the Inca came in 1572 when Manco's son Túpac Amaru led the last native army – just one thousand men strong by then – in defence of Vilcabamba. His golden shield and prayers to the sun god were once more no match for Toledo steel and gunpowder. The Spanish took the city, executed Tupac and left the jungle to cover the ruins of Vilcabamba for almost four hundred years.

In truth by the time Tupac fought his desperate last fight the Inca resistance was already based more on dreams than reality. Once before, it was said, the sacred stones of Peru had come to life to save the Inca in battle, and now the Inca preachers prophesied that the same would happen again:

> *They believed that all the huacas of the kingdom, all those that the Christians had burnt and destroyed, had come to life again… that they were all preparing in the heavens to do battle against God and to conquer him… now the world was completing its cycle, God and the Spaniards would this time be conquered and all the Spaniards killed, their towns swallowed up, and the sea would swell up to submerge them and wipe out their memory.*

But the ancestors failed to return from heaven; no sea swallowed the Spanish, and the world did not end. Only the fragile dream that Peru would once again be controlled by the Inca did. The Land of Four Quarters itself, the great empire built by generations of Sapa Incas, died much earlier, with Atahuallpa in the bloody square of Cajamarca. Died earlier still, perhaps, with Huayna Capac when the mourning amongst the Inca 'was such that the lamentation and shrieks rose to the skies, causing the birds to fall to the ground'. Even Pedro Pizarro believed that had 'this Huayna Capac been alive when we Spaniards entered this land, it would have been impossible for us to win it, for he was much beloved by his vassals.' If the empire lived at all after the Spanish took Cuzco, then it certainly died with the last great Sapa Inca to gather an army of resistance, Manco, at the Inca summer palace in Vitcos.

Of the four Pizarro brothers who had terrorised the country, Francisco and Juan died before Manco's murder and Hernando languished in a Spanish jail at that time. He had been arrested over his role in the execution of Almagro and would only be released after serving some twenty years in confinement. Only Gonzalo, then, was there in Peru to savour Manco's downfall. He too would die a violent death before long

– executed for treason in 1548 after turning against the king and seizing control of Peru.

As the Spaniards fought amongst themselves over who should run the empire of the Inca, other bands of Conquistadors had already embarked on fresh adventures to other lands in the New World. None would encounter such remarkable cultures as the Aztecs or the Incas, but their stories are just as extraordinary, thrilling, and improbable as those of the two main conquests. All were inspired to some degree by the eternal Spanish lust for gold. Though Mexico and Peru had given Spain vast wealth, far from satisfying the Conquistadors, the discoveries of such rich lands only spurred them on to try and find even more fabulous treasures. The conquests of Mexico and Peru had seen much bloodshed and hardship, but no land would claim more lives or break more hearts than the land to which the Conquistadors now turned their attention. It promised gold, glory and even eternal youth. It was a land the Spanish called 'El Dorado'.

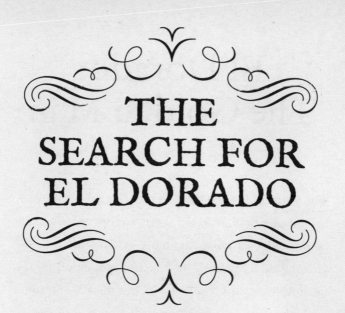

THE
SEARCH FOR
EL DORADO

El Dorado:
The Golden Man

The stories of hidden lands of great wealth had already been shown to be true, yet there was one tale that kept being told by natives in many settlements that the Conquistadors visited. In the land spoken of, lived a fabulously wealthy king – far richer than Montezuma or Atahuallapa – who dressed his body in flakes of the purest gold. This 'Golden Man' gave his name to a land of such extraordinary riches that it beguiled thousands of Conquistadors for hundreds of years. El Dorado was, for the Spanish adventurers gripped with a maniacal lust for gold, a type of heaven: the ultimate prize. Whenever captains looked jealously at the achievements of Cortés and Pizarro, whenever soldiers drooled at the great wealth they themselves had missed out on, they could console themselves that their chance had not yet passed: the greatest of all the lands in the New World was yet to be discovered. El Dorado would make Mexico and Peru look like minor provinces. The first to conquer it would write their names in history and acquire more riches than they could ever hope to spend.

Nobody really knows exactly how the myth of El Dorado came into being. One credible explanation is that it was born from the ceremony held by the Muisca people of Colombia, which involved covering a new king in flakes of gold as part of his initiation. The details of the ritual were given by Juan Rodriguez Troxell in 1638:

> At this time they stripped the heir to his skin, and anointed him with a sticky earth on which they placed gold dust so that he was completely covered with this metal. They placed him on the raft... and at his feet they placed a great heap of gold and emeralds for him to offer to his god.... when the raft reached the centre of the lagoon... they... threw out all the pile of gold into the middle of the lake.

Gonzalo Fernández de Oviedo y Valdés places the origins of the story in Quito, by which time it had already become embellished:

> *They tell me that what they have learned from the Indians is that the great lord or prince goes about continually covered in gold dust as fine as ground salt. He feels that it would be less beautiful to wear any other ornament: it would be crude and common to put on armour plates or hammered or stamped gold, for other rich lords wear these when they wish. But to powder oneself with gold is something exotic and unusually novel, and more costly, for he washes away at night what he puts on each morning, so that it is discarded and lost, and he does this every day of the year.*

But the story was almost certainly born not in the New World but in Spain. It was a story written in blood and the authors were the fanatical priests of the Spanish Inquisition. The methods they used on unfortunate heretics such as Elvira del Campo, the woman tried in

Toledo for not eating pork, influenced Conquistadors such as the Pizarros, who habitually tortured the natives for information. If their victims did not provide the answers they wanted, then the torture continued, just as it did for Elvira who screamed, 'Señor I did it... remind me of what I did not know.' In the New World it was all about gold, rather than heresy, and those desperate to escape from the agonies inflicted upon them by the Spanish would have told the Conquistadors what they knew they most wanted to hear. With each new fire lit beneath the feet of a writhing native chief the legend grew. Each would confirm the extraordinary secret land was real; was just as the Spanish wanted it to be; was close by and would provide them with endless quantities of what they most craved – gold.

Everyone, then, agreed that the land existed: the only problem was that they disagreed about where it could be found. And so it was that expeditions struck forth from Mexico and Peru in every direction, each sure that just beyond the next mountain or through the next dense jungle lay the shimmering dreamland where the king covered himself in flakes of gold.

It should come as no surprise that the man who spearheaded the most famous search for the secret golden land of El Dorado was a Pizarro.

GONZALO PIZARRO, FRANCISCO DE ORELLANA AND THE AMAZON

...in this expedition of Gonzalo Pizarro assuredly very great hardships were endured, for this exploration and conquest of Gonzalo Pizarro, I am bound to say, was the most laborious journey ever undertaken in these Indies, and in it the Spaniards endured hardships, famine and miseries, which truly tried the virtues of their nation.'

Pedro de Cieza de León

Gonzalo Pizarro believed there was gold to be found in the lands that lay across the Andes from Quito, and even if there wasn't, he was certain that he would find vast amounts of another treasure prized by the Spanish: cinnamon. The area was already called 'The Land of Canela' (or 'The Land of Cinnamon') and earlier expeditions had reported that the spice grew in copious quantities there. This was important to Pizarro as the spice trade was worth a fortune in the sixteenth century – indeed it was in order to open a trade route to buy and sell spices that Columbus first set sail in 1492. Gonzalo's expedition was well planned and well supplied: when he left Quito in 1541 he took with him five hundred men, a hundred of them on horseback (each and every one with a spare mount) and three thousand sheep and pigs to feed the army. In addition, he had a force of some four thousand natives to do the heavy lifting and to support his troops should there be a need to fight. He had a considerably larger force than his half-brother Francisco had entered Peru with. Now in his mid-thirties and a veteran of several campaigns in the land of the Inca, Gonzalo was no doubt confident that his mission would add to his already considerable personal wealth.

He would be joined on the expedition by a cousin of Francisco Pizarro, Francisco de Orellana. Having sided with the Pizarros in the recent wars between the Spanish in the New World, Orellana had been rewarded with the governorship of Guayaquil in Ecuador. The loss of an eye in a skirmish with the Inca had not affected his ability to fight and to lead, and having proven his loyalty when the Pizarros most needed it, he was no doubt a welcome addition to the Gonzalo's retinue. Orellana's small party of twenty-three men on horseback arrived in Quito late, and hurried after Pizarro's main force, catching up with them around a month or so after they had departed.

By the time Orellana joined the expedition it was already in deep trouble. This part of South America lay beyond the Inca's 'Land of Four Quarters' which meant there were no roads suitable for such a large entourage of men and animals. The Conquistadors and their native conscripts had to hack their own path through the thick vines and wade across swamps that stretched for miles. Bridges had to be built across rivers, and narrow mountain passes negotiated. The intense cold of the Andes froze the lightly clothed men, particularly at night. At lower levels incessant rain turned every trail into a mud-bath. Progress was desperately difficult, desperately slow. The native prisoners, chained together day and night and forced to do the most exhausting work, had by far the worst of it. They were quite literally worked to death, and many more succumbed to disease. There was a short respite at the valley of Sumaco, but Gonzalo pushed on further inland and soon ordered the main force to join him. He had found the 'Land of Cinnamon' – a few small scattered trees that could never hope to turn a profit. Despite the ruthless torture of scores of native men and women, Gonzalo could find nothing more, because there was nothing more. He pushed on, felling trees to cross the Coca river and then followed its course until eventually he reached a point where the rapids were less tumultuous. The Conquistadors had been trudging through the hostile landscape for seven months by now. Most of the natives they brought with them were dead, and those that remained were sick and weak. The Land of Cinnamon was far behind them, and ahead was only countless miles of impenetrable woodland. The land of El Dorado was nowhere to be seen. The men who still survived were at breaking point and begged Pizarro to turn back. But Gonzalo had a new plan: he would build a boat.

San Pedro set sail down the Coca river on 9 November 1541, with Gonzalo and twenty-five of the sickest men on board, along with the heavier supplies. The rest of the Conquistadors continued to hack their weary way along the river bank, further into the unchartered territory. No doubt at every turn they hoped against hope to find a settlement or a source of food. But every new bend in the river presented them with the same view of an endless jungle, almost entirely uninhabited by humans. Any fleeting glimpses of local natives were accompanied by arrows fired with deadly accuracy. The days turned into weeks, and the Coca river turned into the Napo. They finally halted sometime just before 25 December. Ruthless he may have been, but even Gonzalo Pizarro knew better than to ask a Spaniard to work on Christmas day.

DO WHAT YOU THINK IS BEST: THE EXPEDITION DIVIDES

The men were starving, and the native guides insisted there were no settlements in the area where they could resupply. Mutiny was in the air. It was clear to Orellana that things could not go on like this, and he had a plan which he now put to Pizarro. Orellana would take the boat, along with sixty or so men, and sail downstream to look for food and water. If he found any, he would return within three days. If he didn't, then the main expedition should not wait for him any longer. Pizarro responded by wearily telling him to 'do whatever he thought best'. And so Orellana took the boat and left Pizarro and the bulk of the men on the riverbank.

At least, that's how Orellana later told it. Gonzalo Pizarro had a different recollection of the events. In his version, he ordered Orellana to return with the boat, come what may, within twelve days. Under no circumstances was he to sail beyond the junction of the two rivers, which the natives predicted lay slightly further downstream. Orellana solemnly pledged that he was not about to sail off and leave Pizarro and his men to starve to death in the middle of nowhere. Which is what – according to Pizarro – Orellana promptly did. At the very least we can suppose that there was some kind of fundamental collapse of leadership at this crucial point in the expedition, as it seems highly unlikely that Pizarro would agree to allow Orellana to sail off with his only boat and a good deal of precious supplies. Orellana also took with him a large percentage of the weapons and ammunition, leaving the main expedition largely defenceless.

Later cast by Pizarro as the worst of traitors, Orellana sailed away from the main force on 26 December 1541. He soon encountered a native settlement, where he and his men were welcomed and given food. There they rested and recovered, but decided that the natives could not support them or the main party for any sustained period of time. After carefully making notes about the language that the natives used, Orellana returned to the ship and resumed his voyage. A few days further on the river was joined by a second river in a mighty confluence and Orellana made the fateful decision that it was now impossible for him to turn back. He sailed on, down the new river and into the unknown. It would take him on an extraordinary journey and for a brief period the river would bear his name in honour of his achievements. Today we know that the river in question is the longest in the world and it is famous by its later name, the Amazon.

THE AMAZON RIVER

The river's modern day name comes from the legendary tribe of fierce female warriors who were said to live there. Such legends predate Orellana's mission by hundreds of years and thus might be dismissed as utter fiction, and yet there are intriguing reports that some kind of all-female tribe may indeed have lived along the banks of the mighty river. Indeed, Orellana's men claim to have fought against them: tall, pale skinned and pale haired women who were as dangerous in combat as any men. They were said to use long bows, with copper-tipped arrows, firing so many at the Spanish that their ships were said to resemble porcupines after the skirmish. Nearby settlements paid homage to the Queen of the Amazons by providing her with brightly coloured parrot and macaw feathers, which the Amazons used to line the roofs of their temples and decorate their garments. Elsewhere, however, it is reported that Orellana was only told about the women but never encountered them directly. Agustin de Zarate states quite directly:

> ...*in a province further on he fought and conquered the Indians; and here he received a report that some days' journey inland was a country inhabited only by women, who fought and defended themselves from their neighbours. He listened to this news but went on his way, finding neither gold nor silver nor any trace of them in the whole land... He reported the existence in this territory of a very rich land inhabited only by women, and from this fable the country received the name by which it is now generally known: 'the conquest of the Amazons'.*

Amazons or no Amazons, what is certain is that Orellana was sailing into hostile territory, and he would fight frequent battles with the natives who dwelled on the banks of the great river. At least, having learned some of the language, Orellana was able to communicate peaceful wishes, which helped to calm a good number of potentially dangerous situations. In taking this approach he stands in marked contrast to his former captain Gonzalo Pizarro, who lay very firmly in the 'shoot first, ask questions later' camp of diplomacy. That approach had served him well in Peru, but now lost in the Amazonian forests what the Conquistadors needed most was help. Orellana had no idea where he was going, or where the river might take him – he simply had to go with the flow. For food and water he was almost entirely reliant on native settlements along the river bank, and had he not been able to befriend them his party would surely have perished. As it was, Orellana managed to gain their trust and in February 1542 he and his men stayed with friendly local villagers for a period of two months. It marked a new phase of their adventure, for they were able during that time to build a new ship, more suited to the vast river that they now found themselves sailing down. And indeed more suited to fighting any future battles with less friendly natives further down the river:

> *Very often great numbers of canoes came out into the river, and they [the Conquistadors] were so tightly packed in the brigantine that they had difficulty in fighting them.*

Orellana believed that worse was to come, for the natives told him that further down the river lay lands inhabited by the Machiparo and Omagua tribes; relatively advanced cultures who protected their territory fiercely. The new boat was fashioned from the wood they chopped down in the nearby environment, with vines being used for rigging and gum for making the planking watertight. It was a makeshift affair, out of necessity, but it was considerably more robust than the earlier vessel. The local men helped with the construction and the women brought the visitors food each day. It was a rare moment of co-operation and harmony between the two alien worlds.

The Victoria was finally ready in April 1542. She was hauled into the great river and Orellana, leaving gifts behind for his guests, sailed once more into unknown waters.

Almost at once they began to see the sprawling settlements of the much feared Machiparo tribe, which continued for many miles along the river banks. The soil in this part of the Amazon basin is rich in nutrients, constantly replenished by deposits of alluvium from the river when it floods. The result is *varzea* (fertile soil) in which crops can be grown in abundance, making the area perfect for human settlement. The Machiparo's crop surpluses brought them huge wealth, and this helped transform them from subsistence farmers into a sophisticated society particularly known for fashioning fine pottery. They also guarded their precious territory closely, and the unfamiliar Spanish brigantine was immediately identified as posing a threat to them. Orellana and his men were attacked repeatedly by Machiparo forces, and if their later reports are to be believed they were obliged to fight for three days and nights without rest in order to resist the onslaught. Father Gaspar de Carvajal, who was travelling with the party, lost an eye in the battles and many others sustained equally grave wounds. But the ship sailed on, further and further down the river, until it reached the edge of Machiparo territory. There was to be no respite in the furious fighting, however. The land they were now entering was in the hands of the even more warlike Omagua tribe.

The lands of the Omagua would become synonymous with El Dorado, as later expeditions discovered their large urban populations, complete with roads, that allowed them to trade with tribes in the Amazonian interior as well as along the river itself. They dominated an area of over 643.7 kilometres (400 miles), keeping their settlements close to the river banks and island areas around it. Later explorers would describe them as 'such good people and with such reason and political organization and such a rich and prosperous land', and as late as 1639 they were still characterised as 'the best governed of all the indigenous people along the river.' They also fought continual battles against their inland neighbours, however, in order to defend their territory and capture prisoners to use as slave labour. At the time Orellana sailed into the Omagua's waters, they were seeking to expand their territory through conquest, and had well-armed warriors with long experience of conducting battles on land and on water. These warriors were now unleashed upon the newly built *Victoria*.

The ship did exactly the job it was designed to do: protecting the Spanish from the Omagua's war canoes whilst allowing them to deploy their own arms to maximum effect. Although the native warriors fought bravely, they were no match for Orellana's heavily armed men. Having defeated the tribe on water, the Spaniards went ashore to explore the network of roads that led away from the river and into the dark unexplored interior of the Amazon basin.

Perhaps the golden spires of El Dorado rose somewhere amidst the forests, and these warriors fought to defend the 'Golden Man' of the legend. Fine pottery and intricate woven cloths told the Spaniards that this was indeed a sophisticated culture, considerably more advanced than any other they had yet encountered on their travels. But the force was too small to both defend the ship from attack and venture deep into the interior, where the Omagua's armies were surely gathering for another attack. With no idea of the size of any force they might have to face, and no real idea of where they were or how they might to return to Peru, the Conquistadors decided to return to the *Victoria*. El Dorado would have to wait: for now their priority was survival.

They sailed on for several hundred miles through Omagua and Amazon territory, all the while glimpsing well built roads that led tantalisingly away from the river to unknown destinations inland. It was clear to them that this region was densely populated – and it has been estimated that up to four million people inhabited the area at the time Orellana first encountered it.

The Amazon's fertile flood plains supported a whole

network of civilisations that are largely lost to us now. Archaeological excavations carried out in 2010 near Santarem in the Brazilian Amazon revealed glimpses of the vanished world. As well as the remains of ninety settlements, the outlines of reservoirs 100 metres (328 ft) long were found, suggesting very large populations could have been supported during the dry season. Modern-day road-building and agricultural expansion are now threatening to destroy the cities for a second time; if the Golden Man did once live in the interior of the Amazon we will probably never discover any traces of his fabled land.

With more men, perhaps Orellana would have indeed found huge riches in the area, but as it was his fifty or so men had to be content with viewing the new lands from afar whilst fighting off frequent native attacks. The Spanish were forced to make land at regular intervals in order to restock from the riverside settlements, and resistance was generally fierce. The names that the Conquistadors gave to these settlements gives a taste of what the encounters were like: 'The Town of the

Burned' for the village they destroyed when the natives retreated into their houses, and 'The Province of the Gibbets' for the area they passed through which had human heads displayed on gibbets to warn invaders of the fate that lay in store for them.

By the middle of July they had reached the Xingu River, close to the mouth of the Amazon. Here the natives also attacked, their skin stained black and their arrows tipped with deadly poison. After a Conquistator was killed by its lethal toxic effect, Orellana decided to sail as quickly as possible through the region and avoid landing at all costs. For once the bow and arrow was a match for Toledo steel – and it might have been even worse for the Spanish had the natives not insisted on going into battle whilst half drunk. As it was, they successfully negotiated the raging river which now showed clearly the influence of the tides, suggesting to the exhausted party that they must surely, finally, be approaching an ocean. They were: they reached the Atlantic Ocean on 26 August 1542. The tiny exploration party that had been sent out to forage for food had ended up on an epic adventure which had taken them 6,437 kilometres (4,000 miles) and lasted for eight months. In order to return safely to Spain they would now have to cross the Atlantic ocean in their two battered boats: a further 1,931 kilometres (1,200 miles) of open sea.

The boats were patched with whatever could be salvaged or scavenged – all metal was melted down and forged into nails, trees were felled to replank the vessels and they were caulked with grease and cloth. They worked late into the night, surviving largely on snails and tiny crabs, and thus their location came to be named on the maps as 'Starvation Island'. The two makeshift crafts were then hauled into the mighty ocean, prayers were said, and the Conquistadors sailed for home. The journey was as hazardous as they no doubt feared it would be, and one storm that struck the little fleet was so severe that the boats became separated, and each crew firmly believed the other vessel was lost. It was only when the boats were finally reunited two weeks later on Spanish terra firma that each party realised the other had not perished. Their jubilation at surviving the extraordinary journey was short-lived, however. They had been away for the best part of two years, and had left their leader behind in the depths of the South American jungle over eight months ago. Left him there to die, he would later claim.

But, against all the odds, Gonzalo Pizarro had managed to survive too.

PIZARRO'S RETURN TO PERU

In terms of sheer endurance of hardship, Gonzalo's story rivals that of Orellana. When his deputy did not return after three days with the food his two hundred starving men so desperately craved, Gonzalo sent a search party to look for him. To look for food, too, if Orellana himself could not be found. The search party was itself gone for a week. When the anxious men welcomed them back they were dismayed by the news: no food had been found, and there was no sign of Orellana. Most of the remaining animals the expedition had brought had been eaten: one thousand dogs and one hundred horses had already featured on the jungle menus. The men were by now surviving on lizards, snakes and anything else they could catch in the forests. Without food they would all be dead within days. Pizarro sent another search party out in captured native canoes to follow in Orellana's footsteps, making it clear to them that if they did not find food the expedition was doomed.

Led by the experienced Conquistador Gonzalo Pineda, they soon found the spot where Orellana had disembarked in the first days of his journey. Deducing that Orellana must have followed the main course of the river at the nearby confluence, they turned the opposite way and paddled upstream along the smaller river. They travelled with great difficulty against the current for over thirty miles and found nothing but thick forests and swamps. They were on the brink of exhaustion when, miraculously, they stumbled across a native plantation of cassava beside the river. The woody shrubs were hardly considered a delicacy, yet they must have seemed so magical that the Conquistadors probably feared they were a hallucination. Giving thanks to god they feasted on cassava roots and regained their strength. The return journey was another test of endurance as they battled back upstream along the Napo to rejoin the main party in canoes laden with cassava. Their trip to the plantation and back took them, in total, twenty-seven days. When they were finally spotted approaching, they were welcomed as heroes, for by that time Pizarro's men were eating shoe leather to stave off starvation.

Their lives had been saved: for now. Once the cassava was eaten and the ragged band was strong enough to walk, they began the long journey to the cassava plantation on foot. To get there they had to cross the mighty Napo river and trek back upstream along the river Pineda until it reached the Aguarico. It took them another three weeks. They then filled their stomachs with as much of the cassava as they could, grateful to at last have a sizeable supply of food.

After more than a week of joyous feasting, the drawbacks of bingeing on South American shrubs became apparent: cassava is poisonous unless thoroughly cooked. The whole party was struck down with agonising stomach pains, and two of them died as a result of their violent reaction to the plant. Pizarro realised that it was time to move on. Those too sick to move were strapped to the few remaining horses and the rest trudged wearily back into the forest on foot. Three hundred miles of jungles, swamps and mountains lay between them and the safety of Quito. All talk of El Dorado, wealth and fame had been long forgotten. Now they just wanted to get home.

The Aguarico twisted and turned on its way down from the foothills of the Andes, and with no idea of where they were or in which direction they needed to head, the Conquistadors had no real option but to follow it. That meant building countless bridges and wading through swamps, as well as hacking through dense undergrowth. For the rest of the march the men would be made continually sick with the poisonous cassava as well as suffering from the effects of dysentery and fever. The rain poured down on them continually. The last of the horses were eaten, and when they were gone the last of the shoes were eaten, so that many of the men had to walk barefoot. Pineda and a few of the stronger men were sent ahead in canoes to try and summon help. They had no happier time of it than the men who were marching, however: they had to paddle against strong currents and were continually attacked by natives.

The brutal march, the illness, the starvation and the exhaustion took a terrible toll on Pizarro's men. Of the two hundred or so that watched Orellana leave, only eighty lived to see Pizarro lead them back into Quito. The survivors were a pitiful sight, hardly more than skeletons stumbling into the town they had left sixteen months previously with such high hopes of finding a golden land. The entire expedition had been a disaster, and it was only a combination of extreme good fortune and an extraordinary will to live that led to any making it back alive. Even before he had fully recovered his strength Pizarro began to give his version of what went so badly wrong. The blame lay with the traitor Orellana, he claimed. He would soon write a letter to the king outlining his grievance against his former deputy, although he did not at this stage know whether Orellana was alive or dead.

Before long, however, Pizarro's attention would turn once again to control of Peru, the land he believed rightfully belonged to him and his brothers. On learning of Francisco's assassination he took control of Peru and expelled the royal viceroy, putting himself on a direct collision course with the king and the might of the Spanish army. It was an unequal fight that even Gonzalo could not hope to win, and he was executed for treason in 1548. By that time Orellana was already dead. He had ventured back into the wilds of the Amazon in 1545, this time with a much larger and better supplied force. He was confident enough of success to bring his young wife with him – it was a terrible mistake.

Orellana became hopelessly lost, and led his band of

men around in circles as he tried desperately to find a way through the maze of tributaries that fed into the Amazon. The man who had discovered the Amazon river could not find it a second time. Fierce attacks from native armies claimed scores of Spanish lives, and starvation and illness decimated the party. Only forty-four of the three hundred men who accompanied Orellana on the expedition survived. Orellana himself succumbed to illness in 1546.

The dream of El Dorado had claimed hundreds of Spanish lives and left many more with no gold to show for their months of almost unimaginable hardship. Yet despite these savage realities, the myth lived on. And the human sacrifices that the Spanish made to the god of gold went on too. One man in particular would lead such an extraordinarily foolish expedition in search of wealth and fame, that he inspired a novel that has since become a by-word for folly, delusion and misadventure. The man was Gonzalo Jiménez de Quesada: the real life Don Quixote.

The Real Life Don Quixote

QUESADA AND THE CONQUEST OF NEW GRANADA

Quesada, like Cortés, was a lawyer, and wielded rhetoric as enthusiastically as his sword. He grew up in Granada at a time when the newly-conquered Moors were often in revolt. Unlike the Pizarros, he was from noble stock and his social connections soon brought him to the attention of Don Pedro Fernández de Lugo, the governor of the colony of Santa Marta. Quesada sailed for the Colombian town in 1535, at the age of thirty-six. On arrival there he must have wondered whether leaving the genteel surroundings of Córdoba had been the worst decision of his life. At that time Santa Marta was little more than a hovel, plagued by disease and under constant attack from hostile natives: '…one of the cities most combated by evil fortune that was to be found in all the Indies.'

Pedro Fernández de Lugo set about improving matters in Santa Marta by following the example of other Spanish settlers, mercilessly attacking the local population and then stealing their gold. When his son Luis de Lugo fled back to Spain with most of the loot, leaving Pedro to face hundreds of angry unpaid soldiers, he despaired of the men around him and looked for a man of honour to invest authority in. The man he decided to put his faith in was the well-bred lawyer Gonzalo Jiménez de Quesada. Item number one in Quesada's intray would be leading an expedition into the vast primeval forest of Colombia's interior. They would sail down the unexplored river Magdalena: Santa Marta was rapidly becoming uninhabitable and the mountains of the Sierra Nevada blocked any other routes inland.

To say that Quesada faced a major challenge would be an understatement: he had no formal military training or experience, and the only intelligence regarding the lands he was about to enter emphasised the ferocity and hostility of the natives. The lives of six hundred men were in his hands. Two hundred of them sailed the river in brigantines whilst the rest had to hack their way through the dense forests. The expedition could afford only eighty horses — and one donkey named Marobare. This was a sort of mascot for the Conquistadors, having been rescued during one of Pedro Fernández de Lugo's raids on the natives. The Spanish were stunned to discover an animal not native to South America braying at them from the top of a mountain. The mystery of how it got there was solved when they spoke to captured locals: the donkey had swum ashore after a Spanish vessel sank off the coast of Colombia and the amazed locals, believing the donkey to be some sort of sacred animal, had tied it to a pole and carried it in relays to the top of the mountain.

From the very first day, Quesada's men had to fight continuously in order to advance. The native armies fired lethal poison arrows from the undergrowth that found their target without making a sound. Any wound inflicted was likely to kill a man or horse within a few short hours. The conditions made fighting exhausting: severe heat combined with perpetual dampness sapped the men's strength and rotted their cloth armour. The only sources of water were swamps, and as a result large numbers of men fell ill with malaria. Many of those who were not claimed by disease fell victim to the hundreds of alligators that infested the waters. Mosquitos plagued the men during the day and vampire bats drained their blood at night. The terrain was the greatest enemy of all: tangled vines and dense forests had to be laboriously hacked down, and vast rivers crossed with precarious bridges made from the undergrowth. But, unbelievably, the hardship of the four hundred men who moved on foot was dwarfed by that of the two hundred men on the brigantines. When they entered the mouth of the river Magdalena they found it was in flood due to the melting of the snow on the mountains. A severe southerly gale made matters considerably worse, and the homemade vessels were not built to withstand such conditions. Hurled around by swirling currents, hammered by floating debris and battered by howling winds, the boats began to break apart. Three of the five in the small flotilla sank, with the loss of almost all hands. A few that did scramble ashore were killed and eaten by the natives. The remaining two ships only just managed to limp back to Santa Marta. There the governor ordered them to be refitted and for three fresh boats to be hurriedly constructed, because by this time it was known that Quesada's main force was in trouble.

Big trouble, in fact. Camped against the river bank and with swamps surrounding him on all other sides, Quesada was vulnerable to attack and running critically short of supplies. The ceaseless onslaught from the native archers, along with the terrible hardship of the journey thus far had already cost the lives of two hundred of his men. The new fleet sailed from Santa Marta to try and rescue him, but no sooner had it entered the mouth of the Magdalena than it was attacked by hundreds of native war canoes. Eye witness accounts talk of being able to walk across the river on the canoes without ever touching the water, and include claims that more than a thousand vessels took part in the attack. Whilst this is almost certainly an exaggeration, the fighting was undoubtedly fierce and only the savage power of the Spanish cannons saved them from being overrun. Eventually the attackers were driven off, however, and the fleet relieved Quesada's starving men at Chiriguaná.

With their new stocks of ammunition the Conquistadors made further headway against the natives, moving inland in search of a major settlement. At last they reached Tamalameque – the farthest point known by the colonists of Santa Marta at that time, and, if not a major settlement, at least a point at which they could rest. Surrounded once again by deep forest, Quesada decided to try and find the river Magdalena once again and follow its course upstream. Native prisoners had informed him that the next settlement of any size was in the province of Sampollon. It was another murderously arduous slog, and the result was entirely predictable: another one hundred men died before the exhausted party reached Sampollon. There they were met by the rest of the fleet from Santa Marta, who brought provisions, ammunition and letters from home. What the letters did not say was that the man who had organised and paid for the mission, Pedro Fernández de Lugo, had died in Santa Marta. It happened shortly after the fleet sailed, and thus it would be many weeks before the news reached Quesada. Perhaps he would have turned back if he had known; but that seems unlikely. For a nobleman like Quesada, to return home with nothing to show for the expedition would be ignominious in the extreme. And so, rousing his men with a long speech full of promises regarding the great wealth that lay ahead of them, Quesada marched his men, once more, into the dark Colombian forests.

It was to be yet another wretched march. If anything, it was even more brutal than what had come before: no food could be found and soon the men were once again starving and exhausted. At least one Spaniard was carried off in the jaws of a tiger, and another was eaten by an alligator. Several died from eating poisonous plants and berries, so desperate were they to stave off the perpetual hunger. And still the silent, poisoned arrows rained down on them from unseen foes lurking in the undergrowth. By the time they reached the Rio Serrano only two hundred and nine of the original party were still alive. Almost all of the native prisoners they had brought with them to do their heavy lifting were dead too. It is reported that some of the men who died were dragged into the woods by other Conquistadors and eaten raw. Quesada perhaps turned a blind eye to this, but he certainly wasn't prepared to allow his men to eat the precious horses. Not only were they incredibly expensive, they also held the key to conquering native territories. One unfortunate soldier who killed a horse was executed on the spot, and Quesada ordered that in future any horse that died should be thrown into the river rather than eaten. This prevented any repeat of the incident, but the survival of the horses undoubtedly cost the lives of men; another example of the many human sacrifices that the Spanish made to the Golden Man of El Dorado.

They would all have perished within another day or two had they not come across a town, La Tora. It was uninhabited, the entire population having fled in advance, but there were large fields of ripe maize there, which at the time were worth more to the Conquistadors than all the gold in the New World. Quesada had to place a guard over the fields and strictly ration the maize for fear that his men, now so unused to food, would die if they were allowed to gorge on it. As his main force rested, an exploratory party was sent out to search the surrounding area for any further signs of civilisation. They were gone for twenty days, during which time the maize supply at the camp was exhausted. The party found nothing. They returned with the news that were no signs of any cultivated land anywhere nearby. Once again, the Conquistadors were entirely surrounded by dense forests, and were starving.

Mutiny was inevitable. The expedition had spent the vast majority of the last eight months at the very brink of death. One of Quesada's most respected captains,

San Martin, was elected by the men to be the one to tell their leader that it was time to call it a day and make for home. Quesada responded by talking not of home, or safety, but of gold. Small amounts had been found from time to time during the expedition, and captured prisoners had told the Spanish that it came from the interior of the country. Certainly, he argued, it could not have come from the 'rude savages' they had encountered thus far. And so there must be a cultured civilisation living somewhere in the forests, a civilisation that had the knowledge and resources to produce gold. Whatever his men thought, Quesada intended to find it. He ordered that 'this murmuring shall cease, and … Captain Martin shall start at once upon another expedition, to explore the country farther afield.'

Quesada's incredible faith and fortitude was rewarded just two days later, when San Martin made a discovery whilst exploring the Rio de Opon. It was not gold he found, but something that at least told him that ahead lay a culture more advanced than anything they had seen thus far: in a captured native canoe he found salt.

THE LAND OF THE CHIBCHA

Further investigation revealed several huts in which salt, along with fine cloths, were stored; fields of maize grew nearby and roads led further into the interior. Confident that he had at last found evidence of an advanced civilisation, San Martin returned with the good news to Quesada. On his way out of the territory he was attacked by a large army from the local tribe. Though he did not know it, this was a very small taste of things to come. The Conquistadors prevailed in the skirmish, however, and when they returned to Quesada's camp they were greeted as heroes. Joy, mixed with relief, filled the hearts of the weary men and without further ado they made at once for the new settlement that San Martin had discovered.

Once more fate conspired against them, and the journey to the salt huts would take a further twenty days. At one point the river suddenly flooded, washing away all their supplies and leaving the Conquistadors hanging from the branches of trees to avoid being drowned. They managed to resupply from the brigantines and hacked their way along the river back, again resorting to eating the leather from their belts and scabbards to stave off starvation. When they reached San Martin's village they found it deserted, and the fields of maize cut down. It was a crushing blow. The weakest of the men were left behind with Quesada's brother, Hernan, while Gonzalo pushed on with those who could still walk. They followed the largest path towards a range of distant hills. The climb through the Sierra de Opon would further test the determination of the exhausted men. By now many of them were dressed only in rags or animal skins and the fierce cold of the nights made sleep impossible. At least one Conquistador is reported to have gone mad during this part of the journey; he never fully recovered his senses. The path was narrow, steep and rocky, yet Quesada sent messengers to order his brother to bring the rest of the men, along with all of the horses, to meet him.

Finally a stroke of good fortune arrived in the form of a native prisoner who showed them a path through the mountains, and told them of the lands that lay beyond the hills. The people who lived there were the Chibchas; one of many different tribes who were at war with one another in the region. In particular he spoke of the local chief having just married, and told them where he was celebrating with his new wife. Armed with this vital piece of information, the Conquistadors pushed on along the native path and managed to surprise the chief at his honeymoon retreat. After taking him captive, they tried to woo him with presents of glass beads and words of friendship. But the chief simply did not trust the strangers and secretly sent word to his village that they were to attack the Spanish at the first opportunity. The plan was discovered before it could be enacted, however, and the chief was punished for his treachery by having a leather collar placed around his neck, attached to which was a thick rope. He was then forced to show the Conquistadors the path to his village, and was led there like a dog on a lead to ensure he could not betray the Spanish once more. When Quesada reached the village he was so relieved and delighted that he freed the chief. It was not vast wealth or amazing architecture that so excited him, but the broad plains beyond the village that promised easy progress much deeper into the interior. The terrain was also perfect for the horses. This was just as well, as Quesada would very shortly need his cavalry.

THE SPANISH IN BOGOTÁ

Before pushing on, Quesada reviewed his army: of the one thousand men who had either started out with him or joined him as reinforcements, just one hundred and sixty-six remained. For his success at penetrating this far into Colombia he had paid a terrible price. The horses had fared better − not least because Quesada often treated them less harshly than the men he commanded. Sixty remained in good health. Almost all of the gunpowder had been used, lost or rendered useless by the damp conditions. The crossbow strings were so wet that they lost much of their power. Many men had eaten their leather scabbards and replaced them with ones made from animal skins, which failed to prevent them from rusting. Several of the cavalry men had eaten their saddles and their horse's bridles, so they had to ride bareback. Almost immediately, this rag-tag army was thrown into a fierce pitch battle with a native army that numbered several thousand.

They were attacked from all sides shortly after dawn, and the ensuing battle raged all day and much of the night. Quesada moved his men onto the plains where his cavalry could do the enemy the most damage, and in common with Cortés and Pizarro he found that the horse was his ultimate weapon against the New World warriors. Charge after charge decimated the Chibchas' ranks and terrified all but the bravest of their fighters. As the Aztecs and Incas had already discovered, the Conquistadors were all but invincible when the fighting took place in open country. Despite their huge numerical superiority, the Chibchas were defeated. With the way across the plains now open, Quesada led his men across it. They were heading towards the lands of the principal chief in the region, Chief Bogotá. The Spanish would later name the capital city of their new land after him.

Chief Bogotá had many allies, but many enemies too. The Conquistadors had a long tradition by now of exploiting divisions between native tribes, and Quesada would use the tried and trusted tactic of kind words combined with raw power to conquer the new lands. Unusually for a Spanish commander in this period, however, Quesada did seem to treat the native people as fellow humman beings, and he urged his men to do the same, saying:

> *We are now in a settled and well-populated country. Let no one show violence to any man… for after all they are men like ourselves, if perhaps not so civilized, and every man likes to be treated with civility. So will these Indians. Therefore we must not take from them that which they do not want to give. By following this plan, they will give us what we require, whereas by harsh treatment we shall force them to withhold even necessities. After all, even the ground we tread upon is theirs, by natural and divine right, and they allow us as a favour to be here, and owe us nothing.*

These are remarkable words indeed when set beside those of Cortés and Pizarro. Quesada was quite certainly a very different sort of leader, but it is fair to say that he and his men in the coming months would not hold true to the sentiments expressed in the speech he gave before entering Bogotá. Still, his nature was not bloodthirsty and he did not seek to subjugate or humiliate the natives as other Conquistadors did: he simply wanted their gold. To this end, he was fully prepared to fight; and fight he and his men did in the coming days against wave after wave of Bogotá's warriors. By the time they reached the settlement at Sorocota, close to the river Sarabita, the natives had retreated further inland and the Conquistadors were able to rest. They feasted on a crop which was entirely new to them, but which grew in great abundance in this area – the potato.

Though Bogotá himself refused to surrender, his people began to realise that resistance was futile. As with the other great New World cultures, they had legends which spoke of men coming from the east and reclaiming their land. Some natives threw live children down the hillsides towards the Conquistadors, believing that they ate them. Others offered human and animal sacrifices to the 'Children of the Sun' who had so suddenly appeared in their country. Quesada captured one elderly local man and treated him with great kindness, then sent him to tell his people that the Spaniards came in peace and required no sacrifices from them. Just as he hoped, all attacks on his men ceased, and the natives began to emerge from hiding and welcome the curious visitors from another world. When Quesada caught one of his men plundering from a native's home, he had the man executed (though some claim the accusation against him was false). In truth there was precious little to steal – some gold and fine cloths in the wooden Chibcha temples, but not a great deal else. Word reached Quesada that this was because Chief Bogotá had ordered everything of value to be taken away and hidden. It was clear that in order to get at the wealth, Quesada had to get at Bogotá.

He marched his men to Cajicá, Chief Bogotá's last stronghold, and laid siege to the fortified town. The fighting there lasted for eight days, and when the Spanish finally took the town, the only trace of Bogotá was the ceremonial litter in which he had been carried. That was a prize of sorts, since it was decorated with thick gold objects, but the main prize had eluded them: Bogotá had escaped and taken with him the majority of his treasure. All the captured natives testified to the size of Bogotá's wealth, but none knew – or would say – where he had hidden it. If the reports of the great Colombian leader's piles of gold were true, then his hoard still lies buried somewhere in the forests or mountains of that country, as, to date, it has never been found.

Bogotá's great wealth had only recently been acquired, as the Chibcha began to conquer the lands of other tribes and force them to pay tribute to them. Local chiefs were allowed to stay as nominal rulers of their province but all in this region had to bow to Chief Bogotá and pay for his protection. One of the tribes conquered by the Chibcha was of particular interest to the Conquistadors: this was the tribe living beside the sacred lake of Guatavita. There, it was said, the local chief would paint himself in gold flakes before casting treasure and jewels into the waters as a sacrifice to the gods. This was almost certainly The Golden Man who inspired the great legend that the Conquistadors had finally found El Dorado, a city of gold.

And yet, remarkable as this new civilisation was to them, it continued to fall short of their dreams of a kingdom of infinite wealth. They reasoned that it was only a matter of time before they found great treasure: but it was, for now, tantalisingly out of their reach. Even after marching to Chief Bogotá's capital, Muequeta, they saw no direct evidence of fabulous golden temples or silver fountains. They ate well and the local people dared not attack them, and clearly the expedition had met with some small measure of success after such a disastrous start. But in order to find the wealth and glory they so craved, they would have to push on and find Bogotá. Many messages of peace had been sent to him by Quesada, but the Chibcha leader ignored them all. Indeed he sent bands of his warriors to ambush the Conquistadors whenever they left their bases. With no idea of where to find the fugitive chief, Quesada pressed on in the direction that looked to him to be the most promising. In doing so he inadvertantly moved into territory controlled by the king of Tunja, who was called Quemenchatocha. Learning that this man, too, was said to have a huge amount of gold, Quesada resolved to ensure that he could not escape in the way that Chief Bogotá had. He ordered the cavalry to move at a swift trot to the city of Tunja whilst his men ran alongside, a local guide leading the way. It was just before nightfall when they reached the gates of the city. Inside its stockades they could see that from almost every building hung plates of pure gold.

THE CAPTURE OF QUEMENCHATOCHA

It was too much for Quesada to resist: even though the light was fading fast he resolved to enter the city at once. War cries rose from within as ambassadors from Tunja beseeched the Spanish to wait until the morning before entering. As Quesada sliced through the cords that secured the stockades, around ten thousand warriors waved their spears and drew their bows. In a battle on an open plain perhaps the fifty or so Conquistadors who entered the city would have a chance: in the confined streets of Tunja, they would surely be overwhelmed. Yet Quesada strode directly towards the king's throne in an inner courtyard, as the cacophany of war cries sounded all around him. He stationed his men outside the king's home and entered with just his deputy, Antonio de Olalla, as back up. It was perhaps the sheer audacity of this that prevented the native army from attacking: what harm could just two men do when surrounded by so many heavily armed warriors?

The king himself sat on a wooden throne and received the strangers graciously. He was old, and relatively frail, and had learned that violent conflict was best avoided if at all possible. He listened politely as Quesada explained that he was a subject of King Charles of Spain, who sought to bring to Quemenchatocha and his people the one true faith of Christianity. Quemenchatocha responded that he was very interested to hear of the thoughts of the men from the other side of the world, and that he would consider what they had said to him. He asked them to stay for the night in quarters that he had prepared for them, and told them that he would give them a fuller answer to their message in the morning. This must surely have been the very best answer that Quesada could have hoped for, and quite why he would consider it unacceptable is difficult to understand. It was the same response that Cortés had received from Montezuma, and even the fiery Cortés had never expected more of a mighty ruler than a polite response of 'let me think about it'. Perhaps Quesada believed that he was being lured into a trap, and that to hesitate for even a moment would lead to disaster. Or perhaps he simply had a rush of blood to the head, now that he was so close to the fabled riches of El Dorado. Whatever the reason, Quesada suddenly lept forward and siezed the elderly king, holding a sword to his throat and threatening to kill him instantly if he resisted.

It is true that both Cortés and Pizarro captured the powerful leaders Montezuma and Atahuallpa with similar coups. They shared great daring, but even their audacity pales by comparison to Quesada's. Cortés learned a bitter lesson on the 'Night of Sorrows' regarding how difficult it was for even well armed Conquistadors to break out of a city that was heavily defended. Had Quesada and his band of just fifty men attempted to leave Tunja by battling the native army he and his followers would almost certainly have been cut to ribbons within a couple of hours. But the sudden capture of the king threw the Tunja warriors into total confusion: they simply could not believe what was happening. Quesada's men rushed into the king's chamber and quickly reinforced their leader to ensure the king's armed courtiers could not attack. Then the king was led to the outer courtyard and place under guard. As night fell, the powerful Tunja leader was securely confined by the Spanish within his own capital city, and not a single weapon had been raised in his defence. The war cries had melted into the dumb silence of disbelief. Somehow, Quesada's extraordinary act of quixotic impulsiveness had resulted in a staggering triumph against seemingly impossible odds.

King Quemenchatocha himself seemed more stunned than anyone at the extraordinary nature of his downfall. Little is known of the man – if the Chibcha tribe ever did keep records of him and his past achievements, then they have long since been lost. We must assume that since he was a man of considerable power, with a fierce army under his command, he would have been consumed with indignation at the manner in which he was taken prisoner. Unlike Montezuma or Atahuallpa, however, he did not attempt to bargain for his freedom by offering up the riches of his empire: when Quesada suggested that he pay a ransom in return for his release he replied:

> *My body is in your hands, do with it what you choose, but no-one shall command my will.*

This seems to have moved Quesada, for he ordered that the king be released into something resembling house arrest, with his wives and servants in attendance. If he hoped that treating the king kindly would result in him repaying Quesada with gold, then he was mistaken. The elderly Quemenchatocha was dead within a couple of weeks – from a broken heart, according to those who witnessed his demise. Certainly it must have been a shattering blow for Quemenchatocha to witness the ransacking and destruction of his capital city, for – despite all of Quesada's fine words about not plundering native possessions – that is what soon happened. The Conquistadors roamed from house to house, tearing down the gold plates that adorned them and searching everywhere for any treasure that the population had hidden. There were some reports that, despite the best efforts of the invaders, the vast bulk of the gold, silver and precious stones that were in the city were spirited away over the walls of the stockade and hidden in the mountains. These tales of great wealth successfully buried or taken to secret caves occur time and again in the story of El Dorado: part of its fable-like feel stems from great wealth slipping through the fingers of those in search of it. Still, the very real treasures of Tunja amounted to quite a considerable reward for all of the Conquistadors' sufferings. Enough was taken to make the one hundred and eighty-six surviving men rich: it was not gold on the scale of Mexico or Peru, but then they had still not yet managed to track down the great Chief Bogotá. This, the Conquistadors must have imagined, was just a taste of things to come. Already they were being told of a great temple full of gold at a place called Suamos. The dream of El Dorado remained very much alive.

THE FIRE AT THE TEMPLE OF SUAMOS

Quesada wasted no time in setting off for Suamos and made rapid progress to nearby Paipa, where the local chief promised to bring him a great deal of treasure in the morning. Perhaps Quesada had by now come to believe that the natives were indeed docile to the point of imbecility, for he trusted the chief's word. When he woke in the morning he found the village empty, and with a few cat calls from the hills beyond, the people and the treasure vanished into a network of rocky passes. Undaunted, Quesada rode to Suamos, where the sacred temple of the Chibcha stood. Once more he found the settlement deserted, save for an elderly priest who explained that he had spent his entire life in the service of the temple and intended to die there too. Within the temple stood the mummified remains of past Chibcha leaders, their bodies dressed in gold and emeralds. It was clear, however, that much more ornate gold panelling and other artifacts had been spirited away before the Spaniards arrived. Either by design or by accident, the temple was burned to the ground during that night. The elderly priest, and all the remains of the ancient leaders, burned with it.

It must have been a terrible loss for the Chibcha, who had constructed the magnificent structure from hardwood carried from many miles away. The inferno burned for six weeks, taking with it all that was most sacred to the native people. Quesada feared the destruction of the temple might push the local people into rebellion, and so he gathered whatever gold and jewels he could find (and there was a good deal of both, despite the efforts of the local chief to remove as much as he could) and returned to Tunja. He did not know it, but he was riding towards one of the fiercest battles that the Conquistadors ever fought in Colombia; one which would nearly cost him his life.

A local Chibcha chief had organised an army to attack the invaders, and re-take Tunja. Quesada entreated him to make peace, but he was determined to resist with force. Chief Tundama's warriors threw themselves upon the Conquistadors at a place called Bonza, using lances, clubs, swords and slings to try and break the Spanish ranks. As so often before, however, the discipline, courage and superior weaponry of the smaller force prevailed. It was a straight-forward victory in the end, but Quesada's extraordinary story almost ended at the battle of Bonza. In a moment of extremely foolish over-enthusiasm, he rushed headlong into the very deepest ranks of the native army and was predictably overwhelmed by their numbers. A blow from a club threw him from his horse, and the Chibcha warriors moved in for the kill as the dazed Quesada staggered back and forth shouting curses at them. He was rescued from certain death by the bravery of a single Spanish soldier who hacked his way through the Chibcha fighters and dragged Quesada back onto his horse. With their leader safely out of harm's way, the Conquistadors got on with the job of systematically butchering the native army, then robbing their dead bodies of any valuables.

The rebellion firmly crushed, Quesada rode to Suesca, a beautiful part of Colombia both then and now. The region appealed to the Spanish captain from the start. There was no major urban settlement, but at a nearby village named Teusaquillo stood the chief's holiday residence. It was a sheltered spot with a good water supply. Quesada planted his sword in the soil and announced that here, on this pleasant plain 2,625 metres (8,612 ft) up in the mountains, he would build the capital city of his new country. Quesada's land was to be called New Granada, and its capital city was to be called Bogotá.

THE FOUNDATION OF BOGOTÁ

Most would have chosen Tunja, which was already well developed, as their capital. But Quesada had a vision of a brand new city rising on the mountain plain. The nearby town of Muequeta had been the historical capital of the Chibcha kings, and there was a plentiful supply of stone to build a modern city. From just a couple of straw huts, the settlement was rapidly expanded to include a church and residences for the Conquistadors. Today it is known as 'The Athens of South America' and over 8.5 million people inhabit the sprawling metropolis. The cathedral of Bogotá stands where the first straw church was built. All of this was nothing more than a dream in the head of an eccentric general who waved his sword in the air on 6 August 1538 and decreed that at this location should be built a city that was fit for his valiant band of Conquistadors. Initially twelve huts were built, to symbolize the twelve apostles. Almost as soon as they started on the construction, however, word reached Quesada of another shimmering city which had a temple built on pillars of pure gold. The great capital of Bogotá would have to wait: the promise of great wealth at Neiva was too mouth-watering a prospect for Quesada to resist.

But once more the golden city turned out to be nothing more than a dream. At Neiva they found no temple on pillars of gold, just huts and fields. They did have one stroke of good fortune, when a single native swam across a great river to greet them, carrying a bundle of gold plates. He returned later with more, and the pieces were of such purity that they were enough to make Quesada and all of his men rich. Had their ambitions been more modest, then the expedition might have been classed as a great success: but Quesada's head was filled with the vision of El Dorado, of limitless wealth, and he became increasingly frustrated that the fabled city continued to elude him. With this in mind, he resolved to renew the search for Chief Bogotá, who he now knew to be hiding amidst the remote, impenetrable marshes of Facatativá.

THE DEATH OF CHIEF BOGOTÁ

Two of Bogotá's spies were captured and tortured for information on how to pick a way through the marshes protecting the great king. The elder native refused to talk, and died in agony without revealing his secret. His younger companion, however, cracked under the torture and agreed to lead Quesada's men to Bogotá's fortress at Facatativá. A large party of Conquistadors set out the very same night and surprised Bogotá and his forces, who fled without a fight. Bogotá was badly wounded in the shoulder by a crossbow bolt as he ran. Streaming with blood, he was carried into the woods by his followers and despite an extensive search the Spanish never found him. His kingdom was lost, but he took the secret of his treasure to the grave with him. Unlike Montezuma and Atahuallapa, Bogotá never allowed himself to be captured, even after his own death.

So once more the truth about El Dorado eluded Quesada – though he must have contented himself with the notion that, with Chief Bogotá out of the way, his forces would no longer threaten the Spanish.

Bogotá had been the undisputed leader in the region, and now that he was dead the native armies began to fight amongst themselves for control of the territory. Just as Cortés and Pizarro had done, Quesada exploited the divisions in his enemies' ranks in order to conquer a land that might otherwise have been impossible for him to take. He began by siding with Chief Bogotá's successor, the warrior general Sagipa, in his battle with the neighbouring Panche tribe. Sagipa agreed to become a vassal of King Charles in return for the protection of the Spanish against the hereditary enemies of the Chibcha people. A large army of Chibcha warriors marched with the Spanish to take on the Panche in their homeland at Tocarema. The mountainous terrain did not allow Quesada to deploy his cavalry, however, and the Conquistadors soon learned why Sagipa had found it so difficult to defeat the Panche army. They defended their positions so ferociously that the Chibcha army was routed and the Spanish themselves driven back by a hail of poisoned arrows. In a second attack, Quesada managed to lure the Panche into an ambush, finally gaining control of the battle by drawing his enemy into the open where his cavalry could smash through their ranks. With so many of their fighters slaughtered, the Panche had no option but to sue for peace.

With the enemy now subdued, Quesada turned his attention to his new ally, the Chibcha leader Sagipa. He had not forgotton the tales of Bogotá's great wealth and the golden palaces of El Dorado. When friendly enquiries regarding the location of El Dorado failed to provide much information from Sagipa, Quesada had him thrown in chains. As there was no reasonable justification for doing so, Quesada concocted a story that Sagipa had taken Bogotá's position unjustly, and had no right to his former king's treasures. If Sagipa had imagined that by agreeing to become a vassal of Spain he would be treated as a friend and ally, then he must have rapidly realised his terrible mistake. At first he stalled for time, claiming he knew where Bogotá's treasure was, but that it would take forty days to gather it together from its assorted hiding places. He told Quesada he would have the gold brought in sack loads and since the Spanish had posted a strong guard outside his quarters, he suggested it should be deposited there. The first load did indeed arrive, but it was removed the same night so that Sagipa's followers could return with the same small load of gold day after day. A naïve trick, and one which inevitably failed to deceive the Spanish for long.

Quesada's ruthless streak now showed itself: gone were the kind words of respect for the native people and their possessions. He had Sagipa flogged, and the more minor chiefs were rounded up, tortured mercilessly, then executed. The horrified Chibcha leader offered to take the Spanish directly to the treasure, no doubt hoping to escape the brutal torture suffered by his subordinates. He was led through the mountains with a rope tied around his neck. In desperation, when they reached a high pass with a steep drop on one side, Sagipa dived into the abyss, hoping to end his life. But the soldiers holding the rope hauled him back up. Sagipa was denied the quick and relatively painless death he sought. Instead his death would be slow and agonising at the hands of Quesada's torturers, another human sacrifice to the god of gold. Despite their savage cruelty, however, he did not reveal the location of the treasures of Bogotá. The gold, if it ever existed, was never found. Any hope of discovering the secret city of El Dorado vanished into the thin mountain air with Sagipa's dying groans.

THE THREE AMIGOS

Quesada may have failed to find El Dorado, but he had nonetheless achieved a great deal in founding Bogotá and conquering the native population of Colombia. Aside from the matter of discovering great wealth, his achievements rivalled those of Cortés and Pizarro. He knew he would require reinforcements in order to travel any further, as his own force was too small to even hold the territory he had already gained. He resolved to return to Spain and petition the king for governorship of the new land, and to ask permission to raise a new force that might push further into the interior – and perhaps to the promised land of El

Dorado. He still did not know that the man who had sent him on the expedition, Pedro Fernández de Lugo, had died in Santa Marta. Clearly he wanted to cut his patron out of the picture, much as Cortés had done when he sailed for Mexico. As it transpired, however, Quesada's plans were thrown into disarray by one of the most extraordinary episodes in the entire story of the conquest of the New World.

Messengers brought Quesada word that a Spanish army had been sighted moving towards Bogotá. It must have seemed like a strange dream to him, so deep into this new country, to suddenly hear of another band of his fellow countrymen in the region. But incredibly, at almost the same time, he received a second message, this time reporting another Spanish army marching towards Bogotá from an entirely separate direction. After years of hacking their way through jungles and clambering over mountains, two different expeditions, one having set out from Peru and the other from Venezuala, were converging on Quesada's remote capital city at the very same time. The town in the middle of nowhere was suddenly the scene of a highly improbable meeting between three exhausted armies of Conquistadors, none of whom previously knew that the others existed. Each of the three parties struggled to comprehend the surreal collision of their expeditions in the vast, wild interior of Colombia. Quesada had started out from Santa Marta on the Caribbean; the two men facing him explained that they had begun their journies from Quito on the one hand and Coro in Venezuela on the other.

Quesada's men were dressed in uniforms reduced to torn and rotten rags by now, and the party from Coro, who had fared even worse, was dressed in animal skins. Only the party from Peru was still resplendent in fine Spanish clothing, as their journey had been the shortest and least arduous. They were led by the dashing and charismatic Sebastián de Belalcázar, governor of Quito and trusted general of Francisco Pizarro. The army reduced to wearing animal skins was led by Nicolaus Federmann, a German who was the lieutenant-general of the governor of Venezuela. Each of them had set out on their journeys with the same ambition: to find and conquer the fabled city of El Dorado. In the case of Federmann, the search had already lasted for three years and cost the lives of three hundred of his men. All three generals had invested huge amounts of blood, sweat and tears to journey this far, and none wanted to return home empty handed. They were all used to battles, and for a while it seemed as though they might have to now fight one another for control of the spoils of Colombia. Quesada, having only just built his capital, was certainly in no mood to yield to the claims of others. It was decided, in the end, that all three should return to Spain and place their claims before the king. A gentleman's agreement between them suggested that Belalcázar and Federmann should claim the lands they had journeyed through to reach the plains of Bogotá, while Quesada would claim the new capital and its surrounding lands.

THE RETURN TO SPAIN

Quesada had returned from the dead, as far as the

settlers at Santa Marta were concerned. He had been away for two years and had sent no letters back, and so was quite naturally assumed lost in the wilds of Colombia. When the new governor of Santa Marta, Jeronimo Lebron, learned of Quesada's conquests he immediately requested that Quesada give him a full account of the new land. But Quesada argued that it was Pedro de Cieza de León who had sent him on his quest, not Lebron, and he could now only answer to the king. And so Quesada, Belalcázar and Federmann sailed first for Cuba and then on to Spain.

Given the importance of the petitions they intended to place in front of Charles V, it is not surprising that Belalcázar and Federmann made directly for the palace. Whole countries were at stake, after all. But Quesada was cut from a different sort of cloth, and given to seeking adventure whenever an opportunity presented itself. He sailed to Lisbon, and there met with Hernando Pizarro, the volatile yet charismatic brother of Francisco. The two hit it off at once and began to frequent the gaming halls and brothels of the city in order to quench their thirst for excitement. Quesada appears to have forgotten that he was supposed to be asking the king for permission to rule over the country he had just discovered. Instead, his reckless gambling landed him in prison, with his new friend Pizarro at his side. This allowed another man to visit King Charles' court and usurp Quesada's claim to Bogotá. The man in question was Alonso Fernández de Lugo, the disgraced son of the former governor of Santa Marta, Pedro. Incredibly, due to his excellent connections in the court of King Charles, Alonso succeeded in arguing that the new lands legally belonged to his father, not Quesada, and that he should therefore inherit the governorship of them.

Quesada soon got word of this outcome and hurried to Spain to plead his case. But he was not nearly as well connected as Alonso, and his petitions fell on deaf ears. It is claimed that Quesada insulted the king by visiting him dressed in a scarlet cloak, but the truth appears even more astonishing: there is no reliable record of Quesada ever actually setting foot in Charles' palace. Perhaps his recent disgrace in the gambling halls of Lisbon had made him too much of an embarrasment, or perhaps Quesada thought that others might make a better impression than he would upon the king. Whatever Quesada was thinking, the result was that he lost the governorship. Belalcázar and Federmann were rewarded with the right to rule the countries that they had conquered, but the rash and eccentric behaviour of Quesada had cost him his great prize of Bogotá. It was utterly unjust, after all that he had endured in order to win the land of Colombia for Spain, but the king's word was final. Quesada had lost not just a personal fortune but an entire country at those gambling tables in Lisbon.

Worse still, he was tried for his participation in the torture and death of the chief of Bogotá. By then Quesada had drifted through France to Flanders, in search of new adventures. He was sentenced, in his absence, to five years of exile from Granada. During those years he wandered throughout Europe, and wrote an account of his time in Colombia, which tragically has since been lost. Nothing else is known of what Quesada did in those years, or where exactly he went. But he was destined not to fade gently into the mists of history, for he had one last great adventure ahead of him. Twelve years after he had left Bogotá, Quesada returned, with the permission of the new king, Philip. He was fifty years old, and broke, when he rode back into Bogotá in 1549. The king had granted him a small pension so that he could retire quietly and comfortably in the city he had founded. But in Quesada's heart, a fabulous golden city still called to him from areas of Colombia yet to be explored. After badgering the king with countless letters over the next twenty years, he was finally granted permission, at the age of seventy, to conquer new territory deeper into the interior of Colombia. The search for El Dorado was back on.

QUESADA'S LAST ADVENTURE

The scale of the elderly adventurer's last expedition was truly epic: five hundred men rallied to his call, keen to march with a man whose exploits were already considered legendary. In addition Quesada had agreed to found a whole new colony in the far flung plains between the rivers Pauto and Papamene. At his own expense (and with a little help from friendly investors) he purchased or borrowed 1,000 horses, 1,000 pigs and 300 cows. Around 1,500 New World natives accompanied him as porters. It was an enormous entourage, perhaps the largest that any Conquistador had ever set out with. No-one doubted that this time Quesada would find his golden city and return in triumph.

His earlier expeditions had begun disastrously, and his final one followed the same pattern. Progress was desperately slow due to the huge menagerie of animals that had to be herded across the difficult terrain. They took twenty days to get as far as the river Guejar, where a rest stop turned into farcical misadventure when Quesada's entire stock of gunpowder exploded. Several men were killed and Quesada himself only narrowly avoided the same fate, losing in the end only his tent rather than his life. The force lumbered on to the furthest outpost of Spanish influence at San Juan de los Llanos. The omens for finding a great civilisation in this part of the world cannot have been good: miles of open plains stretched in every direction. Yet still no one doubted that somewhere, just beyond the horizon, lay El Dorado.

They moved through grass that grew many feet above their heads and which was home to countless mosquitoes, flies, venomous snakes and tigers. All of these attacked both the Conquistadors and their livestock. The path they hacked through the plains was soon littered with the bones of men and animals alike. There was not a single sign of human habitation for weeks at a time. Even men who had suffered on Quesada's earlier expeditions begged to be allowed to return home, such was the unrelenting agony and hopelessness of the march. Quesada had to hang deserters as an example to the others in order to prevent outright mutiny. But in truth it was futile: they were chasing an illusion, and there was nothing to find, nowhere to head to. With almost no water and only wild berries for food, the men died in droves.

Still Quesada pushed on, delivering rousing speeches on the nature of the riches that lay just around the corner. After three years of wandering aimlessly, however, his audience had thinned to just forty-five. Twenty of these Quesada allowed to return home, while he continued his search with the twenty-five who still believed in his dream. Nobody knows how much further Quesada and his band of dreamers went in pursuit of the golden city. At some point, most surely when they were on the very brink of death, they turned back. Quesada staggered back into Bogotá with the rest of the survivors, at the age of seventy-three, to face the ruinous debts he had accumulated on his epic misadventure.

THE DEATH OF QUESADA

He had lost all of his money and most of his army in his ill-fated quest, yet Quesada's reputation seems to have survived intact. When Bogotá was threatened with attack by a confederation of native armies, it was to Quesada that the citizens turned to lead the defence. The old warrior could no longer ride a horse for any distance, and had to be carried to the battlefield in a hammock, but he still knew how to inspire men: hundreds volunteered to join his makeshift army. In the series of battles that followed, Quesada's army defeated the New World forces and killed their leader, effectively ending the rebellion. At the front of every charge was the grey and frail Quesada, still urging his troops on with poetry and promises, still rushing towards danger without a thought for his own safety.

Almost as soon as his last mission was successfully completed, Quesada's health finally gave out: he contracted leprosy and retired from Bogotá to Mariquita, where the climate was milder. He wrote poetry and detailed memoirs describing his adventures – tragically all of these volumes have since been lost. Unlike Don Quixote, he never lost faith in the dream he had chased for so long: right up until his death he was making deals with various captains to help him conquer the lands where he still believed El Dorado stood. He died, at the age of eighty, on the

15 February 1579. The man who had conquered an entire country left nothing of material value behind. He still owed huge amounts of money to all those who had backed him in the search for El Dorado. His legacy was the amazing story of his life. The legendary indefatigability of Quesada made him famous both in his own lifetime and long after his death. It inspired soldiers to pick up their swords, and authors to pick up their pens. Because of this, even death could not fully extinguish his extraordinary zeal.

And nor would his failure to find 'The Golden Man' tarnish the shimmering dream that he chased for so long: that legend lived on too, and others would soon follow in Quesada's footsteps in search of El Dorado.

Going Native

ALVAR NÚÑEZ CABEZA DE VACA IN AMERICA

The Land of Flowers – or *La Florida* – was known to the Spanish from a 1513 expedition led by Juan Ponce de León. It was reputed to be the location not just of the 'Fountain of Youth' that de León resolved to find (his death in 1521 no doubt coming as something of a disappointment), but also of great cities of gold which soon became bound up with the myth of El Dorado. The seasoned Spanish commander Pánfilo de Narváez was granted permission to claim the land around the Gulf Coast of what is now the United States of America, on condition that he founded two new cities along the coast. Narváez had set out once before for the New World, with dreams of gold in his heart. He was the man sent to capture Cortés in Mexico, a mission which ended in failure and humiliation – and the loss of an eye. Still, Narváez had no problem raising funds for the expedition: after the return of Cortés from Mexico, rumours were rife of lands to the North that held even greater riches. On 17 June 1527, he left Spain with around six hundred men, including the king's treasurer who had been sent to ensure that the crown got their 'royal fifth' of any gold found. The treasurer's name was Álvar Núñez Cabeza de Vaca, and his story is one of the most astonishing in the entire saga of the Conquistadors.

THE JOURNEY TO FLORIDA

Cabeza de Vaca was of noble birth but of modest means, and whilst his forefather had fought heroically against the Moors he himself had little military experience. He was expected to oversee the accounts, not to lead men to the elusive golden city. While his opinions would certainly be sought by Narváez, they would not necessarily be respected. Narváez was a warrior in the same mould as Cortés, Pizarro and Quesada – he appears to have had little time for paper-pushers such as Cabeza de Vaca. Nonetheless,

Cabeza de Vaca's close ties to the king, and his noble birth, meant that he had a good deal of authority on the expedition, and Narváez placed him in command of one of the six ships in his fleet. The party reached the Canary Islands without much incident, and there resupplied in order to push on towards Cuba. Cabeza de Vaca sailed from there to Trinidad in order to pick up extra horses from a wealthy associate of Narváez, while the commander himself sailed from Santiago around the coast of Cuba to the Gulf of Guacanayabo.

Things did not go to plan. Hurricanes and violent storms roared through the New World at exactly the time that Narváez was attempting to prepare and set sail. The party that sailed for Trinidad was smashed to ribbons and all the provisions were lost. Both ships were wrecked and sixty men drowned. It meant a serious delay, but by February 1528 Narváez and Cabeza de Vaca were reunited at Cienfuegos on the southern coast of Cuba. Despite large numbers of desertions, the force remained strong with four hundred men and eighty horses ready to depart. It was agreed that a stop should be made in Havana in order to restock before the journey to Florida, and a pilot with local knowledge of the coast was hired to lead the fleet through the treacherous sandbars and reefs of the seas around Cuba. His name was Miruelo, and he must have talked a good talk, for he knew next to nothing about the shallow seas they now sailed into. Every single ship ran aground, and the entire expedition was stranded for three weeks, further diminishing the meagre supplies on board. When a large storm brought swells large enough to free the boats, it also forced them past Havana and north towards the coast of North America. There was nothing to do but press on and hope that supplies could be found in the land of Florida, which they spotted in April 1528. While Miruelo led them along the coast in search of a harbour that he absolutely swore was just around the next bend, another ship was lost in stormy weather. Eventually Narváez ordered his men to drop anchor at a small bay and go ashore to explore, whilst Miruelo sailed on along the coast to locate his great harbour. And, perhaps predictably, that was the last the fleet ever saw of their expert pilot.

The men who went ashore found the natives to be peaceable, and they managed to trade their ubiquitous glass beads for articles of much greater value to them: fresh fish and game. But it was when they spotted a small gold bell amongst their fishing nets that the Conquistadors became interested in truly learning how to communicate with the villagers. Narváez sent a raiding party to find out more, and although the natives fled, four of them were caught and interrogated over the source of the gold they possessed:

> *By signs we asked the Indians whence these things had come: they signified to us that very far from there was a province called Apalache, where there was much gold, and an abundance of everything that we greatly valued.*

It was music to Narváez's ears and he resolved to set out at once in search of Apalache, the new land of gold. Cabeza de Vaca cautioned the commander not to leave the ships until they were in a safe port, pointing out that they had very limited supplies, could not speak the language of the natives, and had no real idea of where they were supposed to be headed. As far as Narváez was concerned, these were trifling matters and Cabeza de Vaca was being faint-hearted. And so the treasurer was over-ruled and the party struck in-land to seek their fortunes, while the ships sailed around the shore. Each of the three hundred men and forty cavalry was carrying two pounds of biscuits and a pound of bacon. Not much to walk the length of North America with, as they were about to find out.

THE JOURNEY TO APALACHE

The supplies were exhausted after fifteen days of marching, during which time they had seen no sign of native settlements. When finally they did reach a native village, they were told, with rudimentary yet effective sign-language, to go back where they came from. The natives were seized and forced to lead the Conquistadors to their maize fields, where they finally dined on a biscuit and bacon free menu. It appeared clear to Cabeza de Vaca that tramping aimlessly into the interior with no provisions was a mistake, and he pleaded with Narváez to change tack and head for the coast. Narváez refused point blank, believing they were moving ever closer to the gold the natives had spoken about, but he allowed Cabeza de Vaca to lead forty men in a separate search for the sea, and the ships they hoped to rendezvous with. They found the sea, but no harbour and no ships: there was nothing for it but to push on further into Florida.

The march to Apalache was arduous, and the Conquistadors had numerous skirmishes with the natives before finally arriving at the town. There they found forty or so huts and several fields of maize, but not a gram of the promised gold. A captured chief assured them that the surrounding area was thinly populated and those who dwelt there were even poorer than his own people. The only town of note was Aute, on the coast, around nine days journey away. After twenty-five days of being shot at with arrows whenever they ventured out for water, the Conquistadors decided to leave Apalache and head for Aute. The same lethal native archers harrassed them every step of the way, with deadly consequences for many of the men:

> ...some of our men were wounded, for whom the good armour they wore did not avail; and there were men this day who swore that they had seen two oaks, each as thick as the lower part of the leg, pierced through from side to side by the arrows of the Indians; and this is not so much to be wondered at, considering the force and precision with which they shoot; and I myself saw an arrow that had entered at the foot of an elm the depth of a palm.... The bows they use are as thick as the arm, of eleven or twelve palms in length, which they discharge at two hundred paces with so great exactness that they never miss.

Aute, once they reached it, was even more disappointing than Apalache. The inhabitants, forewarned of the approaching Spaniards, had burnt the place to the ground and fled. The lack of supplies, ceaseless fighting and arduous travelling was starting to take its toll on the health of the men, who were now struck down with a mysterious illness. With so many sick, and nothing but difficult terrain filled with hostile natives behind him, Narváez resolved to build rafts and sail his way out of the miserable land. Five were hastily constructed, each having to hold fifty men. Forty had died of disease, hunger and attacks; the rest boarded the rickety vessels for the perilous journey ahead. Cabeza de Vaca recalled the moment they set sail:

> *After the provision and clothes had been taken in, there remained not over a span of the gunwales above the water; and, more than this, we went so crowded that we could not move: so much can necessity do, which drove us to hazard our lives in this manner, running into a sea so turbulent, with not a single one that went there having a knowledge of navigation.*

Suicidal, surely. And so it proved. The boats were soon separated by a fierce storm, and swept far out to sea. With few provisions the men starved, died of thirst or drowned. Narváez was one of the many killed. Just two of the five crafts made it to land at what the Spaniards would soon name 'The Island of Misfortune'.

THE ISLAND OF MISFORTUNE

It is hardly surprising that the Conquistadors gave the island they found themselves wrecked upon such a doom-laden name: after all, just eighty of those who had set out from the coast at Aute remained alive. Yet, in truth, it was on The Island of Misfortune that the Spaniards enjoyed the greatest stroke of good fortune of the entire expedition, and one which undoubtedly saved the life of Cabeza de Vaca. The shipwrecked men, barely able to lift their heads with hunger and fatigue, were discovered by a party of natives. In a moment of incredible empathy and humanity, the natives approached the unfortunate adventurers with none of the hostility that they had encountered further up the coast:

> *The Indians, at sight of the disaster that had befallen us, and our state of suffering and melan-*

*choly destitution, sat down amongst us, and from
the sorrow and pity they felt for us they all began to
lament, and so earnestly that they might have been
heard at a distance, and they continued so doing more
than half an hour. It was strange to see these men,
so wild and untaught, howling like brutes over our
misfortunes. It caused in me, as in others, an increase
of feeling and a livelier sense of our calamity.*

At the very brink of death, the Conquistadors were
shown a truly extraordinary level of kindness by the
native Karankawa people. They picked the Spaniards
up and carried them back to their homes through the
bitterly cold night, stopping every now and then to
light fires so that the naked and exhausted men could
warm themselves and rest. On arrival at their village,
the men found that a hut had been cleared for them,
with several fires lit to ensure they would not freeze to
death. Fresh fish and clean water was given to them,
and the natives then danced and whooped with joy as
the men began to revive. Cabeza de Vaca admitted the
men themselves feared it was the start of a ceremony

which would end with them being sacrificed to the Karankawa's gods, but in fact it was sheer jubilation, a celebration of life triumphing over death.

Cabeza de Vaca learned from the Karankawa that a second party of Spaniards had also survived, and were living elsewhere on the island. The captains Andrés Dorantes and Castillo had struggled ashore with a handful of men when their boat capsized a little further up the coast. The two parties were reunited amidst much rejoycing, but neither group had any provisions and the weather now began to worsen dramatically. Due to the severe storms the natives could barely feed themselves let alone the shipwrecked men, and as the days went by they began to starve to death. Another group of five Spanish survivors finally resorted to cannibalism: each of them eating the corpses of those that died until only one remained. Cabeza de Vaca named them, and reported that when the Karankawa learned of this act their attitude to the visitors changed, so horrified were they by such a gruesome practice. They also began to suffer sickness, which they blamed on the newcomers, believing they had cursed the island. With only fifteen of the eighty Conquistadors who made land now still alive, the situation looked desperate. Cabeza de Vaca pleaded with the natives not to blame them for the misfortune which had overtaken the island, pointing out that his own men were dying in even greater numbers than the locals. The Karankawa relented, but wanted to put the strangers to work, insisting that they should try and heal their sick people. Despite the protestations of Cabeza de Vaca and his men that they had no power to heal, the locals would not take no for an answer and refused to help the Spanish unless they agreed to become healers:

> *They cure by blowing upon the sick, and by the breath and the imposing of hands they cast out infirmity. They ordered us that we should do this likewise, and be of use to them in something. We laughed at what they did, telling them it was folly, and that we knew not how to heal. In consequence, they withheld food from us until we should do what*

they required. Seeing our persistence, an Indian said to me that I knew not what I uttered in saying that that profited nothing which he knew, for that the stones and other things which grow in the fields have virtue, and that he by passing a hot stone along the stomach took away pain and restored health, and that we who were extraordinary men must of all others possess the greatest power and efficacy.

All living things were sacred to the Karankawa, and the power to heal was not something learned but something the men were born with. The Conquistadors had little option but to do as they were asked, and so they began to live amidst the Karankawa, saying prayers and laying hands upon their sick. And, it seems, their efforts pleased their hosts: before long it was accepted that they were indeed powerful healers. Such was the Karankawa's faith in the power of Cabeza de Vaca to cure them, that the power became real, and the sick became well. The strangers thus began to repay a little of the enormous debt that they owed their hosts – but there was still deep mistrust amongst the Karankawa of any beings who could eat one another. The Spanish decided to swim to the mainland when the weather improved, but Cabeza de Vaca was too weak to join them and instead went to live with the Karankawa. He lived more or less as a slave, and was not treated with the respect we might imagine a holy man would deserve: this was strictly a business transaction, in which Cabeza de Vaca received food and lodging in return for his services as a healer. In the summer he was sent to other communities to barter, as the numerous tribes in Florida had a deep mistrust of one another that often made trade difficult. Over the next six years he earnt the trust of the Karankawa and was allowed to journey great distances entirely on his own.

Cabeza de Vaca dreamed of escaping, and returning once more to Spain. The dream became a concrete plan when he unexpectedly discovered three other survivors of the shipwrecks living with a tribe further along the coast of Florida.

DORANTES, CASTILLO AND ESTEVANICO

The other survivors were being held against their will by a local tribe, and warned Cabeza de Vaca that they would kill them all if they attempted to escape. Dorantes was the more senior figure in the party, and had for many months urged his compatriots to try and flee but they were scared of crossing the numerous rivers in the area. They were also unsure of how they would be received by other tribes they encountered: as a group of two white men and one black man they certainly could not pass themselves off as indigenous. Other Spanish survivors had attempted to walk to freedom and had been pursued and killed. Cabeza de Vaca learned that several other parties had scrambled onto the shore at various locations after the shipwrecks, and all of them had met with gruesome fates – including one party that resorted to preserving the flesh of their dead comrades in order to feed themselves. Such stories meant that the tribes in the area treated the Spanish with contempt, using them as slaves and regularly abusing them. Cabeza de Vaca persuaded them that the locals would treat them kindly if they presented themselves as healers, and that he himself had walked safely through the territories of several different tribes in the last six years. When Dorantes explained that in six months time the tribe he was staying with would move on to pick pears at a different location, allowing them a brief window of opportunity to escape, the four of them agreed to band together and attempt to walk south to the Spanish settlement of Panuco in Mexico.

Disaster struck when the natives holding them fell out with one another. The feud was so bitter that the natives separated, taking their different slave Spaniards with them. Now divided, the Conquistadors were obliged to spend another year living with the natives, waiting for the prickly pear picking season to begin again. It was a particularly difficult time for Cabeza de Vaca:

In this time, I passed a very hard life, caused as much by hunger as the treatment I received, which

was such that three times I was obliged to run
from the masters I had, and each time they went
in pursuit and endeavoured to kill me; but God, our
Lord, in his mercy chose to preserve and protect me
from them.

At last the year passed, and the men were reunited.
They made their break when the native tribe's
attention was focused on picking pears, and the four
managed to escape along a path that led to the sea.
They hoped that following the coast would guide
them, as they had no clear idea of where they were in
relation to Panuco. The mighty Rio Grande, however,
blocked their progress and they were forced to turn
inland in order to cross it. From there they followed
the native trails that led into the interior of what is
now Texas, performing acts of healing in return for
food and accommodation. Perhaps by now Cabeza
de Vaca and the other three believed that god was
working through them to heal the natives: certainly all
their doubts about taking on the role of healers seem
to have left them. News of the unusual gifts that the

strangers possessed spread throughout native villages with incredible speed, as Cabeza de Vaca explains:

> *That same night of our arrival there came some Indians to Castillo and told him that they had great pain in the head, begging him to cure them. After he had made over them the sign of the cross, and commended them to God, instantly they said that all the pain had left; and they went to their houses and brought us many pears, and a piece of venison, a thing to us little known. As the report of his performance spread, there came many others to us that night sick, that we should heal them, and each brought with him a piece of venison, until the quantity was so great we knew not where to dispose of it.*

They wandered on through native settlements, performing their healing acts and managing to secure vital food in return. At one settlement they prayed over a man who was at the very brink of death, and when he later revived they were credited with raising him from the dead. This increased their fame and reputation even further, making them famous throughout the region. Eventually they reached the Sierra Madre mountain range which, at 3,657 metres (12,000 ft) high, they knew they could not hope to climb. The local natives there warned the small band of Spaniards that hostile tribes inhabited the lands to the south, which was the direction they desperately wanted to head in, and so they were forced to turn north instead. It meant a major change of plan: instead of heading to Panuco they would now attempt to reach the Pacific coast, and from there head south to Mexico city. It was all unchartered territory, and they had little idea of the distances involved. Perhaps if they had known how far from Mexico City they were, they would have given up and resigned themselves to living amongst the native tribes of Texas. The journey they hoped to complete was over 3,218 kilometres (2,000 miles) long.

THE JOURNEY TO THE PACIFIC

Many of the natives decided to journey with the band

of healers, carrying water for them and searching out food and settlements ahead of them. At each village, the story of the Conquistadors' achievements was embellished further, so that they became mystical 'children of the sun' who could raise the dead if they chose to. Cabeza de Vaca claims to have downplayed such stories, but there is no doubt that it made their epic journey considerably easier. Although they were often hungry and thirsty, they could almost always count on a friendly reception when they reached the next native village. They managed to acquire animal skins to protect their naked bodies from the intense cold of the nights, but they were still barefoot and under constant attack from mosquitoes and flies. Cabeza de Vaca documented their travels in detail, and it read like a catalogue of hardships. He also wrote vividly of the different tribes that they encountered, many of whom would soon be obliterated forever when European settlers arrived. All of the Conquistadors were by now fluent in half a dozen different native languages and were thus able to easily make themselves understood, which prevented misunderstandings from turning into conflicts. What is extraordinary is that these four men walked entirely defenceless through hundreds of miles of territory that was bristling with war-like tribes, and yet they almost never suffered attack.

Their journey is in marked contrast to all of the others undertaken by the Conquistadors: Cortés, Pizarro and Quesada, who dressed in armour and carried lethal weaponry, were under constant assault. Perhaps the answer to this apparent mystery is that Cabeza de Vaca and the other three Conquistadors had long since forgotten about El Dorado, wealth or glory. They lived hand to mouth, as the natives themselves did, and sought nothing from the people they met other than food and water. They took nothing that wasn't offered to them, they spoke the same language as the natives and they lived in the same manner as them. In modern day parlance we would describe them as having 'gone native'. Doing so seems to have protected them far more effectively than steel shields and chain-mail could ever have.

Faith, then, produced miracles: the miracles worked

by the Conquistadors, and the greater miracle of the journey itself. Four unarmed men were able to walk through mile after mile of fiercely protected territories unscathed. And everywhere they went the miracles continued – the lame walked, the blind could see, even the dead could rise up and live once more, if the stories of the natives are to be believed. Cabeza de Vaca even had a go at rudimentary surgery on one local man, removing an arrow head with his knife and stitching the wound with hair. The entourage walking with the Conquistadors grew and grew as a result of their amazing feats. The natives killed rabbits by hurling clubs at them, and served them to Cabeza de Vaca and the others to alleviate their hunger. The women carried mats which they unfurled at night for the travellers to sleep on. By the time they reached 'a great river' – possibly the Rio Grande or the Conchos – the four Spaniards had been joined by an astonishing four thousand native followers. On the other side of the river, hundreds more stood waiting to meet them, having been told of their imminent arrival. Rivalries and feuds between the tribes were forgotten:

*Throughout all these countries the people who were
at war immediately made friends, that they might
come to meet us, and bring us all that they possessed.
In this way we left all the land at peace...*

They walked towards the setting sun, and towards
Mexico. The settlements they passed through changed
from primitive huts and tents to permanent houses,
surrounded by cultivated fields. They were reaching
the first outposts of civilisation. They did not yet know
it, but these were also the last outposts of 'the land at
peace'. Ahead of them lay a land at war, plagued by
bloodshed and persecution. It was being terrorised by
the most brutal of all the peoples that Cabeza de Vaca
encountered on his journey: the Spanish.

THE RETURN TO MEXICO

The buckle of a sword-belt, worn as a necklace by
a tribesman they met, was the first sign of the Old
World that Cabeza de Vaca's party came across. He
had taken it from a race of gods, he told them, who

had come from the sea and killed two of his fellow countrymen with their lances. As Cabeza de Vaca walked on, further similar reports reached him and he must have known that they were entering a territory on the fringes of Spanish-controlled Mexico. The landscape changed dramatically: no longer were they greeted by local inhabitants bearing food and gifts, asking to be healed. Instead:

> *We passed through many territories, and we found them all vacant; for their inhabitants wandered fleeing among the mountains, without daring to have houses, or to till the earth, for fear of the Christians. It was a sight of infinite pain to us, the view of a land very fertile and beautiful, abundant in waters and streams, with its hamlets deserted and burnt, the fugitives thin and weak, and all gone and concealed. As they did not plant, they appeased their fierce hunger by eating roots, and the bark of trees. We bore a share in this famine on the whole length of the journey, for these unfortunates could but poorly provide for us, being so reduced that they looked as*

though they would willingly die… they related to us how the Christians at other times had entered by land, and had destroyed and burnt the towns, carrying away half of the men, and all the women and boys.

The four Conquistadors that set out to search for El Dorado had come full circle and turned to face themselves, as if travelling back in time. Eight years earlier, they too had been part of that army that terrorised the natives; now, they were more native than Spanish. It is clear that Cabeza de Vaca felt ashamed of his countrymen and their actions. He had experienced so much kindness from the native people across America, and was now confronted with its antithesis: the Spanish lust for gold. He and his fellow companions no longer cared for treasure or wealth; sharing instead the natives' attitudes towards it:

The people…regard silver and gold with indifference; nor can they conceive for what they can be useful.

When he talks of the people who raided the native settlements, he cannot even bring himself to describe them as his own countrymen, referring to them simply as 'this people':

> *We told the natives we were going in search of this people, to tell them not to kill them, nor to make them slaves, nor to take from their country, nor do them other injustice, and of this they were very glad.*

Cabeza de Vaca had dreamed of returning home, of being reuinted with his friends and family and re-joining what he had always thought of as the civilised world. When he finally came to face to face with a group of Spanish slave-traders, however, they barely recognised the king's treasurer as being 'a Christian' like themselves. And Cabeza de Vaca in turn no longer recognised them: where once he had seen brave and noble Christian crusaders, now he saw only plundering savages. It took 'many and high words' for Cabeza de Vaca to even persuade the Spanish Captain, Diego de Alcaraz, not to take the six hundred natives who had followed him as slaves. He risked his life doing so: the slave-traders might easily have killed him in order to get their hands on a lucrative hoard of human treasure. Those natives refused to believe that their healer had come from the same race that now persecuted and enslaved them. Cabeza de Vaca tried to persuade them that it was true, but perhaps he too realised that his experiences had fundamentally changed him, and he really was now more like the native people he had travelled with than the Conquistadors he had set out with. The natives, certainly, perceived a difference between Cabeza de Vaca's ragged band and the Spanish Conquistadors:

> *They cared little or nothing for what was told to them,*
> *and conversed amongst themselves, saying that the*
> *Christians lied, for we had come from whence the sun*
> *rises, and they whence it goes down; that we healed the*
> *sick, and they killed the sound; and that we had come*
> *naked and barefooted, and they in clothing and on*
> *horses, and with lances; that we were not covetous of*
> *anything, but that all that was given to us we directly*

turned to give, remaining with nothing; and the others,
that they had no purpose but to rob whomsoever they
found, and give nothing to anyone.

THE RETURN TO SPAIN

It was the end of Cabeza de Vaca's extraordinary journey. Though other Conquistadors had endured similar hardships on a similarly epic scale, there is nothing in the history books that can remotely compare with his incredible story. The journey he took was as much spiritual as physical: alone amongst the Conquistadors he truly learned to understand the native people of North America. In the end, for all intents and purposes, he became one of them. His account of the journey he took would eventually help persuade those back in Spain that the native people were men like themselves rather than sub-human savages. Yet all of that would take time, and it did not save the people who so kindly and courageously helped Cabeza de Vaca on his odyssey across their lands. He sent them back to their settlements with firm promises that they would not be harmed; no sooner had he turned his back than Alcaraz's men descended upon them and enslaved them. The tyranny would continue for many more years. By then Cabeza de Vaca was back in Spain, writing his story, which tragically few read when it was first published. Had more done so, perhaps the slaughter and injustice would have ended sooner.

But the story of El Dorado's golden pillars had a stronger hold on men's hearts at this time, than any story of simple native people. Incredibly it still haunted Cabeza de Vaca, too. He returned to look for the shimmering city in Paraguay, and led an ill-fated expedition into the wilds of that country which ended with the mutiny of his men. Cabeza de Vaca was later put on trial – it is not entirely clear quite what for, but whatever the charge he was found guilty. He died in poverty and disgrace in the sleepy Spanish town of Valladolid sometime around 1558. A long way indeed from the gold and the glory of El Dorado. A long way too from La Florida, the Land of Flowers, where Cabeza de Vaca had believed the mythical city stood. But his 4,023 kilometres (2,500 miles) journey had shown that there was a vast land to the north of Mexico, the land we now know as the United States of America. That land was easily large enough, it was believed, to harbour the secret city of gold, somewhere within its vast mountains, plains and swamps.

Indeed some believed there was not just one city of gold waiting to be found, but many. Seven, to be exact.

FRANCISCO CORONADO AND THE SEVEN CITIES OF GOLD

In the year 1530 Nuño de Guzmán, who was president of New Spain, had in his possession an Indian, a native of the valley (or valleys) of Oxitipar, who was called Tejo by the Spaniards. This Indian said he was the son of a trader who was dead, but that when he was a little boy his father had gone into the back country with fine feathers to trade for ornaments, and that when he came back he brought a large amount of gold and

silver, of which there is a good deal in that country.
He went with him once or twice, and saw some very
large villages, which he compared to Mexico and its
environs. He had seen seven very large towns which
had streets of silver workers....The guide they had,
who was called Tejo, died....and thus the name of
these Seven Cities and the search for them remains
until now, since they have not been discovered.

So begins Pedro de Castañeda's chronicle of the search
for the Seven Cities of Gold, undertaken by Francisco
Vásquez de Coronado in 1540. We know nothing
more of the native American Tejo, who claimed to
have seen the great cities when he was a child, so it
is impossible to know if he was a reliable witness,
calculating schemer or simple dreamer. The story
that he told seems to have become bound up with the
amazing true tale of Cabeza de Vaca's journey across
America, as rumours swirled that Vaca had seen
'powerful villages, four and five stories high'. Cabeza
de Vaca's 'return from the dead' after eight years of
wandering was so astonishing that it sounded like a

myth, and doubtless the story was embellished each and every time it was re-told. Few ever read his actual account, preferring to hear the tale from the mouths of storytellers. By the time it reached Coronado's ears it was full of fabulous beasts, giants and fabled cities – and gold, always gold, for no story at this time in the New World was complete without a source of infinite wealth. An exploratory expedition was sent to look for 'Cibola', the golden city, with one of the survivors of Cabeza de Vaca's journey, Estevanico, in tow. The result was more tales of golden cities viewed from afar by Friar Marcos de Niza (and more deaths, this time Estevanico, reportedly killed by natives of Cibola). As Castañeda drily remarks at the start of his chronicle, Coronado was certainly told 'things very different from what turned out to be the truth'.

Which explains why he pawned his wife's estates and borrowed vast amounts of money to fund a full expedition to find the Seven Cities. Coronado took a force of three hundred and thirty-five Conquistadors, with eight hundred natives, by land along the same trail the exploratory party had used. A second force under the command of Hernando de Alacron took all the supplies that would be needed by boat along the Guadelope river. The party reached the northernmost Spanish settlement of Culiacan on 28 March 1540, and from there set out to explore the interior: the lands now lying in Arizona and New Mexico. Friar Marcos de Niza led the Conquistadors to the spot where he had seen the golden city of Cibola, and they gazed down at the native settlement in amazement. Amazement that it was so unlike the city Friar Marcos had previously described: nothing more, in fact, than a string of simple huts and a few fields. Needless to say, Friar Marcos was not a popular figure:

> ...*when they saw the first village, which was Cibola, such were the curses that some hurled at Friar Marcos that I pray God may protect him from them.*

A brief skirmish followed, but the natives defending their village were routed in under an hour. Friar Marcos was promptly sent home to Mexico by Coronado:

...because he did not think it was safe for him to stay in Cibola, seeing that his report had turned out to be entirely false, because the kingdoms that he had told about had not been found, nor the populous cities, nor the wealth of gold, nor the previous stones which he had reported, nor the fine clothes, nor other things that had been proclaimed from the pulpits.

Absolutely nothing that the Friar had said was true. Explorations in every direction returned with the same bad news: there was no golden city. Various native settlements were discovered and duly conquered, often after short and bloody battles, but the expedition is perhaps best summed up with the words of Friar Juan, who took over from Marcos and was heard to remark, 'To tell the truth, I do not know why we came here.' They found extraordinary natural treasures in the form of the Grand Canyon and Colorado river, but nothing, crucially, that they could pocket and sell. In the province of Tiguex, they encountered a slave who hailed from Florida who had another story of golden cities to tell. Nicknamed 'The Turk' (because 'he looked like one') he spoke of great piles of gold and silver in the cities further east, and despite having already been led on a giant wild goose chase the Conquistadors could not resist investigating his claims. And so, with the myth of Cibola now disproved, they headed east to search for the latest incarnation of El Dorado, the land of Quivira.

THE JOURNEY TO QUIVIRA

With the Turk guiding them, they moved through the vast flat plains of the mid-West, marvelling at the huge herds of buffalo that roamed there, and meeting the Apache natives who hunted them. Most of the tribes were nomadic, and thus permanent settlements were few and far between. Gradually Coronado lost faith in his guide and appears to have come to realise that the mission was unlikely to deliver on its promise of substantial wealth. His fears were confirmed when the local natives, probably of Wichita ancestry, informed him that the Turk was leading them in entirely the wrong direction: they needed to head north in order to reach Quivira. Thirty days and several violent dust storms later, they reached the promised land. It was indeed a large settlement, with over two hundred houses and fields of corn and beans. The only evidence of wealth, however, was a single tiny copper bell that one of the natives proudly displayed to them. Coronado, listening to its dull tinkle, decided that it was high time that the Turk was garotted. That task satisfactorily completed, he turned his army around and trudged wearily back to New Mexico.

On arrival there he promptly fell off his horse and suffered serious injuries. It was, in the eyes of all who sponsored and took part in the expedition, a complete and utter failure. Coronado was bankrupted by the mission and died very soon afterwards, in abject poverty. Yet the Conquistadors were some of the first Europeans to discover what, in time, would become the richest country on earth. Years later some of them would come to realise that although they had not found the Seven Cities of Gold, they had indeed touched a treasure of a different kind. As Pedro de Castañeda wistfully observes:

I always notice, and it is a fact, that for the most part when we have something valuable in our hands, and deal with it without hindrance, we do not value or prize it as highly as if we understood how much we would miss it after we had lost it, and the longer we continue to have it the less we value it; but after we have lost it and miss the advantages of it, we have a great pain in the heart, and we are all the time imagining and trying to find ways and means by which to get it back again. It seems to me that this has happened to all or most of those who went on the expedition which, in the year of our Saviour Jesus Christ 1540, Francisco Vásquez led in search of the Seven Cities.

Granted that they did not find the riches of which they had been told, they found a place in which to search for them and the beginning of a good country to settle in, so as to go on farther from there. Since they came back from the country which they conquered and abandoned, time has given them a chance to understand the direction and locality in which they were, and the borders of the good country they had in their hands, and their hearts weep for having lost so favourable an opportunity.... I say this because I have known several of those who came back from there who amuse themselves now by talking of how it would be to go back and proceed to recover that which is lost, while others enjoy trying to find the reason why it was discovered at all.

LOPE DE AGUIRRE: TRAITOR, WANDERER, MADMAN

Aguirre earned himself the nickname 'El Loco' primarily due to his actions during an expedition in 1560, following Orellana's trail along the Amazon. Like so many before him, he was searching for El Dorado. Mentally, emotionally, spiritually and physically he was spectacularly ill-suited to the task in hand – but the New World was teeming with such men at this time, and the viceroy of Quito had to find something for them all to do. And so he sent them to look for El Dorado in the lands of the Omaguas:

In these provinces, of which the Indians spoke when they reached Peru, dwelt the gilded man, at least this name was spread about in the land... It so excited the minds of those restless spirits with whom Peru was full, and who were ever ready to credit these rumours, that the viceroy thought it prudent to seek some way by which to give employment to so large a body of turbulent men.

Aguirre was most certainly a turbulent man. He walked with a severe limp after sustaining an injury while fighting for the king in Peru some six years earlier, and seethed with a sense of injustice because of this. He had received precious little reward for his service, and now felt ostracised by those who had no physical impediments. And this was not the sort of man to let bygones be bygones, as the Spanish judge Francisco de Esquivel had learned to his cost in Peru. Esquivel had sentenced Aguirre to be publicly flogged after he found him guilty of breaking new laws designed to protect the native population. It didn't go down well with Aguirre. El Loco pursued the judge relentlessly – on foot – for three years across Peru, in search of revenge. When Aguirre finally caught up with him in Cuzco, the chain mail Esquivel always wore for fear of his dogged pursuer did not help him. Aguirre cut his temples and watched him bleed to death. He then calmly departed, realised he had forgotten his sombrero, returned for it, and departed again. Hiding with various friends, he then lived as a fugitive, until he was pardoned on condition that he fight for the king against the rebel army of Francisco Hernández Giron. It was whilst doing so that he sustained the injury that now made his progress along the Amazon painful and difficult. His commander on the expedition, Pedro de Ursúa, perhaps should have known better than to ask a man with a limp, a grudge and a hugely unstable temperament to hack aimlessly through jungles for months on end. Given Aguirre's track record, it was always likely to lead to a loss of blood from the temples.

The expedition was dogged with problems even before it began: a priest who had promised to lend Ursúa two thousand dollars in order to buy supplies suddenly had a change of heart. Having already spent the promised money, Ursúa was in a difficult situation. The priest was summoned to give the last rites to a man on the brink of death: himself, as it turned out. Firearms were pointed at his heart and he was forced to surrender all of his wealth. That allowed the expedition to at least set out, though the advance party of Conquistadors that Ursúa sent to the province of Tubalosas managed to strangle their captain within a matter of days. Ordering the conspirators to be publicly beheaded, Ursúa must have wondered if it was going to be one of those expeditions. Others warned him of the unruly nature of the men under his command, and mentioned one Lope de Aguirre as a particularly volatile character, but Ursúa hoped that he had now established his authority over the expedition. He was wrong.

Ursúa split the expedition into three separate parties, which were ordered to gather supplies and seek information about the land they were entering, then rendezvous at a certain point on the river. After three difficult months, mutiny was already in the air by the time Ursúa met up with the other two parties to begin the main expedition. When the boats were fully loaded with men and supplies they immediately sprang leaks due to having been built from unseasoned wood. The men had to crowd into the few boats that could be patched, along with forty horses and the bare minimum of supplies. Two hundred and sixty horses, a vast stockpile of arms and the bulk of the food was left behind on the river bank, despite the fact that horses, arms and food had a long history of proving useful when exploring the dark interior of South America. Things became even more uncomfortable when one of the boats' rotten timbers caused her to break up entirely. Her crew had to squeeze in on the remaining boats, leaving them perilously overloaded. Soon the entire party was reduced to sailing on rafts as one by one the Spanish boats sank to the bottom of the river.

Had the rafts sailed down the grand canals of the golden city of El Dorado, no doubt all would have been forgiven. But the expedition found only minor native settlements and no signs of a powerful civilisation or any great wealth. Aguirre and his fellow mutineers decided that they would never be able to return to Peru whilst Ursúa was in command, and so they resolved to murder him. He was stabbed to death and his lieutenant Vargas had a sword rammed through his body so violently that it wounded a man standing behind him. All of those considered close to Ursúa were killed in a similar fashion and the army appeared to risk cutting itself to pieces until the new governor, Fernando de Guzmán, ordered a halt to the slaughter. Guzmán's new deputy was Lope de Aguirre, and from the outset there was tension between the two men. Guzmán wanted to push on and continue the hunt for El Dorado: the limping madman wanted to cut his losses and go home. And when Guzmán drew up a document aimed at explaining and legitimising the murder of Ursúa, a contemptuous Aguirre signed it 'Aguirre the traitor', saying:

Yes, we have all killed the governor... We have all been traitors, we have all been a party to this mutiny, and have agreed that the country (in search of which we are) shall be sought for, found and settled. Now should it be ten times richer than Peru, and more populous than New Spain (Mexico), and should the king draw more profit from it than from all the Indies together, yet as soon as the first chailler or letradillo comes with powers from his majesty to take up his residence amongst us, and to take notice of what has been done by us, I tell you it will cost us all our heads.

When hunger once more struck the Conquistadors a couple of months later, Aguirre was quick to suggest eating the horses and dogs, as he knew that this would hamper any land conquest and make a return to Peru more likely. Still Guzmán pressed on, however, and Aguirre decided to change tactics: rather than trying to thwart and undermine Guzmán, he now pretended to help him. Aguirre proposed that Guzmán should be named 'Prince of Peru', and announced that henceforth he was renouncing his Spanish citizenship and would only be a subject of the new prince. Others joined him in his declaration, and a flattered Guzmán accepted the honours bestowed upon him. A return to Peru was much more appealing to Guzmán now that he had suddenly been elected the leader of the whole kingdom. But the new 'Prince of Peru' would not reign for long.

New brigantines were built, but opinion was still divided over which way they should sail: back to Peru, or onwards to El Dorado. Guzmán decided that the latter course was, on balance, the safest, as if they returned they would surely be put to death for their mutiny. And so he resolved to murder Aguirre, in order to remove the main focus for dissent. Aguirre had developed a nasty habit of killing those who disagreed with him and was by now considered to be more or less ungovernable. When Guzmán told Aguirre that on no account should he make good his threat to murder one of his enemies named Salduendo, Aguirre responded by hacking Salduendo to pieces in front of Guzmán's eyes. It was clear that Guzmán was losing control, but before he could put in place his plan to murder the madman Aguirre, the madman turned the tables and killed Guzmán instead. He was shot and then cut to pieces with swords, along with many of his most trusted companions. When the butchery was over, Aguirre assembled the remaining Conquistadors and explained that the murders were entirely necessary in order to ensure the safe return of the expedition. He elected himself the new leader of the party, ordered everyone into the brigantines, and sailed down the river in search of a way back to Peru.

Paranoid that the men would mutiny against him after his series of brutal murders, Aguirre decided that the only way he could shore up his position was to commit several more. Men were killed simply for being too popular, or insufficiently devoted to him. One had his wounds poisoned by the camp doctor, on Aguirre's instructions, others were cut down with swords or strangled. The luckier ones were simply disarmed and imprisoned. One victim who had been hurled overboard, turned out to be still alive, and Aguirre laughed and joked as the man drowned. The natives who had journeyed for so long with the Spanish were dumped in a village by the river, on the basis that the ships did not have enough room for them. Two Conquistadors remarked that since the natives were certain to die in such a hostile country, perhaps it would be more humane to kill them swiftly. For such monstrous dissent Aguirre had them both strangled on the spot.

With his crew rapidly diminishing, Aguirre finally made it to the mouth of the Amazon and out into the sea. He sailed to the island of Margarita, near Venezuela, where he was welcomed by the governor. Aguirre thanked him for the welcome, then promptly took him prisoner and looted the island of all its supplies. He made his plans clear to his men: they would take a Peruvian province by force, and divide the spoils between themselves. In addition they would execute all monks, bishops, viceroys, presidents, governors, lawyers, men of noble birth and pretty much all women. If the full extent of Aguirre's insanity had not been evident previously, it most certainly was now. Some tried to desert, but it was too late: the island was tiny and they were easily found, and executed. All dissent – real or imagined – was punished ruthlessly: one of Aguirre's captains was left wandering around the island fortress with his brains and bowels hanging out, begging for a priest to hear his confession before he died. Another of Aguirre's soldiers attempted to prove his allegiance by sucking the dead man's brains out and drinking his blood. By all accounts Aguirre commended him on his actions and spared his life. On another occasion a man who turned up late for an appointment with Aguirre was made to shave in front of him using fetid urine. 'El Loco' now had total power over his men and the island on which they resided, and he used that power to amuse himself and to terrify all those who might seek to oppose him.

But word of the lunatic Aguirre's exploits soon reached Venezuela, where the governor immediately summoned troops from all over the New World to deal with the traitor. In August 1561, Aguirre's small fleet sailed away from Margarita aware that mighty armies had already assembled to meet him and his men in battle. The winds did not favour him, and he languished on the flat calm seas for eight days, railing maniacally against god for having sabotaged the weather. Eventually he landed at Burburata, on the Colombian coast. One of his men enquired whether the land was an island or the mainland, and Aguirre responded by immediately murdering him. Then, following the example of Cortés, he burned his ships to prevent any of his followers contemplating retreat. To the sound of drums and trumpets, Aguirre declared war on the King of Spain and all those who followed him. It marked his final descent into utter insanity: King Philip's empire was the most powerful military force on the planet and Aguirre commanded an army of just two hundred ill-disciplined men, with only ninety cavalry and practically no heavy arms. Nonetheless, the fearless Aguirre penned a rambling incoherent letter to the King, outlining his grievances with a truly astonishing degree of defiance:

> *I firmly believe that thou, O Christian king and lord, hast been very cruel and ungrateful to me and my companions... I, and my companions.... regard*

ourselves no longer as Spaniards. We make a cruel war on thee, because we will not endure the oppression of thy ministers... I am lame in the left foot, from two shots of an arquebus, which I received in the battle of Chucuinga, fighting... against Francisco Hernández Girón, a rebel, as I and my companions are now, and will be until death: for we now know, in this country, how cruel thou art, that thou art a breaker of thy faith and word.... Remember, king Philip, that thou hast no right to draw revenues from these provinces, since their conquest has been without danger to thee. I take it for certain that few kings go to hell, only because they are few in number... I believe that you are all worse than Lucifer, and that you hunger and thirst after human blood; and further, I think little of you, and despise you all, nor do I look upon your government as more than an air bubble... because of thine ingratitude, I am a rebel against thee until death.

When he signed the letter 'Lope de Aguirre, the Wanderer', he must have known that he was signing his own death warrant.

Having now started to foam at the mouth, Aguirre marched his forces through rocky mountain passes that made progress slow and difficult. The incessant rain didn't help matters, and Aguirre once again railed against his god:

> *Does God think that because it rains in torrents I am not to go to Peru, and destroy the world? He is mistaken in me.*

The conditions, along with desertions and Aguirre's habit of executing men more or less at random, reduced the size of the force to one hundred and forty men. It would have been reduced by a further forty if Aguirre had had his way and executed all the sick and those he considered of dubious loyalty. A royalist army of almost twice that size faced him outside the small town of Barquicimeto, with five hundred more marching from other provinces to reinforce them. Aguirre sent sixty arquebusiers to attack the king's men by the cover of darkness, and on the following day there were further skirmishes, including one in which Aguirre's horse was shot from under him. The two sides traded insults as well as gunfire, with the royalists calling Aguirre's men traitors and simultaneously urging them to defect from their insane leader. More and more of them chose to do so, and an exasperated Aguirre resolved to retreat back to the coast and try a different route to Peru. But it was too late: the royalist forces had encircled the camp, and the trickle of defections soon turned into a flood. A dejected Aguirre saw the writing on the wall and no longer even attempted to stop his men deserting. There was to be no spectacular last battle: the royalist army stormed Aguirre's quarters and found him leaning over the body of his own daughter, whom he killed when he heard them approach. He had thrown his weapons to the ground, and asked to be taken prisoner, but his own men begged the royalists to shoot him so that he could not reveal the crimes they had committed during the expedition. Two shots from arquebusiers struck Aguirre, the first only grazing him but the second striking him in the heart. He sank to the floor with the words 'That has done the business.'

He was then beheaded before his body was chopped into quarters and thrown into the road. His hands were chopped off and sent as prizes to the towns of Valencia and Merida, which provided the bulk of the royalist troops. Those from Valencia threw Aguirre's left hand to some dogs, who gratefully ate it. Those from Merida tired of the stench of the putrefying right hand and threw it into the river Mototan. The traitor's head was taken to the nearby town of Tocuyo where it was displayed in an iron cage until it rotted to a skull. Aguirre grinned, then, even after the brutal death that had been the inevitable end to a life of violent defiance. There was an element of truth in his extraordinary letter to the king, for much of the wealth that the Conquistadors risked their lives for found its way into the coffers of the king and the noblemen closest to him. Few common soldiers ever saw any of the gold of the New World. And no man ever saw any of the gold of El Dorado. The dream faded with every year that passed, until eventually it was washed from the minds of the Conquistadors like the flakes of gold painted upon the Gilded Man as he dived into his secret sacred lake.

EPILOGUE

The Unconquerable Maya

Many Maya lands had been pacified before Francisco de Montejo led his men into the eastern fringes of Mexico – Cortés had engaged in battles with them on his way to conquer the Aztecs, and Pedro de Alvarado had hacked his way through much of Guatemala and El Salvador – but the Spanish expedition of 1527 was now entering the Maya heartland. They came seeking gold, it almost goes without saying, but also seeking land and slaves – and that most elusive of all prizes, glory. The man who took command of the Yucatán Conquistadors was born in Salamanca in 1479 and had fought bravely alongside both Grijalva and Cortés in their earlier expeditions in the New World. He was thus already a highly experienced soldier by the time the king of Spain made him Captain General of Yucatán and gave him permission to explore there. Given the relative strength of the Maya, when compared to the Aztec empire Montejo had already helped to conquer, it might seem surprising that such a seasoned and professional general struggled to subdue the natives of Yucatán. But this was a very different land, with a different culture, and it required a very different type of campaign from any other that the Conquistadors had embarked upon.

The problem for Montejo was that the Maya were less a single entity than a confederation of separate states, and thus there was no one powerful leader to capture as had been the case with Montezuma and Atahuallpa in Mexico and Peru. Control simply wasn't centralised in Yucatán to nearly the same degree. Instead the Spanish had to break each and every province separately: and they were met with ferocious resistance every step of the way. Córdoba had witnessed the effectiveness of Maya armies in 1517, when eighty of his men were killed at Cape Catoche in one of the first expeditions to the New World. Ten years later Montejo found that the Maya were just as unwelcoming, and his attempt at conquest ended in failure as the Maya adopted 'hit and run' tactics that left the Spanish bloodied and bewildered. A second conquest was attempted in 1531, led by Montejo and his son, and this time they built forts to secure their hard-won positions against the native attacks. After four years of continual harassment, however, the Spanish army had simply had enough, and retreated back to Veracruz in search of easier lands to conquer.

By 1540 Montejo was in his late sixties and so it fell to his son, Francisco Montejo the Younger to lead the final major attempt to conquer the Yucatán. Several Maya states this time sided with the invaders, and the expedition was considerably more successful than those led by Montejo the Elder. Permanent settlements were at last formed, though revolts were frequent and continued for some six years. A major battle between Maya forces and the Spanish in 1546 resulted in victory for the Old World army, and seemed to have finally crushed the native rebellion.

Yet the Maya clung on, in the remote Peten region of what is now Guatemala. The Itza who lived there had pledged loyalty to Spain many years earlier in 1525, but had continued to worship the same gods and remained largely untroubled by the Spanish until 1618 when Franciscan friars arrived to try and convert them to Christianity. When their attempts failed, an army was sent to impose the new faith by force, but the Itza slaughtered them in their island city of Tayasal. In 1624 a second army was sent to deal with the troublesome province. They fared no better than the first, suffering massive losses after an Itza ambush. There were few volunteers to join a third such army, and so the Spanish reluctantly left the Maya to their heretical ways for another seventy years.

In 1695 the Franciscans decided to try again, and the Itza king responded with polite but firm refusals to change his ways. Once more the Spanish sent an army to enforce their will. The result was the now all too familiar carnage and humiliation as the Itza armies forced the Conquistadors to retreat. Finally, in

1697, an army of tens of thousands of Spaniards and their native allies arrived in Tayasal, complete with cannons, horses, and vast amounts of firearms. It took a force larger than that which conquered Peru to seize control of the Itza capital. Once there, the Spanish burnt all of the sacred Maya texts and broke their idols. The last Maya outpost had finally fallen.

The clash between the Spanish and the Maya may lack a little grandeur when set beside the stories of the Aztecs and the Incas, but it makes up for it in intrigue. Above all it hints at what might have been: what might have been for either of those mighty cultures, so strong when the Spanish arrived on their shores, if only they had fought as the Maya did. For although they were a civilisation already in marked decline when the story starts in 1527, they resisted their invaders for an astonishing one hundred and seventy years in total. Twice entire armies were forced to retreat from the lands of the Maya and return to the safer realms previously conquered by Cortés. Even after the third invasion triumphed in 1546, the Maya held on in remote pockets, just as the Inca had tried and failed to do. Indeed as late as 1933 Maya uprisings were still occupying the Mexican army, continuing an uprising that had begun over eighty-five years earlier. The 'Caste War of Yucatán' resulted – albeit briefly – in an independent Maya state, recognised by the United Kingdom until 1893. They may well have taken control of the entire Yucatán peninsula were it not for a swarm of winged ants. As they approached the city of Merida, the Maya noted the ants and knew that their arrival meant that it was time for them to plant their corn fields. They thus returned home (much to the exasperation of their generals) rather than continuing their march. The official end of the war came in 1915, when the Mexican Revolution led to General Alvardo cancelling all 'debt labour', effectively freeing the Maya from three hundred and fifty years of slavery. Chewing gum helped the peace treaty to hold: the Wrigley Company began to gather 'chicle' gum in the area, bringing wealth to a region previously blighted by widespread poverty. By the time hostilities ceased, 247,000 people had reportedly lost their lives in the war.

Today some six million people in modern day Guatemala, Belize and Mexico still refer to themselves as Maya. Their religion is a fusion of Christianity and traditional beliefs: shaman still keep count of the two hundred and sixty-day ritual calendar, and chickens are sacrificed at cave shrines. This tenacious culture, then, was never truly conquered, and never truly disappeared. It is now, as it was then, too disparate and shifting to tie down or even neatly define, and this flexibility and adaptability is the very thing that allowed it to survive the Spanish conquests. The Maya believe that time is cyclical, and that worlds end and begin again on a regular basis, in much the same way as the sun sets and rises. Their own history appears to mirror this cycle, as they have risen and fallen in power and influence, and been apparently destroyed only to be reborn again as something new. For them, the age of the Conquistadors was one moment in an eternal cycle; an age that would pass as all ages must. Their sacred scrolls perished in the fires lit by Friar Diego de

Landa in 1652, but hidden by the smoke the ancient glyphs were already being passed on in whispers that would echo down from generation to generation. The same culture that watched the Spanish empire march into their homelands in the sixteenth century would watch that empire fall, some four hundred years later. Just another small circle completed by the eternal wheel of the Maya calendar, which even Toledo steel could not entirely break.

THE LEGACY OF THE CONQUESTS

The two worlds that collided in the sixteenth century were both changed forever by the sudden and spectacular impact, the effects of which are still felt today. As soon as word reached Spain of the fabulous New World that had been discovered far across the ocean, men rushed from the Iberian peninsula to grab their piece of the new lands. Men, rather than women or families; this was an influx of settlers very different from those that sailed for America in the Mayflower, for example. Native women were taken as wives and concubines by the conquering Spanish men: they were given as prizes, used as currency, each bride a small piece of territory in the eyes of the invaders. The bloodlines of the Aztecs, Incas and other native tribes were diluted as an estimated 240,000 Spaniards poured into the New World.

With them came diseases unknown to the native population: with no previous exposure to the New World plagues the indigenous people were highly susceptible to infection. Because very few animals were domesticated in the New World, the people were not exposed to any diseases which might have provided a degree of immunity. The results were devastating. The most deadly of the new diseases was smallpox. Historians have blamed the virus for the vast majority of the deaths in the New World, though there is some quite compelling recent evidence that suggests that the 'cocolitzli' plague which tore through the Aztec population after the arrival of Cortés may in fact have been a different disease. Similarly, analysis of Inca mummies shows that none display the tell-tale pockmarks left by smallpox before 1558, yet the disease was supposed to have claimed the lives of Huayna Capac and thousands of his people thirty or more years earlier. Contrary to popular belief, smallpox is relatively difficult to communicate across large distances – it requires continuous close human contact and thus tends to spread with ships and horses rather than by men on foot. Once present in a densely populated urban centre such as Tenochtitlan, however, it proves highly contagious, spreading through breath or contaminated garments. Once infected, the strongest warriors are as likely to die as new-born babies, with the rate of mortality estimated at around sixty per cent. Those who do not die might be left blinded or with debilitating sores on their bodies: it is thought around half of the population of Tenochtitlan perished because of the epidemic that struck the city, and many more were left too weak to fight the Spanish invaders. With the water supply cut and food in short supply, conditions in Tenochtitlan allowed diseases to thrive. After the fall of the Aztec capital, much of the remaining population fled or were forcibly expelled, spreading disease much further afield. Soon it ravaged the entire country, with truly devastating consequences: it is estimated that between 1518 and 1585 the population of Mexico fell from over twenty-five million to under two million. Famine and brutal Spanish oppression no doubt played a part in the cataclysm, but disease is believed to be the primary culprit.

The natives that survived were put to work straight away, in order to make their new masters wealthy, under the 'encomienda' system. Although dressed up in the noble idea of educating and protecting the native population, the encomienda was in reality an extension of the Aztec and Inca principle of paying tribute under threat of death. For many in the New World, the difference between life under the encomienda and outright slavery was minimal. Those granted native workers were known as 'encomenderos' – usually Conquistadors or Spanish settlers – and ostensibly they only held rights over their workforce for two generations, after which time the encomendero returned to the crown. In practice this was often overlooked, and the encomienda system was not abolished until 1720, meaning that many of the indigenous people in the sixteenth century had no prospect of freedom within their lifetimes. Since those of mixed race were not subject to the encomienda, the native people often attempted to intermarry with those of different ethnicities – most frequently Spaniards. This further diluted the bloodlines of the native people, and reduced their sense of national and tribal identity.

The great wealth that the encomienda system created, along with the spoils of South America's vast natural resources, brought the Spanish crown a staggering windfall throughout the sixteenth century. The 'Silver Mountain' of Cerro Rico at Potosi produced a total of 35,000 tons of silver – more than previously existed in all of the countries of Europe put together. It was said that a bridge of silver could have been built from the Andes to Spain with that single mountain's produce. It was wealth that was sorely needed, however, as the zealous Catholic King Philip II launched a series of religious wars against the Netherlands, France and England. They proved ruinously expensive, even for an empire with such enormous resources now at its disposal. The sacred relics of the Aztecs and Incas that had been melted down into gold ingots were in turn traded for machines of war. The Spanish Armada, that most potent symbol of Spain's new wealth and power, was defeated by the English in 1588. And so the treasure that flowed from the Silver Mountain in the Andes ended up at the bottom of an ocean on the other side of the world.

In addition, the sudden influx of precious metals resulted in spiralling inflation in Spain, destabilising the economy and ultimately forcing the crown to declare itself bankrupt. The Spanish empire entered a period of steady decline. Other European powers, who had suffered at the hands of the Catholic kings, agitated their populations with lurid tales of how the Spanish had come by their gold. The cruelty of her Conquistadors and her inquisitors was exaggerated and thus the 'Black Legend' of Spain was born. 'La Leyenda Negra' can be traced back to Bartolomé de las Casas's 1552 chronicle *A Short Account of the Destruction of the Indies* which was later printed with lurid copper plate engravings portraying some of the more sensational crimes that the Conquistadors were accused of committing. It became a huge hit across mainland Europe, instilling in its readers a sense that the Spanish empire represented the epitome of repression, cruelty and religious intolerance. In truth, almost all of the major powers in the sixteenth century had an equally poor record with regards to human rights. The Spanish undoubtedly committed countless cruelties against the people of the New World, but it is by no means certain that had any other nation journeyed across the Atlantic the result would have been any more favourable for the indigenous people. In time, criticism of the encomienda system and the associated poor treatment of the natives grew, perhaps fuelled by the Black Legend, and laws were passed to guarantee freedom and justice for the people of the New World.

In 1803, King Charles IV sent the Balmis expedition to distribute smallpox vaccines across the Americas: it is regarded as the first international health-care expedition in history. Hundreds of thousands of people were vaccinated by a new and entirely benevolent party of Spanish adventurers, and the disease first brought to the continent by the Conquistadors was practically eradicated, some one hundred and eighty years before the rest of the world was declared free of the virus.

Disease was one of the more obvious exports from the Old World to the New World, but there were countless others. The conquest of the New World ushered in the age of globalisation, which in time would affect every society on earth. The 'Colombian Exchange', as it came to be known, involved the interchange of plants, crops and animals, but also of human populations and ideas. Ways of life on both sides of the Atlantic were changed dramatically and forever. The potato became a staple food in Europe after its introduction from the Americas, and maize began to be widely consumed for the first time in

Africa and Asia. Avocados, chilli peppers, artichokes, peanuts, pumpkins, pineapples and tomatoes all began to appear on European dining tables. Other exotic imports that found favour in the Old World were chocolate and tobacco. In the New World apples, bananas, carrots, onions and many other imported plants were shown to flourish and became important crops. Chickens, cows, goats, pigs and sheep were bred in Mexico and Peru for the first time in history. Alpacas, turkeys, llamas and guinea pigs travelled across the vast ocean to be bred on the European mainland. The horse, that almost supernatural creature that so terrified the Aztec and Inca armies, became an everyday sight throughout the Americas, along with donkeys and mules.

It is thought that syphilis originated in the Americas and spread from there to the rest of the world: diseases travelling in the opposite direction included bubonic plague, chicken pox, cholera, influenza, leprosy, malaria, measles, scarlet fever and typhoid. The devastation these new diseases wrought upon the populations of the New World was to have severe consequences in turn for Africa: the new territories required vast amounts of labour in order for them to generate wealth for their owners, and when the indigenous population was decimated by disease the Europeans turned to Africa to replace them. The slave trade became one of the most important industries on the planet, bringing abject misery to millions, whilst generating staggering revenues for the European empires. They rose in influence and prosperity, entering the golden age of the Renaissance, whilst the conquered lands sank ever further into poverty and despair.

The Colombian Exchange, then, worked both ways and changed both worlds beyond recognition. But it was never an equal exchange: and the inequalities it brought about are with us even today. The battles fought by the Conquistadors in the sixteenth century determined the futures of entire nations for generations to come. At times a mere handful of Spaniards took to the field: millions across the world, most not even yet born, would win and lose with them.

NEW WORLD MEETS OLD

Conclusion

In El Paso, Texas, stands the largest bronze equestrian statue in the world. It depicts Juan de Oñate, sometimes referred to as 'The Last Conquistador', triumphantly mounted upon his trusty steed. It is fitting that a horse as well as a man should be commemorated, given the importance of the role these animals played in the conquest of the New World. Oñate himself earned his place in history after founding various settlements in the present day Southwest of the United States of America. Not all consider him a hero however. The right foot of the statue was hacked off by Native American protestors keen to remind the world of an incident in which Oñate ordered that the left foot of every native Acoma man aged over twenty-five should be severed. The statue still bears the scar of the attack – a potent symbol of the weeping wound that burns in the memories of all those who suffered at the hands of the Conquistadors.

History, as we know, is written by the victors, and there is no question that the indigenous populations of the New World lost. From the moment that the Spanish sailor Rodrigo de Triana first sighted land from one of Columbus' ships in 1492, the fate of the New World was sealed. Had Cortés and Pizarro failed, as they so nearly did, then others would have surely followed with even larger armies and the same insatiable lust for gold. The fall of the Americas was inevitable: not divinely determined as the Aztec and Inca myths had imagined, but the clockwork advance of a technically superior military machine.

Yet, given the superhuman resistance of the Aztecs and Inca, perhaps it was inevitable, too, that autonomy would one day be won back by the people of South America. The half-Spanish and half-Inca chronicler Felipe Guaman Poma de Ayala saw this as early as 1600, when he began work on an extraordinary 1,200 page letter to King Philip III of Spain. Guaman's life's work, entitled *New Chronicle and Good Government*, looked both backwards and forwards, chronicling the events of the conquest and urging a different approach by the Spanish in governing Peru. In 1615 and at the age of eighty, Guaman walked through the Andes to deliver his manuscript to officials in Lima, in order to assure himself that it would indeed reach the king, across the world in Spain. It outlined a breathtakingly progressive blueprint for the governance of The Land of Four Quarters, drawing on both Catholic theology and the indigenous Inca belief in social justice. Guaman highlights the best of both the Old World and New World teachings to argue that Peru should be governed not as a vassal state but as an autonomous nation protected and guided by Spain. It is a document as remarkable in its own way as the Magna Carta or the United States' Declaration of Independence. The King of Spain, however, never read it.

Resistance to the rule of the Conquistadors continued, though the Aztec and Inca empires had been shattered by the might of the Spanish military. Today tourists flock to visit the ruins that those ancient cultures left behind. You can take a train from Cuzco to Aguas

Calientes, through the Sacred Valley where the fugitive Manco Inca once taunted the Conquistadors from across a river. From there it is a short bus ride to Machu Picchu, the secret 'Lost City of the Incas'. It is a journey now taken by more than three hundred thousand tourists every year. Indeed, the number of visitors is so high that the site has had to be shored up to protect it from landslides. The fortress that endured five hundred years of warfare threatened to crash into the Urubamba river under the weight of pilgrims' footsteps.

Acid air pollutants from oil refineries and power stations along Mexico's gulf coast threaten to erase carved stone murals at El Tajin, a site that pre-dates even the Aztecs. There are, then, new and deadly threats to the last few visible remains of the cultures that once flourished prior to the arrival of the Spanish. Tourism and multi-national companies are, it seems, the new Conquistadors of the Americas. Dreams of gold once more determine the future of the land: this time wealth brought in to the Americas rather than taken from her. Countries on the wrong side of the Colombian exchange, riven by poverty and desperate for investment, reach for the treasure of travellers' cheques and jobs. It would be ironic if the final destruction of the great stone temples and fortresses was caused by an army of holidaymakers armed only with cameras.

But the lands are not undefended: the resistance continues, just as it always has done. A proposal to build a cable car up to Machu Picchu was eventually refused, after ferocious objections over the damage it would do to the tranquillity and spirituality of the site. It is now protected by UNESCO World Heritage designation, along with Cuzco and Lima; the Great Inca Trail that united the Land of Four Quarters is being considered for inclusion on the same list. The treasures of the Americas will not be yielded up easily. The New World countries now know all of the opportunities and threats that being part of a global community can bring. Some four hundred years after Guaman wrote his visionary masterpiece, his dream of an autonomous homeland working in partnership with the Old World powers is finally coming true. The lands that the Spanish conquered are reasserting their right to rule by themselves, and for themselves, and they might yet claim the ultimate prize that eternally eluded the Conquistadors: El Dorado. The Golden Man, after all, was naked once he had plunged into the sacred lake. His gold was never hoarded: it was only hewn from the rock in order to be given away, offered up to something infinitely more valuable than base metals or land. The spirits of the ancestors in the Sacred Valley, the gods that make the sun rise over The Plain of Ghosts: these were always the true jewels of the Americas, and her people kept them safe throughout the centuries. All other riches, all other victories were always an illusion, like the shimmering dream of El Dorado itself. Felipe Guaman Poma de Ayala saw through it all, and knew that the long suffering, courageous, extraordinary people of the New World would have the final word in the story of the Americas.

Timeline of Spanish Invasion

NAME OF CONQUISTADOR	DATES	LAND
Diego de Nicuesa	1506 – 1511	Panama
Juan Ponce de León	1508	Puerto Rico
Juan de Esquivel	1509	Jamaica
Vasco Núñez de Balboa	1511 – 1519	Panama
Diego Velázquez de Cuéllar	1511 – 1519	Cuba
Juan Ponce de León	1513	Florida
Francisco Hernández de Córdoba	1517	Yucatán
Juan de Grijalva	1518	Yucatán
Pedro de Alvarado	1519 – 1521	Mexico
Hernán Cortés	1519 – 1521	Mexico
Pedro de Alvarado	1523 – 1527	Guatemala
Hernán Cortés	1524 – 1526	Honduras
Cristóbal de Olid	1524 – 1526	Honduras
Lucas Vásquez de Ayllón	1524 – 1527	East Coast United States
Diego de Almagro	1524 – 1534	Peru
Francisco Pizarro	1524 – 1534	Peru
Pánfilo de Narváez	1527 – 1528	Florida
Álvar Núñez Cabeza de Vaca	1527 – 1536	South West United States
Francisco de Montejo	1527 – 1543	Yucatán
Hernán Cortés	1532	California
Juan Pizarro	1532 – 1536	Peru
Gonzalo Pizarro	1532 – 1542	Peru

NAME OF CONQUISTADOR	DATES	LAND
Hernando Pizarro	1532 – 1560	Peru
Pedro de Alvarado	1533 – 1535	Peru
Sebastián de Belalcázar	1533 – 1536	Ecuador and
Colombia		
Diego de Almagro	1535 – 1537	Chile
Gonzalo Jiménez de		
Quesada	1536 – 1537	Colombia
Hernando de Soto	1539 – 1542	Florida and
South East United States		
Francisco Vázquez de		
Coronado	1540 – 1542	Arizona and
		New Mexico
Pedro de Valdivia	1540 – 1552	Chile
Inés de Suárez	1541	Chile
Francisco de Orellana	1541 – 1543	Amazon River
Pedro Menéndez de Aviles	1565 – 1567	Florida
Gonzalo Jiménez de		
Quesada	1569 – 1572	Venezuela
Juan de Salcedo	1569 – 1576	Philippines
Antonio de Berrio	1592	Trinidad
Martín de Ursúa	1696 – 1697	Guatemala

Index

Author Biography

John Pemberton is a freelance writer who specializes in ancient and modern history. He grew up in Ireland where he became fascinated by Celtic myths and legends. He has since travelled widely, particularly in Central and South America, where he lived for some time studying the cultural history of the Aztecs and Incas. He currently resides in Tintagel, North Cornwall close to the legendary castle of King Arthur.

Further Reading

The Conquest of New Spain (Bernal Díaz, translated by J.M. Cohen, Penguin Classics, 1963).

The Broken Spears: The Aztec Account of the Conquest of Mexico (Miguel León-Portilla,1962).

The Discovery and Conquest of Peru (Augustin Zarate, translated by J.M. Cohen, Penguin Classics, 1968).

Relation of the Discovery and Conquest of The Kingdoms of Peru (Pedro Pizarro, translated by Philip Ainsworth Means, 1921).

Travels of Pedro de Cieza de León, AD 1532–50 (Pedro de Cieza de León, translated by Clements R. Markham, 1874).

Chronicle of the Narváez Expedition (Alvar Núñez Cabeza de Vaca, translated by Fanny Bandelier, Penguin Classics, 2002).

The Search For El Dorado (John Hemming, 1978).

The History of the Conquest of Mexico (William Hickling Prescott, 1843).

A History of the Conquest of Peru (William Hickling Prescott, 1847).

The Cambridge History of Latin America Vol. 1 and 2 (Leslie Bethell, Cambridge University Press, 1984).

Conquistadors (Michael Wood, BBC Worldwide, 2000).

Images credits in order of appearance: Getty Images, Nick Harris/ Getty Images, Getty Images, Pierre Duflos/Getty Images, Getty Images, Getty Images, Getty Images, Leemage/Universal Images Group/Getty Images, Look and Learn/The Bridgeman Art Library, Lori Epstein/Getty Images, Roc Canals Photography/Getty Images.